Exercise Science
Understanding and Evaluating Physical Fitness and Health

Second Edition

Warren Rosenberg, Ph.D.
Professor of Biology

Ciaran Cullen, D.C.
Doctor of Chiropractic
Adjunct Professor, Iona College

Iona College
New Rochelle, New York

 KENDALL/HUNT PUBLISHING COMPANY
4050 Westmark Drive   Dubuque, Iowa 52002

CONTENTS

FITNESS ASSESSMENT ACTIVITIES

Preface

"If we could give every individual the right amount of nourishment and exercise, not too little and not too much, we would have found the safest way to health."
Hippocrates 460-370 BC

The purpose of this book is to provide individuals who have little or no experience in college-level science with a guided experience through the science of exercise and fitness. While there are many texts for higher-level courses in exercise physiology, kinesiology, and functional anatomy, they require a firm grounding in underlying physical, chemical and biological knowledge that is more characteristic of students majoring in the health or applied sciences. On the other end of the spectrum are found self-help books by the trade publishers that have little or no relevance to college-level study, and which may or may not be grounded in firm scientific principles. While there does exist some books in the middle, very few of them present a comprehensive treatment of the complex interactions between the human body and physical activity along with a series of laboratory-based activities.

We have revised this second edition so that it provides, in essence, an introductory owner's manual of the human body for individuals interested in preserving and enhancing their health through physical fitness and sports as well as for those preparing for personal trainer certification exams and school coaching certificates. In addition to conceptual content material, the book also provides a comprehensive series of physical assessment activities through which students can evaluate the status of their own physical fitness relative to expected norms. Several new assessment activities have been added in this second edition. In combination, these provide the student with the powerful tools of establishing a scientifically based, personalized program for self-improvement with respect to physical fitness and health.

World-Wide Web Resources

Although many books provide references to Web-posted materials, as does this text, the fluid nature of the Web and the rapidly changing sites almost ensure that these printed references will be at least partially obsolete within weeks or months of original publication. For that reason, this book has been created with an accompanying Web site that will continually post updated Web-addresses for referenced and newly created information sites. While all readers of this book may access the Web site for information updates, only registered participants (enrolled students) of the accompanying course will have access to restricted portions of the site such as the discussion board and virtual classroom.

Feedback from the readers and users of this book is welcomed as it provides information for continuous improvement. Comments are best made through the accompanying website. We would like to thank our colleagues and in particular, our students, for the valuable feedback they have provided that has allowed this book to continually evolve.

The accompanying Web site can be accessed at: http://online.iona.edu

WR / CC

Acknowledgments

This book has benefited greatly from the comments and input of several national and internationally known athletic coaches and trainers. Their review of the draft manuscript, their suggestions for improvement and the contribution of their knowledge and experience have vastly improved the content of this book. Their gracious contributions are thankfully acknowledged.

Sorin Cepoi and **Teodora Ungureanu**, Olympic competitors in men's and women's gymnastics for the Romanian national team, now coach men's and women's gymnastics at the Dynamic Gymnastics training facility in Mohegan Lake, NY, and at the U.S. Gymnastics Training Center in Holyoke MA. Trained in anatomy, physiology, sports medicine and elite-level coaching, Coach Cepoi competed in the 1976 Montreal and 1980 Moscow Olympics and was a four-time world championship competitor. Coach Ungureanu was an international competitor for ten years and a three-time medallist in the 1976 Montreal Olympics. The coaching team of Cepoi and Ungureanu have produced national competitors in USA Women's gymnastics for five years in row and were jointly named 1997 Coach of the Year for USA Gymnastics in New York State. Prior to founding Dynamic Gymnastics, Cepoi and Ungureanu were head coaches at LaGrenobloise Gym in France and produced four second place French National Teams along with the 1992 French National Individual Champion and Barcelona Olympic competitor.

Mick Byrne has been Head Coach of the Iona College men's and women's Cross Country and Track & Field programs for 15 years and a member of the coaching staff for 20 years. An accomplished athlete in his own right, Coach Byrne holds the school record as a member of the four-mile relay team at Providence College and, as Head Coach, has lead Iona to four appearances in the NCAA Cross Country Championships, 14 Metro Atlantic Athletic Conference team championships and consecutive NCAA Division I-A top 20 National rankings including a second place finish in the Division I National Championships.

Sam DeRosa is Head Trainer for all of Iona College's NCAA Division I – III men's and women's intercollegiate athletic teams and is a member of the Athletic Department's Sports Medicine staff.

Fred Mariani is Head Coach of Iona's NCAA Division I-AA men's football program. Coach Mariani has been coaching NCAA college-level football for over 20 years including positions at Fordham University and Lehigh University before taking over the Iona College program.

I would also like to thank my editors at Kendall/Hunt Publishing Company, Sue Ellen Saad and Katie Riggs for their patience and helpful comments. Finally, I'd like to recognize the contributions of all of our students who, over the years, have helped us refine our course notes and revisions of this text.

Chapter 1

Introduction

Chapter Contents

- The Need for Physical Activity
- The Risks and Benefits of Exercise
- The Science of Exercise and Fitness
- Professional Organizations and Certifications
- Selected Readings

Learning Objectives

The material in this chapter will allow you to:

- Understand the health-related consequences of a sedentary, hypokinetic, lifestyles
- Understand the benefits of physical activity, exercise and athletic participation
- Understand the risks associated with exercise and athletic participation and how to measure those risks
- Appreciate that scientific research provides the basis for our knowledge about exercise and fitness
- Know about the professional organizations and professional certifications for exercise professionals

2

The Need for Physical Activity

The human body has evolved over a period of several tens of thousands of years into a sophisticated machine, capable of converting energy into motion in order to perform physical work. This living system, the human machine, unlike its more simple mechanical counterparts, is capable of responding to the various levels of workload demanded of it by improving its capacity to perform. The greater the demands placed upon the body, within limits, the greater the improvement in performance. Conversely, body systems that are not utilized, or not stressed, will lose capacity and atrophy.

If we extend this analogy to a mechanical system, we might expect that if we drive our cars consistently fast, engine size and horsepower will increase in response. If we run our air conditioners at maximum output during a long hot spell, we might expect to find the air conditioner's cooling capacity, its B.T.U. ratings, increasing over time. Obviously, this is not the case with mechanical systems. It is with us!

Our modern society, with all of its technological benefits has, to a large extent, deprived the human body of many of the demands once placed upon it. To our detriment, this has resulted in decreases in bodily performance which are reflected in our unacceptably high incidences of heart disease, obesity, osteoporosis, depression and a host of other ills in part attributable to lack of exercise. Our bodies need to work, need to be physically stressed, in order to remain fit and healthy. This concept is not a new one and dates back more than two millennia. Although many have only recently come to appreciate this relationship, it was actually identified centuries ago and constituted, to a large extent, the basic premise of the foundation of modern medicine. Hippocrates, one of the founders of modern medicine, who lived and practiced during the years 460 – 370 B.C. (he is also responsible for the Hippocratic Oath in which physicians commit to, *"First, do no harm"*) observed that, *"If we could give every individual the right amount of nourishment and exercise, not too little and not too much, we would have found the safest way to health."*

> "The preservation of health is a duty. Few seem conscious that there is such a thing as physical morality."
> Herbert Spencer, Philosopher, 1861

Fortunately, more and more individuals, either on their own or under their physician's orders, are taking up exercise to improve fitness, health, or just to have fun. The New York City Marathon now attracts upwards of 20,000 amateur and professional runners per year. Health clubs and fitness centers are proliferating in every community and major corporate office and have become so popular that they often cannot provide enough parking to meet demand. Video stores have racks of exercise, workout and instructional videos produced by athletes, trainers, physicians, entertainment personalities, and just about everyone else! Bookstore shelves are similarly crowded with self-help exercise books. In every department store circular, on most television programs, and in an ever-expanding number of infomercials, there are numerous advertisements for home gym and physical training equipment. Most school systems now offer continuing adult education courses in health and fitness. It has become evident that exercise and fitness are in!

Just what is physical fitness? In its simplest definition, it is a state of well-being associated with a low risk of premature health problems and the energy and ability to participate comfortably in a variety of physical activities. In a more detailed description, it is the state of possessing morphological fitness (body composition), bone strength (density), muscular fitness (strength, endurance, power), flexibility (range of motion), motor fitness (agility, speed, balance), cardiovascular fitness (heart, blood, and blood vessels) and metabolic fitness (respiration, metabolism, hormones).

The health-related benefits of a properly planned and executed exercise program are well documented. In a series of articles in the journal *The Physician and Sportsmedicine*, the concept of exercise as medicine was thoroughly explored. In these articles, supported by research findings, physicians are encouraged to prescribe exercise as they would medicine, to prevent or alleviate conditions such as obesity, osteoporosis (bone loss), coronary artery disease, hypertension, diabetes, arthritis and a host of other *hypokinetic* diseases. Often, the prescription of exercise will prove to be less costly, have fewer harmful side effects, and can address a number of different conditions simultaneously compared with the use of drug therapies. The term hypokinetic refers to those conditions typically associated with a lack of exercise or motion (*hypo* = insufficient or under; *kinesis* = movement or motion).

As the figure 1.1 summarizes, exercise and athletic activity can provide benefit in two separate areas; health-related benefits and skill-related benefits.

Figure 1.1 Benefits of Exercise and Athletics

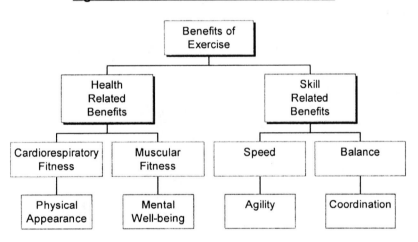

The Risks and Benefits of Exercise

In short, people exercise and athletes train simply because it is good for them. While it is true that regular exercise and athletic participation provide a sure way to better health and fitness for people of all ages, as with the all human activities, exercise and athletics present some degree of risk for injury, illness and, occasionally, sudden death. Such risk shouldn't discourage us from exercising or participating in athletic competition because, with proper knowledge and caution, these risks can be minimized.

4

As with everything we do, exercise is an undertaking that is not without risk. Risk, the statistical chance that something unwanted, dangerous, or unexpected will occur, is something we accept regularly in daily life, often without realizing it. When we choose to drive somewhere rather than walk, we risk injury or death from an auto accident. We chlorinate our public water supplies even though we know that chlorine, and the byproducts formed by its reaction with organic molecules in the water, are harmful to our health. We cook our steaks even though it has been demonstrated that the browning process that occurs during the cooking of meat creates cancer-causing molecules. We accept each of these risks because we have knowledge that the risks are minimal and the benefits gained from these activities are great. Proportionally, the benefits far outweigh the risks and, therefore, we choose to engage in the activity. The situation is similar with exercise. The benefits of exercise, as briefly summarized above, are certain and are great. The risks, although real, occur in only rare circumstances and usually with exercising either too hard, incorrectly, or with pre-existing medical conditions. Among the better-known risks are sudden cardiac death, exercise-induced bronchospasm, menstrual irregularities, gastrointestinal disturbances, hematuria (blood in the urine), and musculoskeletal strains, sprains, dislocations and fractures. For example, research shows us that the relative rate of injury during participation in school-based sports is 8.6 for males, 4.7 for females, when compared with all other non-sleeping activities. Although relatively rare, exercise-related deaths among healthy athletes make for big news stories so that many of us were made aware of the exercise-induced deaths of college basketball star Hank Gathers, Boston Celtic basketball player Reggie Lewis, figure skater Sergei Grinkov and marathon runner Jim Fixx. With the aid of a pre-exercise medical evaluation, proper instruction and technique, a gradual start-up, and appropriate moderation, risks can be minimized and benefits maximized.

Table 1.1. Some Selected Benefits of a Well Planned Exercise Program

Calculating Relative Risk

What is meant by a relative risk of 4.7 for young women participating in school-based sports activities? Relative risk is measurement indicating the ratio of injury incidence during participation in some activity compared with the injury incidence among a comparison group not participating in that activity.

$$\text{Relative Risk} = \frac{\text{injury rate among those participating}}{\text{injury rate among those not participating}}$$

Assume that under normal conditions the incidence of stress fracture among young women is 1 per 675,000 young women per year. This would calculate to a rate of .0000015 (1/675,000). Among those who participate in high school or college sports, the measured rate of stress fracture occurrence was determined to be 1 per 150,000 participants per year, a rate of .000007 (1/150,000).

The relative risk of stress fracture among female school athletes would then be calculated as:

$$\text{Relative Risk} = \frac{.000007}{.0000015} = 4.7$$

A relative risk of 4.7 indicates that, according to these data, a young woman has a 4.7 times greater risk of being injured during a school sporting event than during all other activities combined.

It is important for both the exerciser and the personal trainer to take appropriate steps to minimize these risks and one of the best ways to do so is to first understand the factors that contribute to such risk and at what level each individual's existing risk status is. One of the simplest ways to assess preexisting risk prior to beginning an exercise program is to administer the ***Physical Activity Readiness Questionnaire***, or the ***PAR-Q*** for short, a simple seven question evaluation form developed by the Canadian Society for Exercise Physiology. These questions, answered by either a "yes" or "no", seek to assess the participant's current health status with respect to cardiovascular, musculoskeletal, neurological conditions.

If any one question in the PAR-Q is answered with a "yes", then the person should not begin a training program without first obtaining professional medical clearance. The PAR-Q test can be found in Activity 1 at the end of this book and can be found at the Canadian Society for Exercise Physiology's web site, *www.csep.forms.asp*.

As an alternative to the PAR-Q, The American Heart Association (AHA) in cooperation with the American College of Sports Medicine (ACSM) have developed a 33 question, self-administered, evaluation form known as the ***AHA/ACSM Health/Fitness Facility Preparticipation Screening Questionnaire***. The AHA/ACSM questionnaire seeks information about a person's medical history, current cardiovascular disease symptoms, other current health issues, and current cardiovascular risks including activity level, blood pressure and cholesterol levels, and family history of heart disease. As with the PAR-Q, answering yes to any one of the questions will require a physical examination and physician's clearance prior to beginning an exercise or athletic training program. A copy of the ***AHA/ACSM Health/Fitness Facility Preparticipation Screening Questionnaire*** can be found at the ACSM website, *www.acsm-msse.org/pt/pt-core/template-journal/msse/media/0698c.htm*.

While the PAR-Q is quick and easy to administer, and while the AHA/ASCM Health/Fitness Questionnaire is only slightly more complicated, a much more comprehensive screening instrument exists which may provide a more valid estimate of risk. Considered to be the gold standard of such risk assessment instruments is the American College of Sports Medicine's (ACSM) ***Risk Stratification*** protocol. The ACSM Risk Stratification protocol involves taking a history of information as with the PAR-Q and AHA/ACSM Preparticipation Screening Questionnaire, categorizing risk into one of three levels, or strata (thus, risk stratification), and limiting exercise intensity to specific levels depending on the risk stratification category.

Among the risk factors considered in the ACSM Risk Stratification protocol are family history of cardiovascular disease including heart attack (***myocardial infarction***), heart bypass operation, or any death from cardiovascular disease in a male relative 55 years of age or younger or female relative 65 years of age or younger. Other cardiovascular risk factors include smoking habits (either current smoker or having quit within only the past six months), blood pressure (***hypertension***), and high cholesterol levels (***hypercholesterolemia***). In addition being overweight (classified by Body Mass Index -discussed in Chapter 3), and exercise habits (not currently exercising) are seen as additional risk factors. In addition to the above history,

TheACSM Risk Stratification process also checks for any current symptoms of cardiovascular or respiratory disease including chest pains (***angina***) or shortness of breath when resting or under only mild exertion, dizziness or fainting (***syncope***), painful breathing while lying on your back (***orthopnea***), or while sleeping (***dyspnea***), swelling of the ankles (*edema*), abnormal heartbeats, sometimes so powerful that they can be felt by an individual within their chest (*palpitations*), or a rapid heartbeat at rest (*tachycardia*).

Table 1.2. ACSM Risk Stratification Factors

Risk Factors	
Family History	Family History of Cardiovascular Disease
	Cardiovascular related death in male relative ≤ 55 years
	Cardiovascular related death in female relative ≤ 65 years
Smoking	Current smoker or quit within past 6 months
Overweight Status	Body Mass Index of ≥ 30 or waist circumference of ≥ 100 cm
Hypertension	Systolic Blood Pressure ≥ 140 mmHg, or Diastolic ≥ 90 mmHg or taking blood pressure lowering medications
High Cholesterol	Total cholesterol ≥ 200 mg/dL or LDL ≥ 35 mg/dL or taking cholesterol lowering medications
Diabetes	Fasting blood glucose ≥ 110 mg/dL
Lifestyle	Sedentary lifestyle with no exercise or regular physical activity
Signs or Symptoms	
Angina	Pain in chest, neck, jaw, arms
Pulmonary	Shortness of breath at rest or under mild exertion
Orthopnea	Painful breathing while lying on back
Dyspnea	Painful breathing during sleep
Syncope	Dizziness
Edema	Swelling of ankles due to fluid build-up
Tachycardia	Rapid heart beat
Palpitations	Abnormal, powerful heartbeats felt in the chest

Once the screening process has been completed, the individual's risk level, or strata, is determined. Table 1.3, below, can be used to classify the risk category. If an individual has no symptoms (asymptomatic) and if they have no more than one risk factor an, if they are male and 45 years of age or less, or female and 55 years of age or less, they would be classified as low risk. Individuals would be classified a moderate risk if they were any male, 45 years of age or older, any female 55 years of age or older, or anyone, regardless of age, with two or more risk factors. Any person, regardless of age or risk factor, with even one sign or symptom of a cardiovascular, respiratory, or metabolic disease would be classified as high risk.

Table 1.3. ACSM Risk Stratification Categories

Risk Stratification	Based Upon the Presence of the Following Risk Factors
Low Risk	-Men under 45 or women under 55 -With no symptoms -And no more than 1 risk factor
Moderate Risk	-All Men 45 or older and women 55 or older -Or anyone with 2 or more risk factors
High Risk	-Anyone with one or more signs or symptoms -Or any existing cardiovascular, respiratory or metabolic disease

Finally, based upon the ACSM Risk Stratification category, an individual's exercise or training program would carry the following restrictions.

Table 1.4. ACSM Risk Stratification Outcomes

	Low Risk	Moderate Risk	High Risk
Engage in Moderate Exercise	Approved	Approved	Physician's Clearance Recommended
Engage in Vigorous Exercise	Approved	Physician's Clearance Recommended	Physician's Clearance Recommended
Submaximal Evaluation Test	Not Necessary	Not Necessary	Recommended
Maximal Evaluation Test	Not Necessary	Recommended	Recommended

For the purpose of the Table above, moderate exercise is defined as any activity performed at the level of 3-6 METs or that can be comfortably sustained for 45 minutes. Vigorous exercise would be considered to be activities conducted at a level of greater than 6 METs or which are sustainable for only 20-30 minutes.

The submaximal evaluation test consists of a treadmill test conducted at a plateau of no more than 80% of the predicted maximum heart rate. In maximal evaluation testing the level of challenge is continually raised eventually approaching the predicted maximum heart rate.

Summary of Benefits

While there are, of course, risks associated with exercise and athletic performance they are certainly outweighed by the numerous, demonstrated benefits, among which are the following.

Musculoskeletal Benefits
Increased muscular strength
Increased bone density (Calcium storage)
Increased flexibility
Increased muscle blood supply (collateral vessels)
Increased muscle mitochondria and aerobic enzymes
Increased myoglobin, ATP, creatine phosphate
Increased resistance to muscle and skeletal injuries
Increased lean body mass (less fat - more muscle)

Cardiac Benefits
Increased heart muscle strength (myocardial efficiency)
Increased cardiac muscle blood supply (size and number of blood vessels)
Decreased resting heart rate
Decreased exercising heart rate
Reduced susceptibility to abnormal rhythms

Blood and Blood Vessel Benefits
Increased red blood cell volume
Increased blood oxygen content

Reduced clotting (heart attack and stroke)
Reduced serum triglycerides (fats), cholesterol, LDL's
Increased HDL's
Reduced blood pressure

Respiratory System Benefits
Increased pulmonary blood supply
Increased diffusion across alveolar wall
Increased functional capacity (volume) of lungs
Decreased residual volume (nonfunctional capacity)

Endocrine System Benefits
Increase Glucose tolerance
Increase thyroid gland function
Increase pituitary growth hormone production
Increased plasma insulin concentration
Increased hormone receptor binding sites
Decreased plasma glucagon concentration

Neural Benefits
Increase tolerance to stress
Increase satisfaction with life
Reduce tendency for depression

Other
Reduction in the incidence of cancer
Improved bowel function
Improved body temperature regulation
Decreases severity of allergic reactions

The Science of Exercise and Fitness

The development of new knowledge about the influence of exercise on human health and fitness and the refinement of training techniques to enhance athletic performance are ongoing processes being carried out in laboratories and training centers around the world. As with the development of new scientific knowledge and the testing and dissemination of new medical procedures, the results of this continuous improvement in the science of exercise and fitness are published in peer-reviewed research journals. Each year, approximately 10,000 research papers on exercise and fitness are published in over 300 journals. Found in these publications are a variety of reports ranging from the presentation of original scientific and clinical research findings to comprehensive review articles synthesizing and summarizing the results of several original reports on a focused topic area.

Table 1.5 highlights some of the more notable research journals referenced by professionals in the exercise and fitness fields.

Table 1.5. Selected Research Journals

American Journal of Sports Medicine
Applied research in Coaching and Athletics
British Journal of Sports Medicine
European Journal of Applied Physiology
Exercise Physiology
International Journal of Physical Fitness
International Journal of Sport Nutrition
Isokinetics and Exercise Science
Journal of Aging and Physical Activity
Journal of Applied Biomechanics
Journal of Applied Sport Psychology
Journal of Athletic Training
Journal of Physical Education, Recreation and Dance
Journal of Sport and Exercise Psychology
Journal of Sports Sciences
Journal of Strength and Conditioning
Medicine and Science in Sports and Exercise
Physician and Sportsmedicine
Sports Medicine
Sports Science Reviews

Some of what we know about the benefits of exercise and athletic participation come from epidemiological studies in which populations of people are evaluated, either on a one-time basis (cross-sectional study) or repeatedly over a long period of time (longitudinal study). Three of the more well-known and well-referenced studies are the *Framingham Heart Study* the *National Health and Nutrition Examination Survey (NHANES), and the Nurses' Health Study*. The Framingham Heart Study was begun in 1948 and identified a representative sample of just over 5,000 people between the ages of 30 and 60 who were residents of Framingham, Massachusetts. For over fifty-two years these Framingham residents have been studied in order to follow the development of any cardiovascular diseases and to try and determine their cause. These 5,000 participants have undergone regular physical examinations, blood tests, X-rays and electrocardiograms and have had almost all aspects of their diet and lifestyle analyzed. It was through the Framingham Heart Study that we observed the links between heart disease and smoking, high fat diets, blood pressure, cholesterol level, HDL/LDL cholesterol carrier ratio, and lack of exercise. In 1971, 5,000 children of the original study group members and their spouses became part of the Framingham study and will provide data into the study's second century.

In 1971, the first of four National Health and Nutrition Examination Surveys (NHANES) was undertaken in order to provide information about the state of health and the diet of the American people. The study, which involved physical examinations and clinical testing of approximately 5,000 people, continued for three years. Follow-up studies were conducted between 1976-1980 (NHANES II) and 1988-1994 (NHANES III). NHANES IV began in 1999. Begun in 1976 with phase I and renewed in 1989 with phase II, the Nurses' Health Study involved 117,000 female nurses and studied the long-term impacts of diet and lifestyle on health.

Professional Organizations and Certifications

Professionals involved in the exercise and fitness industries are represented by a number of professional organizations and have a variety of professional certification options. Within the ever-expanding spectrum of such organizations and certifications, several are generally recognized as being the most legitimate and prestigious. In alphabetical order, these are:

American Council on Exercise (ACE): The American Council on Exercise is committed to promoting active, healthy lifestyles and their positive effects on the mind, body and spirit. ACE pledges to enable all segments of society to enjoy the benefits of physical activity and protect the public against unsafe and ineffective fitness products and instruction. The ACE offers examinations and certification for *personal trainers, clinical exercise specialists, group fitness instructors,* and *lifestyle and weight management consultants.* The Council produces two publications, *ACE Fitness Matters* and *ACE Certified News.* More information on ACE can be found at their web site: *www.acefitness.org*

American College of Sports Medicine (ACSM): The goal of the ACSM is to promote and integrate scientific research, education and practical applications of sports medicine and exercise science to maintain and enhance physical performance, fitness, health and quality of life. The ACSM provides training and certification in the following categories: Exercise Specialist, Exercise Leader, Health/Fitness Instructor, Health/Fitness Director, Advanced Personal Trainer, Exercise and the Older Adult, and Nutrition and Exercise. The organization publishes the very highly regarded journal, *Medicine and Science in Sports and Exercise.* The ACSM web site is: *www.acsm.org*

Aerobics and Fitness Association of America (AFAA): The AFAA provides educational workshops, home study programs and certifications for aerobics instructors, personal trainers, step instructors, weight training instructors, and kickboxing instructors. Over 145,000 fitness professionals have been certified by the AFAA. The association publishes the *American Fitness Magazine.* More information can be found at the association's web site : *www.afaa.com*

IDEA:The Health and Fitness Source: When first established, IDEA was an acronym but has since come to be simply the organization's name. IDEA's mission is to support the world's leading health and fitness professionals with credible information, education, career development and leadership to help enhance the quality of life worldwide through safe, effective fitness and healthy lifestyle programs. IDEA publishes a monthly magazine for fitness professionals titled IdeaSource. The organization's web address is *www.ideafit.com*

International Fitness Professionals Association (IFPA): The IFPA is an organization dedicated to providing the most practical and scientifically based fitness education and fitness certifications for the fitness professional and the general public. The IFPA provides training and certification as *certified master trainer.* Information about the IFPA can be obtained from the association's web site: *www.ifpa-fitnes.com*

International Sports Sciences Association (ISSA): The ISSA is committed to setting and developing standards within the fitness industry and on providing access to the highest quality certification and continuing education programs. The ISSA offers ten specialized certification programs for fitness professionals including specialties for children, senior citizens and the physically challenged. More information can be found at the association's web site: *www.FitnessEducation.com*

National Strength and Conditioning Association (NSCA): The National Strength and Conditioning Association is an educational organization established to provide resources and opportunities for professionals in the strength and conditioning field and to serve as a clearinghouse for the dissemination of strength training and conditioning and personal training information. The association's web site is: *www.nsca-cc.org*

Selected Readings:

Elrick, H., **Commentary: Exercise is Medicine**, *The Physician and Sportsmedicine*, Vol. 24, No. 2, February 1996, http://www.physsportsmed.com/issues/feb_96/elrick.htm

Roos, R.J., **The Surgeon General's Report: A Prime Resource for Exercise Advocates**. *The Physician and Sportsmedicine*, Vol. 24, No. 4, April 1997, http://www.physsportsmed.com/issues/1997/04Apr/roos.htm

Gettman, L.R., **Economic Benefits of Physical Activity**, *President's Council on Physical Fitness and Sports Research Digest*, Series 2, No. 7, September 1996, http://www.indiana.edu/~preschal/digests/sept96/sept96digest.html

O'Connor, F.G., J.P. Kugler and R.G. Oriscello, **Sudden Death in Young Athletes: Screening for the Needle in a Haystack**, *American Family Physician*, June 1998, http://www.aafp.org/afp/980600ap/oconnor.html

Chapter 2

Adaptation to Exercise

Chapter Contents

- The General Adaptation Syndrome
- Exercise Intensity and Volume
- Overtraining and Rest
- Sleep
- Timing of Exercise Sessions
- Aerobic vs. Anaerobic Exercise
- An Idealized Exercise Program
- The Importance of Warm-up and Cool-Down
- Patterns of Training
- Exercise and the Immune System
- Medical Clearance for Exercise and Training
- Selected Readings

Learning Objectives

The material in this chapter will allow you to:

- Understand the body's response to physical stress and exercise through the General Adaptation Syndrome
- Understand the components and design of a well-planned exercise program including both the active and resting stages
- Understand why too much exercise is not a good thing
- Understand the various ways of quantifying and measuring exercise
- Plan an exercise or training program to accomplish specific goals
- Understand the need for medical consultation

The General Adaptation Syndrome

The body is a dynamic system that is capable of sensing and responding to the demands of its environment. The body will, in general, respond to an environmental stress by developing the ability to better cope with that stress in the future, a mechanism that allowed our ancestors to survive under conditions of adversity. The purpose of exercise or athletic training programs is to stress the body or a bodily system so that it responds in a positive, predictable way, a phenomenon known as *adaptation*. For this to occur, the stress must be of sufficient magnitude to overload the system, but not so great as to push the body to the point of injury or tissue damage.

Stress is a normal and expected part of life; one which we have evolved mechanisms to cope with. Stress refers to any situation that threatens to disrupt the body's well-being, stability, or homeostasis. Stress can be caused by environmental factors, physiological factors, and mental factors. Any specific factor that causes stress is known as a *stressor*.

Environmental Stress: heat/cold; noise; toxins; radiation; disrupted light cycles

Physiological Stress: pain; hunger; infection; heightened work load

Mental Stress: fear; anxiety;

Like so many other things in life, small amounts of stress are actually beneficial while large amounts of stress, or small stresses experienced over a prolonged period of time, are not. Stress which is positive, resulting in actual anatomical and physiological improvements in the human body are referred to as *eustress*, and may be caused by physical stressors such as resistance exercise, aerobic exercise, calorie deprivation, all of which can improve physical fitness; mental stressors such as studying for an exam the desired result of which will be new long-term memory storage; or environmental stressors such as chicken pox infection which will bring about long-term immunity.

Negative stressors, resulting in physiological harm are referred to as *distress*, and may include any of the above, in excess.

An example of the body's response to a stress can be seen by looking at the result of repeatedly lifting weights, as is done in strength training. The stress that this places on the musculoskeletal system results in the enlargement (hypertrophy) of muscles so that they are better able to deal with that stress (heavy weights) in the future. In karate training, participants often perform push-ups on their knuckles rather than on the palms of their hands. This stress results in the development of calluses (thicker skin) on the knuckles thereby hardening the striking surface of the fist and also stressing and overdeveloping the muscles, tendons and ligaments of the wrist and forearm. Prolonged aerobic exercises such as running or swimming stress the muscular, cardiovascular and respiratory systems which can adapt to the stress by synthesizing new energy-releasing muscle enzymes, thereby increasing the muscular strength of the heart, enlarging the existing blood vessels, developing new ones, and increasing lung capacity.

The phenomenon of adaptation as described above was named the *General Adaptation Syndrome (GAS)* by Dr. Hans Selye, a prominent physiologist. The GAS consists of three levels of response to a stress, these being:

1. **Alarm Reaction**: The initial response of the body to the stress that involves the mobilization of bodily systems to cope with the stress. For example, an increased heart and respiratory rate during strenuous or aerobic activities. The alarm reaction is most often mediated through quick-acting, short-term, nervous system responses.

2. **Resistance Development**: The body improves its ability and builds reserve capacities to better resist the stress in the future. This will only occur if the stress is above a critical threshold or load level. Examples would be the development of larger muscles, a stronger heart and more circulating red blood cells. It is this level, resistance development, which is the goal of an exercise or training program. The longer-term and slower-onset resistance development changes are most often mediated through hormonal responses.

3. **Exhaustion**: As a result of overtraining, the body suffers from soft tissue injuries, sprains, strains, fractures and distress.

The basic doctrine of training and exercise is known as the *overload principle*. As described above, to achieve the goal of resistance development, the body must be stressed above a critical threshold or load level, that is to say that the stress must be taken to the point of overload. There are four factors through which we can measure or quantify the amount of stress or load in exercise activities. These include:

Load : increasing the weight, speed, distance, etc.

Repetitions: increasing the number of times the load is administered in an exercise session

Rest: decreasing the time interval between repetitions

Frequency: increasing the number of training or exercise sessions per week

There are three important characteristics of the general adaptation syndrome and of the overload training principle which are important in developing or understanding an exercise or training program. These are:

Specificity: Stressing a particular system or part of the body will not develop another system or part of the body. For example, performing curls with the right arm will do nothing to develop the left biceps muscle.

Reversibility: Inactivity for a period of time will lead to a progressive decline in capacity and performance.

Individuality: The adaptation to a particular stress will differ among individuals.

Therefore, we can simply summarize the purpose of exercise or athletic training as being the process of stressing the body in specific ways and in specific amounts so as to push it into specific modes of resistance development.

The characteristic response to stress as described by the general adaptation syndrome is sometimes referred to as the *SAID* principle. SAID is an acronym that stands for <u>S</u>pecific <u>A</u>daptation to <u>I</u>mposed <u>D</u>emands. Once again we see that the benefits derived from an exercise or training program are specific to the stress or demands placed upon the body. Any well-planned exercise or training regimen must take these factors into consideration.

Blisters and Calluses: The General Adaptation Syndrome at Work

The General Adaptation Syndrome (GAS) is characterized by both short-term (alarm reaction) and long-term (resistance development) responses of the body to stress. Let's look closely at one particularly characteristic response. When the hands are subjected to the vigorous stressful forces of friction, compression, and abrasion, as might occur when chopping wood with an axe, the initial and immediate response is the formation of a blister. The blister, a fluid filled pocket that develops between layers of the skin, forms rapidly – within minutes – and represents the body's attempt to cushion the fragile underlying structures (blood vessels, nerves, connective tissues) from being damaged by the stresses of friction, compression and abrasion. In addition, the blister causes pain when compressed providing the body with a reinforcing signal to stop the stressful activity. The blister is an example of the alarm reaction stage. If the stresses continue to be applied with frequency and intensity over time, the body will respond with a longer-term adaptation that will enhance its ability to deal with this stress in the future. Genetic signals within the lower layers of the skin will promote the start of cell division and form stronger adhesions between the skin cells. Connective tissues under the skin will become denser and stronger. A thick, tough callous will develop, characteristic of the resistance development phase of the GAS.

Exercise Intensity and Volume

The level or severity of exercise or training is frequently measured in terms of the training *intensity*, *volume*, *frequency*, and *mode*.

The exercise or training intensity refers to the amount of physical work performed during a single exercise or training session, for example, the weight that is lifted, the speed at which laps are run or swam, or the magnitude of the elevation of heart rate. Intensity is therefore synonymous with the parameter of load as described above.

Training volume refers to the quantity of training that is performed, for example, the number of repetitions and sets that are lifted, regardless of weight, the number of laps run or swam regardless of the speed at which they are performed, or the total number of calories expended. Training or exercise volume encompasses the parameters of repetitions and rest described above along with the duration of the training session.

Frequency, as described earlier, refers to the number of training sessions per week.

Mode refers to the specific type of activity that was performed, for example, isotonic or isometric contractions, jogging or sprints, backstroke or butterfly, aerobic or anaerobic.

The intensity of an exercise or training session can be quantified in several ways. Table 2.1 indicates three such ways that correlate exercise intensity level with either heart rate, rating of perceived exertion (RPE), or metabolic equivalent (MET).

It is common experience that our *heart rate (HR)* increases upon exertion or activity in a proportional manner, that is, the greater the amount of exertion or activity, the greater the heart rate will be elevated. Heart rate during exercise is typically measured by taking either the radial (inside of the wrist) or carotid (side of the neck) pulse rate. Such measurements of heart rate can be used to help determine the intensity of an activity. Low levels of activity will be associated with near-resting heart rates, typically around 60-70 beats/minute (30-35% of maximum heart rate). Very strenuous activities will elevate the heart rate to near maximum, typically around 180-200 beats/min.

The *rating of perceived exertion (RPE),* measured on a scale running from 6 to 20 developed by the psychologist P. Borg, is a self-assessment that individuals can use to determine how hard they are working. One needs to simply pick the number on the scale that corresponds best with the amount of they feel they are expending. On this scale, your perception of exerting minimal if any effort would be rated at six; at twenty your perception would be that you are exerting yourself as hard as you can. The Borg RPE range of between 12 and 18 corresponds to an exercise level of approximately 60%-90% of maximal effort. In fact, the Borg scale was developed so that it closely corresponds to your predicted heart rate at various levels of exertion; adding a zero to your RPE should give you your estimated heart rate. Therefore, an RPE of 6 should reflect a 60 beat/min heart rate while an RPE of 18 should reflect a 180 beat/min heart rate.

Fig. 2.1 Borg Rating of Perceived Exertion Scale

6	7	8	9	10	11	12	13	14	15	16	17	18	19	20
very, very light			very light			fairly light		somewhat hard		hard		very hard		very, very hard

The *metabolic equivalent (MET)* provides a way of measuring exercise intensity as a function of the exercise-induced change in the body's metabolic rate. The metabolic rate, which will be explained in greater detail later on, is a measure of the rate at which the body converts the energy stored in the foods we eat into a useable form for our muscles. Since this conversion is performed as a "just-in-time" process, the metabolic rate will fluctuate in direct proportion to the exercise or workload. If the resting metabolic rate is considered to be the baseline, or 1, the exercise-induced increases in metabolic rate are considered to be multiples of 1. A level of exertion that requires three times the energy at rest will raise the metabolic rate by three times and be referred to as 3 METS.

The **maximum volume of oxygen utilized (VO$_2$ $_{max}$)** during exercise is yet another way of determining the exercise intensity. As working muscles contract at increasingly faster rates the volume of oxygen they use increases as does both the heart rate and respiration rate. VO2max can be measured directly, or calculated from treadmill or running exercises.

Table 2.1 – Classification of Physical Activity Intensity

	Maximal H.R.	R.P.E.	M.E.T.
Intensity	%		
Very Light	<30	<9	1
Light	30-49	9-10	2-5
Moderate	50-69	10-12	6-9
Hard	70-89	13-16	10-13
Very Hard	90-99	17-19	14-16
Maximal	100	20	17+

Overtraining and Rest

The previous sections stressed the importance of working out at the appropriate frequency, and with sufficient loads or at sufficient intensity, so as to stress the body in a positive way. While overload of this type is essential for improvement, or resistance development, training with too high a load or at too great an intensity will be counterproductive. If sufficient time is not allowed for rest between exercise or training sessions, or if training load or intensity is too high, *overtraining syndrome* may result. The results of overtraining are typically a high frequency of injury at its worst, or by lingering joint and muscle soreness, general lethargy, altered mood, and altered immune status. In fact, the general symptoms of overtraining closely mimic the condition of a lack of physical fitness.

Figure 2.2 illustrates the relationship between the relative benefit and harm associated with increasing exercise intensity and volume. The graph presents an analysis of the expected results (solid lines) in response to a continually increasing exercise intensity and volume. Initially, there is little performance and little risk of injury that can be expected from exercise with a very low intensity and volume.

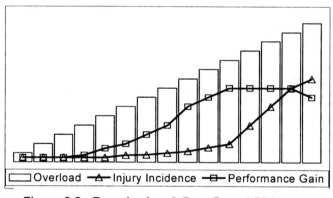

Figure 2.2. Exercise Load, Benefit and Risk

As the quantity of exercise is increased (represented by the bars on the graph) performance gain also increases, in relative proportion to the increasing exercise. As intensity and volume are further increased, the risk of injury also begins to increase and, when the maximum effective intensity and volume are surpassed, performance gain drops and injury risk increases tremendously.

While it is important to exercise and, after a period of acclimation, to exercise hard, an equally important part of a well-balanced exercise or training program is the provision for adequate rest. Rest, as referenced here, pertains to both the time off from training (non-training or rest days) as well as sleep.

The stresses placed on the body's systems, organs, and tissues during an exercise or training session often result in minor, microscopic trauma or damage. It is during the natural repair process that the body develops the adaptive changes that allow it to better respond to these stresses in the future. Therefore, we can see that the general adaptation syndrome is a two-stage process, stage one being the application of the stress (during exercise) and stage two being the development of the adaptive changes (during rest). *Simply stated, exercise and training will break you down and make you weaker; it is the period of rest that follows the training session that will build you up and make you stronger.* The process of rebuilding the body's tissues following a damage-inducing period of exercise is known as *adaptive reconstruction* and occurs during the periods of rest that follow an exercise or training session. Therefore, in a well-balanced exercise or training program, rest should be considered as important as exercise. It is generally recommended that the work : rest ratio should be 1 : 1, that is one day during which training is performed and one day off that follows.

Sleep

Recent studies have shown that insufficient sleep may adversely affect overall health in a number of ways including the impairment of the ability to process glucose, excess insulin secretion, increased body fat storage, elevated secretion of the stress hormone cortisol, and impairment of immune function. Growth hormone, secreted by the pituitary gland and contributing to tissue repair and growth, is an important mediator of the benefits of exercise. The secretion of growth hormone declines naturally with age and this decline parallels certain characteristic age-related changes including the reduction in lean body mass (muscle loss), an increase in body fat percentage, and increased levels of harmful LDL cholesterol. The secretion of growth hormone is stimulated by exercise and by sleep. Sleep deprivation can therefore lead to a premature onset of these age-related changes and can counterbalance any benefits gained through exercise.

Human sleep patterns consist of five phases; Stage 1, Stage 2, Stage 3, Stage 4, and REM sleep. *Stage 4 sleep*, also known as *deep or slow-wave sleep*, and which occurs approximately 30-45 minutes after initially falling asleep is an important phase for tissue growth, maintenance and healing. It is during Stage 4 sleep that muscle blood supply increases and growth hormone is released in large quantities. Research has shown that following periods of vigorous physical activity the length of time spent in Stage 4 sleep increases as the body's tissues repair themselves under the principles of the general adaptation syndrome. A Stage 4 sleep cycle will last for approximately 30 minutes after which you begin to drift back through Stage 3 and Stage 2 sleep. About two hours after first falling asleep you will have passed back through Stage 2 and will enter *REM sleep*, so named because it is associated with **r**apid **e**ye **m**ovements and generally heightened brain activity. It is during REM sleep that most dreaming occurs and where the brain reviews the activities of the day, categorizes and organizes information that it received during the day, makes sense of what it perceived or learned, discards useless information, and develops new nerve cell connections that consolidate information into memory.

The sequential repetition of patterned muscle movements will result in the development and strengthening of neuromuscular pathways and the development of "*muscle memory*", the ability of the nervous and muscular systems to perform specific activities more quickly and more precisely after training. Recent studies in psychology and neurobiology laboratories have shown that our exposure during the day to new experiences and items of information will not result in long-term learning without the important step of *"consolidation"* that occurs during the deeper phases of the sleep cycle. It follows that our training activities during the day are consolidated into long-term improvements in athletic skill only during the deep phases of sleep.

It is easy to see how adequate amounts of quality sleep form an important part of an exercise or training program and how inadequate sleep, either by disrupted sleep patterns or simply not getting enough sleep, can render a good exercise program useless.

Figure 2.3. Sleep Stages and Implications for Exercise and Training

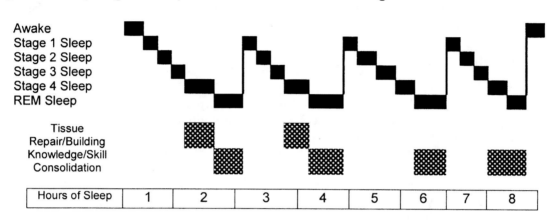

Timing Exercise Sessions

There is some evidence, although not undisputed, that exercising or training at different times of the day, for example in the morning rather than the evening, may influence the effectiveness of the exercise or training session. All living systems appear to be regulated by an internal clock that is set to a cycle of about 24 hours and, in humans, is believed to be located in a region of the brain known as the hypothalamus. The natural body rhythms that follow this clock, sleep and wake cycles, body temperature, blood pressure and hormone release among others, are said to follow a *circadian rhythm* (derived from the Latin *circa* = about, and *dia* = day). As explained elsewhere in this chapter, warmer body temperatures are beneficial to exercise and training and provide one of the reasons why a pre-exercise warm-up period is recommended. In the circadian rhythm of body temperature, the lowest temperatures are found in sleep, during the period of approximately 1 – 3 hours before waking up. Body temperature gradually rises throughout the day and reaches a peak in mid-to-late afternoon, declining through the evening and through the early parts of sleep. Exercise during the afternoon period of peak body temperature has been shown to be the most productive with respect to exercise-related gains. It is during this period that resting heart rate and blood pressure are low, body temperature is elevated, muscles, tendons and ligaments are warm and flexible, nervous system reaction time is quickest, and ratings of perceived exertion for specific activities are lowest. The benefits of a late afternoon exercise, although real, are minimal for those who are not elite athletes and should not overly influence the timing of your exercise. Because of the rerouting of blood flow to the digestive organs and, therefore, away from the muscles following a heavy meal, heavy exercise should be avoided during the period from approximately 90 minutes before a heavy meal to approximately two hours after. Given that any exercise is better than no exercise, and that more exercise is better than less exercise (to a limit), what is important is that you exercise. With the complicated schedules most of us live with it is, quite simply, easier for some to exercise early in the morning - before work, later in the morning – after the kids are off to school, during a mid-day break, or later in the evening - after the events of a hectic day have passed. The simple and proper advice is: exercise when it suits you.

NSAIDs, COX Inhibitors and Pain Relief

As stated earlier, the actual physical stresses of exercise and athletic training will actually damage and physically break down body tissues such as muscle, bone, and connective tissues. It is the repair process that occurs during both active rest and sleep that leads to the build up of strengthened tissues and performance enhancement. Associated with this break down and repair process is physical discomfort and soreness, often referred to a delayed onset muscle soreness (DOMS) but which is also felt in bone and other connective tissue structures as well. A large industry of pain relief medications, including popular over-the-counter painkillers such as aspirin (Bayer, Anacin), naproxen (Aleve), and ibuprofen (Advil, Motrin) and prescription drugs such as Celebrex, are targeted towards athletes and exercisers. While these medications are effective at their intended purpose, the relief of pain and discomfort, they have an unexpected, and unwelcome, side effect that many don't know about. They inhibit the tissue repair and rebuilding process as effectively as they inhibit pain and discomfort.

These agents, classified as non steroidal anti inflammatory drugs (NSAIDs) work through their inhibition of an enzyme known as cyclooxygenase and are therefore referred to as cyclooxgenxase inhibitors (COX inhibitors, for short). Unfortunately, the enzyme these medications inhibit is responsible for both the pain and discomfort mechanism as well as the tissue repair and building mechanism. A growing body of research is showing that athletes who engage in vigorous and well-designed exercise programs and who get the proper forms and amount of rest will not show the expected benefits if they took NSAID or COX inhibitor medications to alleviate post-exercise soreness.

Fig 2.4. NSAID Action

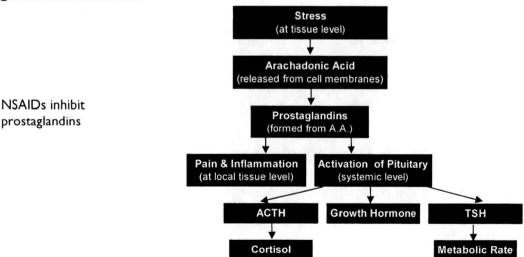

Aerobic vs. Anaerobic Exercise

The single most beneficial type of exercise is that which has positive impacts or benefits on the heart, circulation and respiratory systems in addition to muscular, skeletal and psychological benefit. This type of exercise is called *aerobic exercise* for reasons that will be explained in more detail in the chapter on bioenergetics. Briefly, aerobic exercise involves a shift in the way the body releases energy to fuel the activity. In aerobic exercise, oxygen is utilized to completely breakdown fuel molecules releasing energy and giving off carbon dioxide as a waste product. Aerobic exercise is characterized by a noticeable increase in the rate and depth or respiration, by a pronounced increase in the heart rate or pulse, and by an increase in the amount of body heat generated and subsequent sweating. Examples of aerobic exercise are distance running, bicycling, and cross-country skiing. *Anaerobic exercise* involves an alternative pathway for fueling muscle contraction that does not require oxygen and does not generate carbon dioxide. For this reason, anaerobic exercise does not typically result in prolonged elevated respiration, heart rate, and sweating although these effects may occur briefly. Examples of anaerobic exercise include weight lifting, springboard or platform diving, and yoga.

To be of measurable benefit, aerobic exercise must be performed for at least twenty minutes, three times a week. Increasing the total exercise time from one hour each week to three hours each week brings with it increased benefit but, beyond three hours per week, there is no additional cardiovascular benefit.

For an ideal exercise session, strength building and stretching activities should be added to the aerobic workout.

A Well-Designed Exercise Program

The concept of a single, ideal exercise program for everyone is a fallacy. An exercise program will differ from individual to individual based upon the specific goals that are desired. An exercise program tailored for weight loss will differ from one designed for increasing muscle mass. A program designed to enhance flexibility might differ from one designed to improve cardiorespiratory performance. Some people seek solitary forms of exercise such as distance running while others prefer group or competitive sports such as basketball or martial arts. The information provided in the following chapters should prove to be of value in understanding and planning an exercise regimen targeted towards your own specific goals.

While it is true that the specifics of an exercise program will vary among individuals, there are certain generalities that most exercise programs should have in common in order to maximize their benefits and reduce the risk of injury.

An exercise program should consist of three phases as detailed in Figure 2.5 and illustrated graphically in Figure 2.6.

Figure 2.5. <u>Suggested Components of a Well-Balanced Exercise Program</u>

<u>**Warm-up and stretch**</u>
> 5 - 10 minutes of slow exercise and stretch to warm muscles,
> > improve flexibility and increase circulation

<u>**Exercise to overload**</u>
> (a) *muscular strength*: at least two 20 min. sessions per week
> > exercising all the major skeletal muscle groups with resistance exercises
> (b) *muscular endurance*: at least three 30 min. sessions per week which
> > include repetitive exercises such as calisthenics, push-ups, sit-ups, etc.
> (c) *cardiorespiratory endurance*: at least three 20 minute workouts of
> > continuous aerobic activities such as swimming, running, rope-jumping,etc.

<u>**Cool down and stretch**</u>
> 5 - 10 minutes of low-level exercise and stretching to return heart
> rate to normal, prevent muscle soreness and enhance flexibility

Figure 2.6. <u>Graphic Display of a Typical Exercise Session</u>

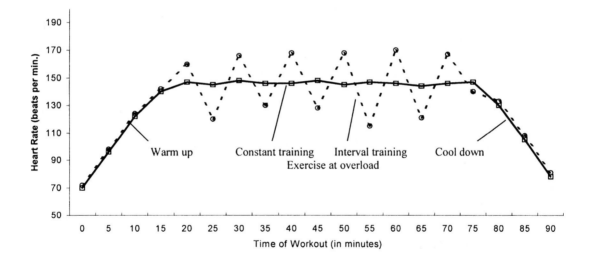

The Importance of Warm-up and Cool-Down

As seen above, a well-designed exercise program should include an initial period of warm-up prior to engaging in vigorous exercise, and a period of cool-down following the exercise. The reasons for this are varied. At its simplest, warm muscles, tendons, and ligaments are more supple, pliable and flexible at warmer temperatures and benefit from an increased blood flow as small vessels dilate. The recommended activities of gentle movement and stretching as part of a pre-exercise warm-up, by increasing the temperature of these structures, will make exercising more comfortable and lessen the likelihood of injuries. In addition, the chemical reactions that provide the energy for muscle activity are more effective and progress more rapidly at warmer temperatures. Oxygen, carried in the blood by the hemoglobin protein, is released more readily at warmer temperatures. Thus, the pre-exercise warm-up can provide more energy during exercise, allow you to work more vigorously and longer, and increase the benefits of the exercise session. Finally, muscles warmed to over 38 °C (normal body temperature is 37 °C), contain less of the waste lactic acid which contributes to muscle fatigue and is produced during intense muscle activity. Full warm-up is reached in about 15 minutes and the effects of the warm-up will remain for about 45 minutes if not immediately followed by exercise or, throughout the exercise period.

Similarly, a period of cool-down, where body temperature, blood pressure, and heart rate are allowed to return to normal gradually rather than rapidly, helps to flush lactic acid from the muscles, prevent blood pooling in the muscles, and allow the stress hormones released during exercise to gradually return to resting levels putting less strain on the heart. The activities during cool-down should be less vigorous than during exercise, include stretching, may be either continuous or intermittent, and should last for approximately 15-20 minutes.

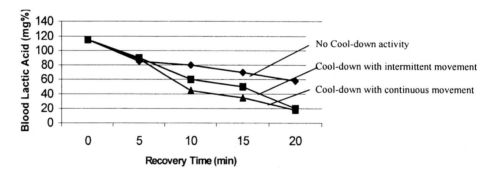

Fig. 2.7. Cool-Down. A cool-down period with low-level activity clears lactic acid faster than with no activity. The activity during cool-down can be continuous or intermittent.

In 1998 The American College of Sports Medicine (ASCM), a professional society of physicians and scientists who practice and study sports medicine published a set of revised guidelines for improving physical fitness. The guidelines recommend that an effective physical fitness program include the following:

Figure 2.8. ACSM Guidelines for Exercise

Aerobic Component: (Using large muscle groups)
<u>Frequency</u>: 3 - 5 times per week
<u>Duration</u>: 20 - 60 minutes of aerobic activity dependent upon intensity
<u>Intensity</u>: 50 - 85% of maximal O_2 uptake or 65 - 90% of maximal heart rate
<u>Activities</u>: Bicycling, Jogging, Rowing, Stair Climbing, Stepping
Resistance Component:
<u>Frequency</u>: 2 - 3 times per week (minimum)
<u>Intensity</u>: 1 set of 8 - 12 repetitions (minimum)
<u>Activities</u>: Free weights, weight machines or calisthenics working the major muscle groups
Flexibility Component:
<u>Frequency</u>: 2 - 3 times per week (minimum)
<u>Activities</u>: Static and/or dynamic stretching of the major muscle groups

In the 1990 revision of their 1978 guidelines, the ACSM included the resistance training component that had not been previously recommended. Prior to this, resistance training was seen as having benefit primarily for those whose interest was increasing muscle mass and muscle strength and it was not believed to have significant health benefits. The 1978 guideline revision reflected the new understanding that resistance training was important to strengthen bones and to retain muscle mass. In the 1998 revision a flexibility component was added. The relative benefits of aerobic exercise and of resistance exercise are summarized in Table 2.2 below.

Table 2.2. Relative Benefits of Aerobic and Resistance Exercise

Function / Improvement	Aerobic Exercise	Resistance Exercise
Muscle Strength	+2	+3
Bone Mineral Density	+2	+2
Body Fat %	-2	-1
Serum HDL	+2	+1
Serum LDL	-2	-1
Resting Heart Rate	-2	0
Cardiac Stroke Volume	+2	0
Resting Blood Pressure	-2	-1
VO_2max	+3	+1
Basal Metabolic Rate	+1	+2
Endurance Time	+3	+2

Adapted from ML Polock and KR Vincent. The President's Council on Physical Fitness and Sports Research Digest, Series 2, No.8, Dec 1996

Table 2.2 demonstrates that aerobic exercise has it greatest impact on increasing cardiorespiratory capacity (decreases resting heart rate and blood pressure, increases cardiac stroke volume, VO_2max, and endurance time), improving blood chemistry (increases good cholesterol [HDL] and lowers bad cholesterol [LDL]), reducing body fat and, through muscular tension on the skeleton, increasing bone density and strength. Resistance exercises have their primary benefit on improving muscle strength, enhancing bone density and increasing the resting, or basal, metabolic rate. This last factor is an important one in weight control. Muscle, being a much more active and energy requiring tissue than fat has a high energy demand, even at rest. As the percentage of one's muscle mass increases, the result of resistance training, the total body metabolic rate increases. Each pound of muscle mass added will burn between 35-50 additional Calories per day. Research has shown that men and women who participate in a resistance training program of both the upper and lower body muscles require 15% more calories per day just to maintain their body weight after 12 weeks of training. A program of resistance training, one that replaces fat body tissue with muscle, can help facilitate further body fat loss and weight reduction through the higher metabolic rate. A twelve week study using three groups of overweight men showed that while a diet program alone with moderate calorie restriction was effective at decreasing weight, the weight loss represented a loss of both body fat and body muscle tissues. A combination program of diet and exercise, consisting of both aerobic and resistance activities, led to a decrease in body weight, an increase in muscle strength and a protection against muscle tissue loss, and an increase in aerobic capacity.

Patterns of Training

Among those training for specific athletic or sport activities, or in the recreational exerciser looking for a wide range of health and skill-related benefits, a long-term training routine is typically developed that varies over time with different phases dedicated to developing different capabilities. This technique of varying the training activities over a period of time is known as periodized training, or *periodization*.

An individual workout, perhaps occupying two hours on any given day may consist of a 15 minute period of warm-up, 45 minutes of aerobic activity, 45 minutes of resistance training, and a 15 minute period of cool-down and stretching. This would be referred to as a single *training session*. An athlete may engage in four training sessions per week, each with a slightly different emphasis, for example, on days one and three the resistance training component would be exclusively for the upper body musculature and on days two and four, for the lower body and abdominal musculature. We might even see a variation in the aerobic component, on days one and three perhaps a stationary cycling class (spinning), and on days two and four a session on the Stairmaster. A group of these four slightly different sessions, repeated on a weekly cycle, would constitute a *microcycle*. If an athlete was training for a specific sport, for example baseball, the microcycle above may take place only during the first two months of the off-season. As we near the next playing season, the training sessions will shift to emphasize the incorporation of more sport-specific skill training such as hitting, fielding and agility drills. We might refer to these as training sessions 5, 6, 7 and 8. This change in the nature of the microcycle activities would represent a new phase of training for example, the first phase was to build strength and cardiovascular endurance (training sessions 1,2,3 and 4), the second phase is to build sport-specific abilities (training sessions 5,6,7 and 8). A repeating pattern of microcycles, if one occurs, constitutes a *mesocycle*. On an annual or seasonal basis, the pattern is referred to as a *macrocycle*.

Figure 2.9. Training Cycles

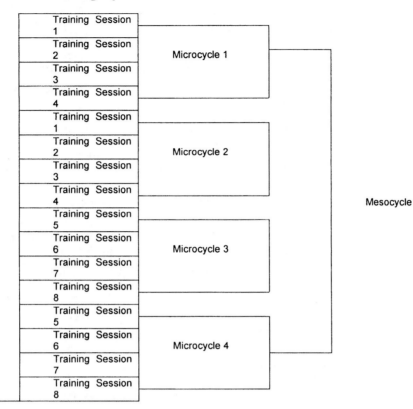

In a typical periodized training program, a competitive athlete would begin formal training during the off season by emphasizing exercises that are targeted towards developing greater muscle mass, or hypertrophy. Hypertrophy training may be continued for 8-12 weeks and generally involves resistance exercises performed with moderate weights and at relatively high repetitions. The specific details and techniques of muscle training will be reviewed in a later chapter. The intent during this initial phase of hypertrophy training is to develop a sufficient muscle mass and muscle endurance to maximize the benefits of strength training which will follow. This period of hypertrophy training would comprise one mesocycle.

Once adequate muscle mass has been developed, the athlete will then move on into a phase of strength training; the next mesocycle. In strength training the exercises are modified to incorporate heavier weights lifted at lower numbers of repetitions. Strength training would then be followed by power training using plyometric exercises as the athlete approached the beginning of the competitive season.

Strength training which follows a period of hypertrophy training has been shown to improve overall strength gains by up to 50% over a strength training program alone.

28

Exercise and the Immune System

Among the beneficial effects of exercise, many of which promote health and longevity, are those relating to the enhancement of immune system function. Numerous research and epidemiological studies conducted in recent years have shown that a program of regular moderate to high intensity exercise will bring about immune system changes that lower our susceptibility to infections as well as reducing the incidence, progression, and spread of cancerous tumors.

The warm, moist, nutrient-rich tissues and fluids of the human body provide bacteria, fungi, viruses and other pathogens with the ideal condition for living and reproducing. Although our skin and mucous membranes provide an effective mechanical and biological barrier to the entry of these pathogens, some still occasionally gain entry through wounds or through other means of penetrating this barrier. Working constantly and vigilantly to protect us when such pathogens attack is our immune system, a network of fixed structures, wandering cells, and an arsenal of chemical agents. The immune system also provides protection against rogue cellular attacks from within, for example, when our own cells become cancerous.

As described in the General Adaptation Syndrome, the exercise-induced benefits on immunesystem function are proportional to exercise intensity, rising gradually with increasing exercise levels and dropping off as the exercise intensity level moves into the overtraining zone as illustrated in Figure 2.9 below.

Figure 2.10. Immune System Effects of Varying Exercise Intensity

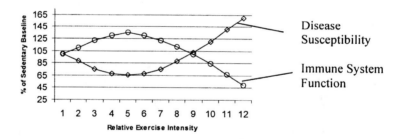

Medical Clearance for Exercise and Training

As described earlier in this chapter, exercise is intended to stress the body's systems so that they adapt in a positive way. This stress can however, prove harmful to individuals with musculoskeletal or cardiorespiratory impairments. Certain individuals should have a medical checkup and receive clearance from a physician before beginning an exercise program. As suggested by the President's Council on Physical Fitness and Sports, a medical clearance is recommended for individuals who meet the following criteria:

    Over 35 years of age
    Inactive for several years
    High Blood Pressure
    Heart Trouble
    Frequent Dizzy Spells

Extreme Breathlessness after mild activity
Arthritis or other bone or joint problems
Severe muscle, ligament or tendon problems
Other known or suspected diseases
Family history of early stroke or heart attack

Selected Readings:

Hopkins, W.G., **Measurement of Training in Competetive Sports**. *Sportscience*, Vol. 2, No.4, 1998, http://www.sportsci.org/jour/9804/wgh.html

Hatfield, F.C., **How They Train: Conditioning Methods of World Champion Boxer Evander Holyfield**. *Sportscience*, September-October 1997, http://www.sportsci.org/news/news9709/hatfield.html

Pollock, et al. **The Recommended Quantity and Quality of Exercise for Developing and Maintaining Cardiorespiratory and Muscular Fitness, and Flexibility in Healthy Adults**. *Medicine and Science in Sports & Exercise*. Vol. 30, No. 6, pp. 975-991, 1998.

Related Fitness Assessment Activities:

Activity 1. Exercise Readiness Assessment

Activity 2. Evaluating Exercise Activity Level

Activity 3. Rating of Perceived Exertion

Chapter 3

Body Type and Composition

Chapter Contents

- Cells and Tissues
- Anatomical Terminology
- Anthropometry
- Body Fat Content and Ideal Body Weight
- Hormones
- Genes
- Selected Readings

Learning Objectives

The material in this chapter will allow you to:

- Understand the structure of the body with respect to cells and tissues
- Understand the use of proper anatomic terminology when referring to body structures
- Understand the various ways of quantitatively describing the body's physical attributes through anthropometry
- Understand the ways in which the body stores fat and the various ways of measuring fat content
- Understand the relationship between body structure and athletic talents
- Understand the relationship between body structure and health
- Understand the influence of hormones, genes, and exercise on body composition
- Understand the need for medical consultation

Cells and Tissues

The human body consists of a mixture of several types of different tissues including *epithelium, fat, muscle* and *bone*. Variations in the relative ratios of these tissues, as well as differences in their structure and distribution, provide each of us with a slightly different body shape and physical appearance. To some extent, these characteristics are genetically determined although exercise training can exert a significant influence. Figure 3.1 shows the variety of different tissues that are found, for example, in a cross-section through the upper arm.

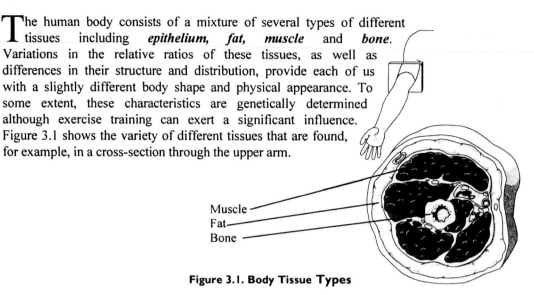

Muscle
Fat
Bone

Figure 3.1. Body Tissue Types

At the most basic biological level, the body is composed of cells, independent living units capable of taking in raw materials, synthesizing new molecules, using energy to perform work, and reproducing to allow for growth and repair. In complex organisms cells come in a wide variety of specialized types, each genetically programmed to carry out one or more vital functions.

Our skin is composed of layers of epithelial cells that protect us from extreme conditions in the environment. As cells from the upper layer are lost due to friction, injury or just aging, new cells, which regenerate from the lower layers rise up to replace them. It is these regenerating cells that are responsible for wound healing. The skin also contains glandular tissue (sweat and sebaceous glands), muscle tissue (arrector pili muscle which causes hair to stand up when chilled), and connective tissue to bind all these structures together.

"All parts of the body which have a function, if used in moderation and exercised in labors to which each is accustomed, become thereby well-developed and age slowly; but if unused and left idle, they become liable to disease, defective in growth, and age quickly."
Hippocrates, 460-370 BC

Our muscles are composed of cells capable of shortening, or contracting, when stimulated, pulling on the bones of the skeleton and resulting in movement. Although a single muscle is made up of tens to hundreds of thousands of cells, it is able to function as a single unit and it might not be apparent that this movement is a cellular phenomenon. Our bones are produced by cells called *osteoblasts*, degraded by cells called *osteoclasts* and then resynthesized by other osteoblasts. In this way old bone is removed and fresh bone deposited in its place. Our skeleton is a dynamic system of ever-working cells. Cells throughout the body are involved in similar processes and are responsible for both our body composition and function.

A cell is a living system capable of sensing, responding to, and interacting with its environment. The General Adaptation Syndrome, the mechanism by which exercise benefits the body, also works at the cellular level. The materials that make up the cell are ordered into a very highly complex arrangement. In order for the cell to accomplish this high degree of organization it must utilize energy obtained from its environment. Using energy and raw materials from its environment, a cell can build new living matter where none previously existed, a process known as synthesis. It is through this process, stimulated by exercise, that we build new muscle proteins, produce new bone matrix and synthesize new aerobic enzymes.

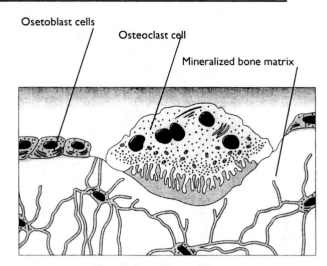

The Cells of Bone Tissue

A cell is capable of reproducing itself. Through a process known as mitosis a cell is able to produce an exact copy of itself. In a slightly different process, meiosis, sex cells produce copies that are not all exactly alike.

Since the inside of this living system is so different from its surroundings (ordered versus disordered) some physical barrier is necessary to keep the two apart. The barrier must not be absolute however, since the selective exchange of materials between the two compartments is necessary. For example, oxygen in the environment must be able to enter the cell and carbon dioxide produced within must be able to leave. The complex regulatory barrier between the intracellular (within the cell) and extracellular (outside of the cell) environments is the *plasma membrane*.

The plasma membrane surrounds all cells and controls the flow of substances into and out of the cell. The plasma membrane also possesses receptors that detect molecules in the environment and allow the cell to "be aware" of what is going on around it. It is through these receptors that our cells can sense and respond to hormones, neurotransmitters, drugs and other molecules. Plant, and some bacterial cells, have an additional cell wall surrounding the plasma membrane. The cell wall provides structural support and acts as an additional barrier between the cell and its environment.

Within the plasma membrane is a viscous, highly ordered material called *cytoplasm*. The cytoplasm contains many enzymes and substrate molecules necessary for the chemical reactions that sustain life. Suspended within this cytoplasm are numerous organelles or cellular substructures with specific functions. Among these are the mitochondria which produce the energy carrying ATP (adenosine triphosphate), lysosomes which contain digestive enzymes important to cellular feeding and nutrition, endoplasmic reticulum which is the machinery on which new protein and fat molecules are synthesized and the nucleus, the repository of the cells genetic information.

Cells can exist as unicellular organisms, that is an animal or plant composed of only a single cell, or as multicellular organisms. An example of the former would be the unicellular amoeba and of the latter, a human being, a complex organism composed of some 75 trillion cells.

A Typical Cell

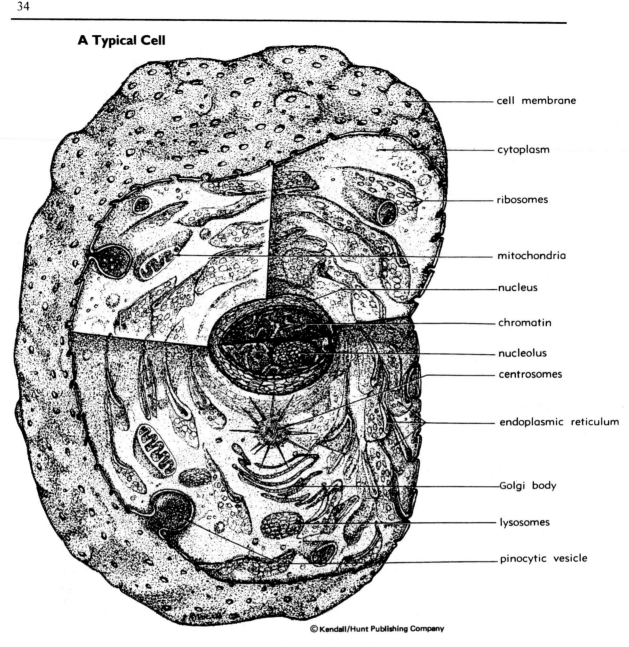

cell membrane

cytoplasm

ribosomes

mitochondria

nucleus

chromatin

nucleolus

centrosomes

endoplasmic reticulum

Golgi body

lysosomes

pinocytic vesicle

© Kendall/Hunt Publishing Company

Anatomical Terminology

As we begin to move further through a study of the human body we will encounter the new language of anatomy. The human body can be divided into regions, including the head, neck, thorax, abdomen, pelvis, and extremities. Each of these contains tissues and organs including bone, muscle, nerve, blood vessels, storage fat and skin; components of the various functional systems. We can also view the body as a collection of functional systems, each consisting of tissues and organs and each contributing a critically important function.

When we refer to various structures of the body we typically do so using a standard set of directional reference terms and a *standard anatomical position*. In the standard anatomic position, the subject of interest is standing upright and facing the observer with feet together and parallel, arms hanging at the sides with palms facing forward and with eyes focused straight ahead. An alternate to the anatomical position which is commonly used by some biomechanists is the *fundamental position*. This position is identical to the anatomical position except the hands lie more naturally – facing the body.

In reference to the anatomical position, the following reference points apply:

Anterior (or ventral)	the forward facing (or belly) side
Posterior	the rearward facing (or back) side
Superior	nearer to the top or head of the body
Inferior	farther from the top or head of the body (nearer to the feet)
Cephalic	toward the head
Caudal	toward the feet
Superficial	nearer to the body's surface
Deep	farther from the body's surface (nearer to the deep interior)
Medial	nearer to the midline of the body (center line running down from between the eyes to between the feet
Lateral	farther from the midline of the body (nearer to the sides or position of the arms)
Ipsilateral	on the same side
Contralateral	on the opposite side
Proximal	nearer to another point of reference
Distal	farther from another point of reference

For example, the eyes are lateral and superior to the bridge of the nose, the brain is located deep to the skull and, relative to the shoulder, the elbow is the proximal joint and the wrist is a distal joint.

Systems of the Body

Skeletal System: *bone, cartilage, joints, ligaments*

Muscular System: *muscles that move the body*

Circulatory System: *heart, blood vessels, blood*

Respiratory System: *lungs, air passageways, nasal apparatus*

Nervous System: *brain, nerves, sensory receptors*

Digestive System: *stomach, liver, esophagus, oral cavity, intestines*

Urinary System: *kidneys, bladder, urine passageways*

Endocrine System: *internal glands*

Reproductive System: *ovaries, testis, uterus, passageways*

Immune System: *lymph nodes, spleen, white blood cells, thymus*

Anthropometry – The Science of Body Measurement

By the Numbers
The average human body consists of 60-65% water

For years, coaches and athletic trainers have attempted to predict the potential athletic ability of individuals by observing their physical appearance, body type or body composition. Although these early attempts were largely qualitative, exercise physiologists are now making quantitative correlations between body type and athletic ability. This discipline is known as ***anthropometry***. While anthropometry is concerned with static measurements of body composition and form, the study of human movement as it is affected by body composition is known as ***kinathropometry***.

The Somatotype Dispersion Index

To arrive at a quantitative description of body type, the anthropometrist records measurements of height, weight, body fat percentage and the length, width and circumference of different body parts such as the arms, legs and torso. In one of the more popular quantitative models, the ***somatotype dispersion index***, individual measurements are taken of various body qualities, and converted into three numerical scores ranging from 1 through 7. According to the somatotype model, there are three basic human body types, ***endomorphic, mesomorphic***, and ***ectomorphic***. The ectomorphic body type is generally considered to be slender and lanky. There is relatively little body fat, the musculature is well toned but not overly developed. The mesomorphic body type is described as having a well-developed and well-proportioned musculature. The body fat content is low and the body mass is lean. The endomorphic body type is characterized as rounder (less angular) with a higher body fat percentage and a less well-defined musculature.

The somatotype distribution index determines the degree to which an individual possesses each of these three body type characteristics by ranking each one on the 1-7 scale. For example, someone who was a pure endomorphic body type, high in body fat content with little muscular development, would rank 7 on the endomorphic scale, 1 on the mesomorphic scale, and 1 on the ectomorphic scale. This person's somatotype would be a 711. A pure mesomorph would rate as a 171 and a pure ectomorph as a 117.

Between these three extremes are intermediate body types. For example, an ecto-mesomorph would be an individual with a tall and slender but well muscled body appearance (rated as a 146), perhaps the body type of a professional basketball player. An endo-mesomorph might be a strong and muscular individual with a high body fat percentage and more rounded appearance (rated as a 461). An Olympic weight lifter or an NFL offensive lineman might qualify for this category.

It is quite common in the professional literature of exercise physiology to find papers correlating success in different athletic events with specific somatotypes. This of course makes a good deal of sense. Certain body types and physical characteristics tend to be preferable for certain sports or athletic events.

Individuals who prove to be excellent runners, as a group, have legs that are longer in relation to overall body height than in the general population. Sprinters tend to have a narrow pelvis. This results in less side to side swaying of the hips when running and translates into a more direct forward line of movement for the legs. Of course, basketball players are preferentially taller and thinner individuals (ectomorphic) than gymnasts who find a shorter, more muscular body type (mesomorphic) to be preferable. The endomorphic body type is more common among swimmers and football linemen. To the swimmer for example, a high body fat percentage lowers the body's density and makes it more buoyant, more prone to floating. Less energy needs to be expended to keep the body afloat and therefore a greater percentage of the energy expended is converted into forward motion. The somatotype dispersion chart is shown in Figure 3.4 and indicates the predominant body types found to excel in four different activities.

While the somatotype index is the most all-encompassing quantitative measure of body type, there are others. These would be more useful when just comparing one parameter of body type rather than a combination of many.

Figure 3.4. Somatotype Dispersion Chart

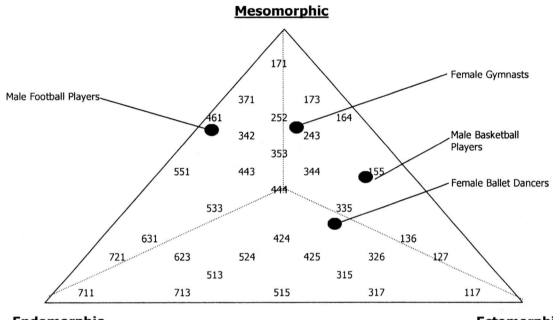

Other Anthropometric Indices

Androgyny Index:
The androgyny index provides a measure of the degree of masculinity of the torso. As the body becomes more "V" shaped (i.e., small waist and broad shoulders) the androgyny index increases. An index of 70 shows a high degree of masculinity. The androgyny index is also referred to as the acromio-iliac index in that shoulder breadth is measured as the bi-acromial distance (distance between the right and left acromion processes of the shoulder) and pelvic breadth as the bi-iliac distance (distance between the right and left iliac crests of the pelvis).

$$\text{Androgyny Index} = \frac{\text{pelvis breadth(cm)} \times 100}{\text{shoulder breadth (cm)}}$$

Ponderal Index:
The Ponderal Index is a measure of the linearity of the body. It also provides an index of the thickness of the body.

$$\text{Ponderal Index} = \frac{\text{Height (cm)}}{\text{Weight (kg)}^{1/3}}$$

Index of Manouvrier:

The Index of Manouvrier provides a measure of the relationship between leg length and torso length.

$$\text{Index of Manouvrier} = \frac{\text{leg length (cm)}}{\text{sitting height (cm)}}$$

Cormic Index:

The Cormic Index provides a ratio indicating the relationship between torso length and overall height.

$$\text{Cormic Index} = \frac{\text{sitting height (cm)}}{\text{standing height (cm)}}$$

Crural Index:

The Crural Index provides a measure relating the respective lengths of the foreleg and the upper leg.

$$\text{Crural Index} = \frac{\text{tibia length (cm)}}{\text{femur length (cm)}}$$

Brachial Index:

The Brachial Index is similar to the Crural Index in that it relates the length of the forearm to the upper arm.

$$\text{Brachial Index} = \frac{\text{forearm length (cm)}}{\text{upper arm length (cm)}}$$

Arm-Leg Index:

The Arm-Leg Index provides a measure comparing the relative lengths of the arms and the legs.

$$\text{Arm-Leg Index} = \frac{\text{arm length (cm)}}{\text{leg length (cm)}}$$

Forearm-Tibia Index:

The Forearm-Tibia Index provides a ratio comparing the relative lengths of the forearm and foreleg,

$$\text{Forearm-Tibia Index} = \frac{\text{forearm length (cm)}}{\text{tibia length (cm)}}$$

Arm Length-Height Index:

The Arm Length-Height Index provides a comparison arm length relative to total body height.

$$\text{Arm Length-Height Index} = \frac{\text{arm length (cm)}}{\text{height (cm)}}$$

Brugsch Chest Stature Index:

The Brugsch Chest Stature Index provides an indication of the relationship of the chest size to total body height.

$$\text{Brugsch Chest Stature Index} = \frac{\text{chest circumference (cm)}}{\text{height (cm)}}$$

2D:4D Ratio:

The 2D:4D ratio is used to compare the relative lengths of the index finger (the 2nd digit, or 2D) and ring finger (the 4th digit, or 4D). In women, this ratio tends to be close to 1, with the index finger and ring fingers being about equal in length. In men, the index finger is about 96% of the length of the ring finger giving a 2D:4D ratio of .96. Lower 2D:4D ratios have been associated with greater assertiveness and visual judgment. Professional football players have lower ratios than the general public and skiers with lower ratios have faster slalom times.

$$\text{2D:4D Ratio} = \frac{\text{Length of } 2^{nd} \text{ digit (cm)}}{\text{Length of } 4^{th} \text{ digit (cm)}}$$

Muscle Circumference and Area:

As seen in figure 3.1, a cross-sectional image of the arm shows it to consist of a variety of tissues and structures including bone, skin, subcutaneous fat, and muscle. In determining a person's maximum strength potential it is necessary to know what the amount of muscle is within the limb. This can be calculated from the following formulae.

AC = circumference of the arm in cm
TS = triceps skinfold measurement in cm

$$\text{Muscle Circumference of the Arm (MCA}_{cm}) = AC - \pi TS$$

$$\text{Muscle Area of the Arm (MAA}_{cm}{}^2) = \frac{(AC - \pi TS)^2}{4\pi}$$

O-Scale Physique Assessment

The O-Scale Physique Assessment uses 20 different body measurements to prepare a proportional comparison of the subject's body physique relative to a standard normal value and presented on a percentile scale. Measurements used in the O-Scale include height, weight, skinfolds (tricep, subscapular, supraspinatous, abdominal, thigh and calf), circumference (arm relaxed, arm flexed, forearm flexed, wrist, chest, thigh, calf flexed, ankle), and biepicondylar widths (humerus, femur).

Body Fat Content and Ideal Body Weight

As noted earlier, our bodies are composed of a number of different tissue types including muscle, bone, epithelium, and fat. Fat, which is also known as adipose tissue, plays an essential role in storing energy, providing thermal insulation, and cushioning vital organs from blunt trauma. Regardless of its site or purpose, fat is stored as droplets within cells known as *adipocytes*. The number of adipocytes present varies from about 30 billion in lean individuals to as many as 100 billion in obese individuals.

Essential fat is typically stored around our vital internal organs as visceral fat, within our bone marrow, and sheathing our nerves. Non-essential fat is typically deposited under the skin as subcutaneous fat (see Figure 3.1) the pattern varying between males and females as will be described later.

Table 3.1. Body Fat Storage Categories

Essential Fat	♂ 2 - 4 %of total body weight
	♀ 6 - 8 % of total body weight
Non-essential Fat	♂ 13 - 15% of total body weight
	♀ 22 - 25% of total body weight

While a certain amount of body fat is normal and natural, in fact it is considered vital, an excess of body fat has been clinically and experimentally shown to pose serious health risks. Several indicators of overall body composition are available and include: *ideal body weight, body mass index and body fat percentage*. The *ideal body weight* is an indicator that compares body stature (height and frame) with body mass (weight). Statistical tables provide us with data that show there is potential harm in being either overweight or underweight.

Body Mass Index:

The body mass index is a ratio of body weight to height. The body mass index is calculated from the formula below:

$$BMI = \frac{weight\ (kg)}{height^2\ (m)}$$

A body mass index greater than 30 is considered to be an indication of obesity. The BMI is considered by many health professionals to be a more reliable indicator of overweight than the more commonly used height and weight tables. In fact, studies have shown correlations between high BMI's and many diseases, particularly those with cardiovascular implications. Caution must be taken when interpreting calculations of BMI for individuals with a high degree of muscularity, for example, body builders. Because of the high proportion of dense (heavy) muscle tissue, these individuals will be relatively heavy for their size (high body density), and show a high BMI. The BMI of these individuals may be high enough to push them into the obese category on the BMI scale when, in fact, they are not and may have very low body fat levels.

Using data collected in the The National Health and Nutrition Examination Survey (NHANES III), a report in the journal Medicine & Science in Sports and Exercise cited the following increases in disease risk for individuals with BMI's of 30 and greater as compared with the population in general. For example, an individual with a BMI of 30 or greater has an 11 times greater risk of developing diabetes and a 4 times greater risk of developing cardiac disease when compared with the average physically fit individual.

Table 3.2. Body Mass Index and Clinical Classification

BMI	Classification	Disease Risk
< 18.5	Underweight	Increased
18.5 - 24.9	Normal Weight	None
25.0 - 29.9	Overweight	Increased
20.0 - 34.9	Clinical Obesity - Class I	High
35.0 - 39.9	Clinical Obesity - Class II	Very High
> 40.0	Clinical Obesity - Class III	Extremely High

Adapted from: Grundy, S.M., et al. Physical Activity in the Prevention of Obesity and its Comorbidities. Medicine & Science in Sport & Exercise. Vol. 31, No.11, Nov. 1999

Table 3.3. Body Mass Index and Disease Risk

Condition	Relative Risk with BMI >30
Diabetes	11
Cardiac Disease	4
Hypertension	4
Gall Bladder Disease	5.5
Breast Cancer	1.3
Uterine Cancer	2.5
Colon Cancer	1.5
Ostoeoarthritis	2.1

Adapted from: Grundy, S.M., et al. Physical Activity in the Prevention of Obesity and its Comorbidities. Medicine & Science in Sport & Exercise. Vol. 31, No.11, Nov. 1999

Body Fat Percentage

Another way of measuring the amount of body fat is to determine what percentage of an individual's total body weight is contributed by body fat content alone. This is referred to as the body fat percentage. For males, fat should account for no more than 15-17% of the body's mass. Females, who normally carry a slightly thicker layer of fat under the skin, should have a body fat percentage of between 20% and 24%.

Body fat content is most accurately determined by comparing an individual's weight when measured on land with the weight when submerged in water (hydrostatic weighing). Since fat is lighter than water and tends to float, an individual will weigh less in water than on dry land. The greater the body fat percentage, the greater will be the difference between the two weights.

A less cumbersome method of estimating body fat percentage involves the use of skinfold calipers. Skinfold calipers are used to measure the thickness of the fat layer under the skin (subcutaneous fat). Measurements taken from specific areas are subjected to an equation or nomogram to calculate the body fat percentage. A procedure to measure body fat percentage with skinfold calipers is included in the chapter on physical assessment.

A third alternative way of measuring body fat percentage is through the determination of bioelectric impedance. Water and lean body tissues such as muscle, being high in water and electrolyte content, are generally good conductors of electricity. Fat on the other hand, because of its low water and electrolyte content is a poor conductor of electricity. When a small electric current is passed through the body it is transmitted through the lean tissues and body fluids with relatively little resistance, or impedance to its flow. Due to the poor conducting properties of fat, the presence of adipose tissue restricts, or impedes the flow of current. By applying a small electric current to the body and measuring the impedance to its flow, a ratio of lean to fat body mass can be determined. From this ratio, the body fat percentage can be calculated.

Table 3.4. Typical Body Fat Percentages

	Male	Female
Elite Athletes	5 – 10%	10 – 15%
Good	11 – 14%	16 – 19%
Acceptable	15 – 17%	20 – 24%
Too Fat	18 – 22%	25 – 29%
Clinically Obese	25% +	32% +
Minimal Fat Level	8%	15%

Waist-to-Hip Ratio

Body fat, no matter where it is found, is stored in the cells of adipose tissue. Men tend to store fat in abdominal adipose tissue (android pattern obesity) whereas women are more likely to store fat under the skin of the thighs and buttocks (gynoid pattern obesity). Sometimes this is referred to as the apple or pear body structure. Apples, which are round and thickest in the middle, would represent the android pattern fat. Pears, which are thicker on the bottom and thinner in the middle, would represent the gynoid pattern fat. Males and females can however store varying amounts of fat in both of these regions and there are many instances of males with gynoid pattern fat deposits and women with android pattern fat deposits. Research has shown that fat is lost more easily from the internal abdominal adipose tissue than from the subcutaneous adipose tissue of the thighs and buttocks. Because the abdominal fat is more easily released into the bloodstream, individuals with android pattern obesity tend to suffer from more fat related cardiovascular disease. In essence, those with large abdominal fat stores rather than buttocks and thigh fat stores are more prone to cardiovascular disease. In this case, pears are healthier than apples! An apple may in fact not keep the doctor away.

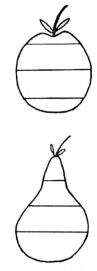

Figure 3.5. Bodyfat Distribution

The waist-to-hip ratio is an indicator of android pattern fat storage and is calculated as follows:

$$\text{ratio} = \frac{\textbf{waist measurement (in or cm)}}{\textbf{hip measurement (in or cm)}}$$

The measurements should be made with a flexible measuring tape on the bare skin. The hip measurement should be made at several different points around the buttocks and the largest measurement should be used in calculating the ratio.

In females, the average ratio is between 0.70 and 0.90. In males, the average lies between 0.90 and 1.00 although it is not uncommon for values to be found above and below these ranges. Waist-to-hip ratios in women that exceed 0.86, and in men exceed 0.95, have been correlated with increased cardiac risk.

Hormones

As was discussed in Chapter 2, the long-term responses to exercise and athletic training, those that result in the bodily changes characteristic of resistance development, are largely influenced by hormones and genes. Many of the body's important hormones are produced in a collection of glands that make up the *endocrine system* (*endo* = internal, *crine* = secretion). The endocrine system refers to the glands and the hormones that are released directly into the blood stream. Changes in muscle mass, bone density, tendon and ligament strength, body fat content, and metabolism are all influenced by endocrine hormones. Hormones are released by the endocrine glands in response to various environmental factors including the stress of exercise activities. Hormone molecules are released into the bloodstream and make their way to target tissues, the tissues upon which they act, throughout the body. Hormone molecules that are built from proteins or protein subunits (polypeptides) exert their effects by interacting with external receptors on the target cell membranes and ultimately activating or inhibiting internal enzyme catalyzed chemical pathways. Hormones built from steroid molecules (a type of fat) act by entering the target cell, traveling to its nucleus, and activating genes which bring about the desired response.

Table 3.5. Hormones and Their Response to Exercise

Gland	Hormone	Stimulus	Exercise Response	Tissue Affected
Pituitary	Growth Hormone	Resistance exercise Low carbohydrate diets	Increased protein sysnthesis;lean tissue repair and growth; Utilization of fat as an energy source	Bone Muscle Tendons/Ligaments Adipose Liver
Thyroid	Thyroxine	Moderate, intense exercise	Increased metabolic rate	All tissues
	Calcitonin	Resistance Exercise	Calcium uptake and retention in bone; increased bone density	Bone osteoblasts
Pancreas	Insulin	Moderate, intense exercise High protein diet	Decreased insulin release Reduced fat storage	Adipose tissue Muscle tissue
	Glucagon	Prolonged exercise	Increase glucose synthesis	Liver
Testis	Testosterone	Resistance exercise Stress High protein diet (*endurance exercise suppresses testosterone*)	Increased protein synthesis Aggression	Bone Muscle Tendons/Ligaments Nervous System
Ovaries	Estrogen	Light-to-moderate exercise (*Prolonged exercise decreases estrogen prod.*)	Increases fat metabolism Inhibits glucose use	Muscle Adipose
Adrenal Cortex	Cortisol	Prolonged exercise Stress	Decreased protein synthesis Increased protein degradation Increased glucose synthesis Anti-inflammatory Increase abdominal visceral fat	Muscle Adipose Liver
Adrenal Medulla	Epinepherine (adrenaline)	Moderate, intense exercise	Glycogen breakdown Increased blood pressure	Muscle; Adipose Nervous
	Norepinephrine	Moderate, intense exercise	Glycogen breakdown Fat breakdown Increased metabolism Increased Heart Rate, Stroke Volume, Blood Pressure	Heart Liver Adipose Nervous
Liver	Insulin-like Growth Factor (IGF-1)	Heavy eccentric resistance training Growth Hormone	Increases protein synthesis Promotes growth	Muscle Bone Cartilage

Genes

Although exercise, diet, and other environmental factors can influence our body composition and affect the way in which we respond to exercise and training, much of our anatomical and physiological characteristics are genetically determined. While we are aware of the genetic influence on outward characteristics such as gender, hair color, and skin pigmentation there are many other genetically-influenced characteristics that directly influence our adaptive response to exercise and our ability to perform well in certain athletic events.

Although training will always result in some degree of improvement, the nature, rapidity, and magnitude of the response will ultimately be determined by genetics. The table below summarizes some of the genetically determined characteristics that influence the adaptive response and athletic potential.

Table 3.6 – The Influence of Genes on Sport-Related Characteristics

Characteristics	Genetic Influence
Stature (height)	Large
Relative length of bones -Arm length - height index -Brachial Index -Crural Index -2D : 4D Ratio -Ponderal Index	Large
Weight -Body mass index -Body fat percentage -Waist-to-hip ratio	Small
Muscle size	Large
Muscle Fiber Composition -Fast-twitch : Slow-twitch ratio	Large
Mitochondria number -Oxidative (aerobic) capacity	Small
Lung size -Vital Capacity	Large
Air Flow in Respiratory Passages -Forced Vital Capacity -Peak Flow Rate	Moderate
Heart Size -Stroke Volume	Large
Resting Heart Rate	Large
Flexibility	Large
Balance	Small
Reaction Time	Small to Moderate

Adapted from: Genes and Sport: Are Your Parents Responsible for Your Wins and Losses? Gatorade Sports Science Exchange, Volume 14, 2001.

Selected Readings:

Kerr, D.A., T.R. Ackland, A.B. Schreiner, **The Elite Athlete-Assessing Body Shape, Size, Proportion and Composition**, *Asia Pacific Journal of Clinical Nutrition*, Vol. 4, No. 1, 1995 http://www.monash.edu.au/APJCN/Vol4/Num1/41p25.htm

Andersen, R.E., **Exercise, and Active Lifestyle, and Obesity**, *The Physician and Sportsmedicine*, Vol. 27, No. 10, October 1999, http://www.physsportsmed.com/issues/1999/10_01_99/andersen.htm

Skinner, J.S. **Do Genes Determine Champions? Gatorade Sports Science Exchange,** Volume 14, No. 4, 20, http://www.gssiweb.com/reflib/refs/298/sse_83.cfm?btid=1

Related Fitness Assessment Activities:

Activity 4. Evaluating Body Mass Index

Activity 5. Evaluating Body Fat Percentage

Activity 6. Evaluating Body Fat Distribution

Activity 7. Somatotype Analysis

Final Essay →
      lab sheet
            Your Current Value -
      Goal   # # you got
BMI   19-25
B.F.%   15-24

Current Value   (+)(-)(√)   Your Goal
   #I got   above, below, right   what it should be
                  where supposed to be

for all (-) become a personal trainer
   ↳ create an exercise program
         -how to recommend you fix it

ex: running fast uses carbs (over 65)
    running slow burns fat (under 65)

- don't have to know scientific reason
  but create a work out ex: 3x a week for
  45 min.

- tables at bottom of sheet give ways to
  fix the (-)

Nutrition test: 58 points

Chapter 4

Bioenergetics and Nutrition

Chapter Contents
- Fueling Exercise Activities
- Nutrition and Fitness
- Carbohydrates, Fats, Proteins, Vitamins, Minerals, Water
- Metabolic Rate
- Calories
- Nutritional Energy Balance
- Weight Management
- Nutrition for Exercise and Athletics
- Fluid Requirements for Exercise and Athletics
- Selected Readings

Learning Objectives

The material in this chapter will allow you to:

- Understand the biological need for a continuous energy supply
- Understand the sources and uses of various forms of energy required for different activities
- Understand the basic metabolic processes and their relationship to various exercise and athletic activities
- Understand the biochemical structure and metabolic use of the nutrient molecules, carbohydrate, fat and protein
- Understand the principles of good nutrition and the application of nutrition to training and competition

Fueling Exercise Activities

All exercise activities, be they running, swimming, skiing, weight lifting, martial arts or ballet require the contraction of muscle. Movement and coordination depend upon the skeletal muscles; the muscles attached to our bones. Cardiovascular function depends upon the contraction of cardiac muscle, making up the walls of the heart, and smooth muscle, lining the blood vessels. Breathing is dependent upon the respiratory muscles of the chest wall and diaphragm.

The efficiency with which muscle can perform these tasks, the power which can be developed, and the duration for which it can be maintained all depend upon the ability of the muscles to convert the chemical energy stored in the foods we eat into the mechanical energy of contraction. In other words, the human body functions as a machine converting one form of energy into another and performing work in the process.

The contraction of muscle for normal activities or for exercise requires energy. As with all systems performing work, and in keeping with the laws of thermodynamics, the energy must be supplied from some external source. Light bulbs require energy in the form of electricity, our cars require energy stored within the bonds of gasoline molecules. The energy for muscular contraction is supplied by the energy stored in the bonds of the molecule adenosine triphosphate (ATP). In simple terms, ATP is the fuel that our muscles burn.

The bonds attaching the last two phosphate groups to this molecule are so called high-energy phosphate bonds, each storing approximately 11,000 calories (11 kCal) of energy. The calorie is a unit used to measure energy, one calorie being the amount of heat energy required to raise on cubic centimeter (or 1 ml) of water one degree Centigrade. When one of these phosphate bonds is split from the ATP molecule, 11,000 calories of energy (or 11 kilocalories) are available to power muscular contraction. The removal of this phosphate group converts the ATP into ADP (adenosine diphosphate). Removal of the second phosphate groups also frees 11,000 calories of energy for use in contraction and converts the ADP to AMP (adenosine monophosphate).

Adenosine~P~P~P →• Adenosine~P~P + P + ENERGY (11 kcal)

Adenosine~P~P →• Adenosine~P + P + ENERGY (11 kcal)

The concept of storing energy within chemical bonds is one, which we should find readily understandable. You are probably familiar with the energy stored in the bonds holding atomic nuclei together. Breaking apart these bonds, or fissioning the atomic nucleus, releases great amounts of energy, commonly known to us as nuclear fission energy. Gasoline is a molecule in the class known as hydrocarbons. This is because gasoline consists of an arrangement of hydrogen and carbon atoms held together by atomic bonds. These atomic bonds contain energy, the same type of energy utilized by the cell. When we break apart the gasoline molecule (by burning it in the presence of oxygen) we release the energy and make it available to do work, such as move the car.

Energy is not always found in the form of atomic and sub-atomic bonds. Energy is found in many forms such as electrical energy, mechanical energy, thermal energy and light energy.

Energy can be converted from one form to another as we well know. Light bulbs convert electrical energy to light energy. Your home furnace converts chemical energy (bond energy in gas or oil) to thermal (heat) energy. Your hair dryer converts electrical energy into thermal energy (heat) and mechanical energy (blower motor). The cells found in living organisms convert chemical bond energy into mechanical, thermal and electrical energy.

The laws that govern energy use in the cell are the same laws of physics that govern energy use in any system. The first law of thermodynamics states that THE TOTAL AMOUNT OF ENERGY IN THE UNIVERSE IS CONSTANT; IN ANY PHYSICAL OR CHEMICAL CHANGE, THE TOTAL AMOUNT OF ENERGY IN THE UNIVERSE REMAINS CONSTANT. In other words, energy can neither be created nor destroyed; this is the law of CONSERVATION OF ENERGY. When cells or living organisms absorb energy from the environment to perform useful work, they must return an equivalent amount of energy to the environment, usually in the form of heat.

ATP is the fuel that is produced by the cells of the body from the nutrients that we eat. The amount of ATP fuel that can be stored in muscle is very small indeed. The muscle of even a well-trained athlete contains only enough stored ATP to fuel only 5 - 6 seconds of maximal activity. Muscles must therefore have the ability to replenish or form new ATP supplies continuously in order to sustain muscular activity. One of the limiting factors in long distance or endurance events is the efficiency of these ATP regenerating and synthesizing mechanisms. There are three such mechanisms, or pathways, which muscles utilize for the production of ATP, these being;

-the phosphagen system

-the glycogen-lactic acid system

-the aerobic system

The Phosphagen System: One of the ways to replenish ATP in the muscle cell is to transfer a new phosphate group and its high-energy bond onto an expended molecule of ADP. This requires the presence, in the muscle cell, of some other molecule with a high-energy phosphate group to serve as the donor. This molecule is *creatine phosphate* (or phosphocreatine). The phosphocreatine molecule can decompose into a high-energy phosphate group and a molecule of creatine and transfer the phosphate group to ADP in a fraction of a second. This system of ATP regeneration is known as the phosphagen system. The amount of phosphocreatine in the cell is limited however and can only provide ATP to sustain maximal muscle activity for 10 - 15 seconds. Because no oxygen is required for this process it is referred to as an anaerobic energy supply.

$$\text{Creatine~P} + \text{ADP} \rightarrow \text{Creatine} + \text{ATP}$$

The Glycogen-Lactic Acid System: Another source of potential ATP for muscular activity lies in the form of the stored carbohydrate glycogen. Carbohydrates ingested in the diet are stored in the body's cells as glycogen. Through a series of biochemical steps, glycogen is broken down in a process known as glycolysis, yielding ATP and pyruvic acid. The chemical reactions of glycolysis do not require the presence of oxygen or air and are referred to as anaerobic metabolism. The ATP yield of this system is limited and is sufficient to fuel muscular activity for only an additional 30 - 40 seconds above the 10 - 15 seconds fueled by the phosphagen system. This is also an anaerobic energy supply system in that no oxygen is required for its operation.

The pyruvic acid that results from this process can itself be used to form additional ATP if oxygen is available in sufficient quantities to the muscle. In the absence of sufficient oxygen, the pyruvic acid is converted to lactic acid which is released from the muscle into the blood. This lactic acid is believed to be partly responsible for the phenomenon of muscular fatigue. The lactic acid released into the blood can be converted by the liver into glucose which can then reenter the pathway and supply further energy. This liver based pathway for the recycling of pyruvic acid is known as the *Cori cycle*.

The Aerobic System: The aerobic system of ATP production is one that follows the glycogen-lactic acid system. The oxidation of pyruvic acid formed during glycolysis results in a tremendous amount of ATP available for muscular activity. This system requires the presence of oxygen, or air, and is therefore called aerobic. The aerobic system is capable of supplying ATP to the muscles for an indefinite time or as long as the nutrient supply lasts. Once the stored glycogen has all been used, this system can go on fueling itself with the body's fat reserves.

These three energy-supplying systems of skeletal muscle, due to their different capacities and restrictions, play specific roles in various types of exercise activities or sports. The tables below highlight the differences between the various systems with respect to endurance values, maximum rates of power generation and activities in which they predominate.

Table 4.1 Endurance and Maximum Generation Potential of ATP Generating Systems

System	Endurance	Maximum Power
Phosphagen	10 - 15 sec	4 M of ATP/min
Glycogen-Lactic Acid	30 - 40 sec	2.5M of ATP/min
Aerobic	unlimited	1 M of ATP/min

Table 4.2 Energy Supply Systems Used in Various Athletic Activities

System(s)	Activities
Phosphagen System (exclusively)	Diving, Jumping, Weight Lifting, 100m dash Football pass play, Shot put, baseball bat swing
Phosphagen and Glycogen Lactic Acid System	Baseball triple, ice hockey dash, Basketball full court dash and lay-up, 200m dash
Glycogen-Lactic Acid System (mainly)	400m dash, 100m swim, tennis volley, soccer, karate kata
Glycogen-Lactic Acid and Aerobic Systems	800m dash, 200m swim, 1500m run, 1500m skating, 1 mile run, 2000m rowing, round of boxing
Aerobic System (exclusively)	Marathon run, 10,000m skating, cross-country skiing, long-distance bicycling, 30 min aerobics

Figure 4.1 graphically illustrates the role that each of these energy supply systems play in powering athletic performance. In the first seconds of activity most of the energy is supplied by the phosphagen system. As the contribution of the phosphagen system drops, the contribution of the glycogen-lactic acid system increases reaching a maximum at about 30 seconds. After this, the glycogen lactic acid system contribution decreases gradually and is replaced by the aerobic system that supplies all of the energy after about 5 minutes.

Figure 4.1. Energy Supply Systems

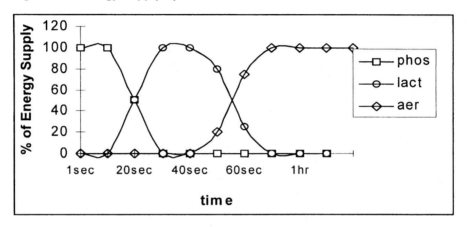

Metabolic Rate

As described above, the living cell contains a complex system of chemical reactions some of which break down large ingested nutrient molecules to release the energy stored within then while other chemical reactions synthesize new macromolecules from smaller, simpler precursors. The sum total of all of these chemical reactions is referred to as *metabolism*. Metabolism, therefore, consists of both reactions that break substances down, the sub-process known as *catabolism*, and the reactions which build new substances, the sub-process known as *anabolism*.

The catabolic process includes those reactions, discussed above, that are responsible for breaking down glucose molecules and releasing the stored energy which can be captured in the form of ATP. ATP can then transfer this energy to the working muscles to allow for the variety of activities that drive exercise and athletic performance. The anabolic process includes, among others, the reactions which build protein and create new muscle from small amino acid molecules as well as the reactions that synthesize new fat from excess nutrient molecules. In a normal, healthy and fit individual, the rate of catabolic reactions should be equivalent to the rate of anabolic reactions. The rate at which these metabolic reactions occur is referred to as the *metabolic rate* and is measured in *calories*. The concept of the calorie will be explored later in this chapter.

For an individual at rest, the metabolic reactions will be running at a minimal level known as the *basal metabolic rate (BMR)*. As one begins to move and become more active, the muscles require additional energy in the form or ATP requiring the catabolic reactions to speed up. If no additional nutrients are consumed, existing energy stores in the form of glycogen and fat will be broken down to provide the necessary energy. If a person remains sedentary, or inactive, and consumes a large amount of nutrients, the excess matter and energy will be stored in the form or additional body fat.

As we all know, aerobic exercise consumes large amounts of energy and can be an effective way of temporarily increasing the metabolic rate. The additional calories consumed by one hour of aerobic exercise performed 3-5 times per week can be quite effective at reducing stored body fat. What may not be as commonly known is the effect that resistance training exercise can have on metabolic rate and fat loss. Following a period of resistance exercise, the muscle repair process requires tremendous amounts of energy, accounting for up to 20% of the total resting metabolic rate. The elevated RMR persists for 48 hours following an acute session of resistance training, peaking at about 24 hours after the exercise session. Strength training burns carbohydrates during the exercise period; fat is primarily consumed after the training session.

Metabolic Rate, Exercise, The General Adaptation Syndrome and Aging

Paradoxically, the most efficient pathway for supplying our energy needs, the aerobic pathway, is the one which produces harmful oxygen byproducts believed to contribute to the aging process. In the terminal step of aerobic respiration, high-energy electrons are transferred to an oxygen molecule (O_2) creating a charged and highly reactive molecule known as the superoxide anion free radical. This free radical is known to damage both cellular membranes and cellular DNA leading to premature cell death. In fact, animals with the highest levels of oxygen consumption and metabolic rate typically have the shortest of all natural life spans. Thankfully, nature has provided us with built-in free radical scavenger molecules, or antioxidants, which help control free radical damage. At first thought it might seem that exercise, particularly aerobic exercise that increases metabolic rate and oxygen consumption, can lead to premature aging by causing the production of excess oxygen free radicals. Although this is in part true, the body can adapt to this added oxidative stress, as it does to all stresses, through the general adaptation syndrome. Individuals who train regularly and subject the body to repeated oxidative stress have been shown to develop a heightened antioxidant system, a form of resistance development predicted by the general adaptation syndrome. This may in fact result in an enhanced resistance to the normal aging process that is brought about by free radical oxidation in our cells.

Nutrition and Fitness

The development and maintenance of a healthy, physically fit body requires a steady input of the proper and appropriately balanced nutrients. A nutrient is defined as any substance, obtained from food, drink or otherwise ingested, that is used by the body for growth, synthesis, repair or as an energy supply. There are six basic classes of nutrients required by the human body to maintain general fitness and good health as well as to provide the fuel for exercise and athletic activities.

Six Classes of Nutrients Required by the Human Body

Carbohydrate
Fat
Protein
Vitamins
Minerals
Water

CARBOHYDRATES are required, primarily, as an energy source. Carbohydrates should account for between 55% and 70% of the energy supply in humans and their usage is described in the chapter on bioenergetics and metabolism. The body's energy demands are large, even without exercise activities. The human brain requires between 400 - 600 Calories (a measure of energy, really kilocalories as will be described in the chapter on bioenergetics) each day to drive its function. The precise amount that carbohydrates should contribute to the diet is influenced by the typical daily energy requirements (more are required for intense exercise) and dietary goals (less is required for weight loss). Each gram of carbohydrate contains 4 kcal of energy.

To a lesser extent, carbohydrates are also required as building blocks of larger molecules including the gelatin-like substance of connective tissues, cell membrane coverings and the mucus secreted by digestive and respiratory system linings. Carbohydrates stimulate the growth of our intestinal bacteria that provide us with our main supply of vitamin K (needed for proper blood clotting), and also provide the fiber, or bulk, required in our diets.

Carbohydrates occur in two general forms. In one form, the carbohydrate occurs as small, single molecules (monomers) called **sugars**, also known as **monosaccharides** or **simple carbohydrates**. More complex forms of carbohydrates exist as long, linear or branched chains of sugar molecules (polymers) and are alternatively known as **starches**, **polysaccharides** or **complex carbohydrates**.

Figure 4.2. Carbohydrate Structure

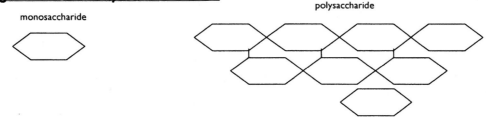

The rate at which carbohydrate-containing foods are digested and the carbohydrate monosaccharides absorbed into the blood stream varies and is dependent upon a variety of factors. Those that are rapidly digested and absorbed and which can provide a rapid but short-term energy burst are said to possess a high **glycemic index** (**GI**). The glycemic index scale runs from 0 (no glycemic value) to 100 (the equivalent of pure glucose). Breads, cakes, refined pastas and bananas are examples of high glycemic index foods and will have a GI index of closer to 100. Foods in which the carbohydrates enter the blood stream more slowly and provide a longer-lasting energy supply are referred to as moderate glycemic index foods and include whole grain breads, oatmeal and corn.

GLYCEMIC INDEX OF SOME SELECTED FOODS

Food Item	GI
Instant Rice	91
Donut	76
Honey	73
Bagel	72
Carrots	71
Orange Juice	57
Cheese	45
Eggs	38
Lentil Beans	29
Peanuts	14

FATS serve primarily as a secondary energy source and, to a lesser extent, also function as building blocks for larger molecules such as those found in cell membranes and hormones. Fats provide a very concentrated source of energy, approximately two times the energy per gram as compared with carbohydrates (9 kcal/gm).

One common class of fat, lipids, also known as neutral fats, are composed of a backbone molecule of glycerol with three fatty acid molecules attached. Because of this structure, neutral lipids are often called *triglycerides*.

Figure 4.3. Triglyceride Structure

```
  H
H-C- O –CH2-CH2-CH2-CH2-CH2-CH2-CH2-CH2-CH2-CH2-CH2-CH2-CH2-CH2-CH2-CH2-CH3
  |
H-C- O –CH2-CH2-CH2-CH2-CH2-CH2-CH2-CH2-CH2-CH2-CH2-CH2-CH2-CH2-CH2-CH2-CH3
  |
H-C- O –CH2-CH2-CH2-CH2-CH2-CH2-CH2-CH2-CH2-CH2-CH2-CH2-CH2-CH2-CH2-CH2-CH3
  H
```
    glycerol   3 fatty acids

As seen in the illustration above, the carbon atoms (C) which form the long chain backbone of the fatty acids each attach to the adjacent carbon atoms and to two hydrogen atoms (H). This is because each carbon atom has 4 bonding sites. A carbon chain such as that found in a fatty acid molecule, having hydrogen attached to each of its two free bonding sites, is said to be a *saturated fatty acid*.

If hydrogens are not present at these two free sites, the carbon will satisfy its need to have four bonds by double bonding with the adjacent carbon atom. This would be known as an unsaturated site. A fatty acid with one such site would be called a *monounsaturated fatty acid*; one with several unsaturated sites would be a *polyunsaturated fatty acid*.

Figure 4.4. Fatty Acid Structure

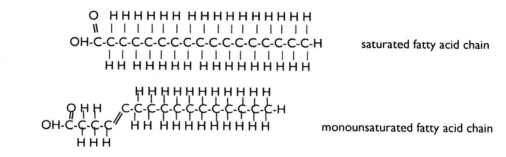

saturated fatty acid chain

monounsaturated fatty acid chain

Saturated fats, made from glycerol and saturated fatty acids and contained in foods from animal sources, tend to be very dense and solid at room temperature. Mono and polyunsaturated fats contained in foods from plants are less dense and are liquid at room temperature. The heavy, dense saturated fats are the ones which help precipitate the blockage of arteries, contribute to heart disease and stroke, and should be avoided.

Another important form of fat is based on the cholesterol molecule and is known, as a class, as **STEROIDS**. Although most people assume that cholesterol is a "bad" fat, and it is in large amounts, it is also required for many reasons. Hormones such as estrogen, progesterone, testosterone and aldosterone are all made from a cholesterol building block. Cholesterol also plays an important role in the function of cell membranes. The body however, can synthesize cholesterol so its importance as a nutrient is minimal.

PROTEIN, if necessary, can serve as a tertiary (3rd order) energy source but only during periods of starvation or in conditions of abnormal metabolism. For the most part, protein is required to provide building blocks, in the form of **AMINO ACIDS**. Amino acids are the basic molecules from which proteins are built. There are twenty such amino acid building blocks that we use to build new protein. These amino acids, some obtained from the protein we eat and others synthesized by the body itself, are required for the production of other proteins such as enzymes, connective tissue fibers, and the contractile elements of muscle.

Although the body can synthesize 11 of the twenty amino acids, nine must be obtained from the diet or through dietary supplements. These are known as the essential amino acids.

Essential Amino Acids
Lysine
Histidine
Tryptophan
Phenylalanine
Threonine
Valine
Methionine
Leucine
Isoleucine

VITAMINS are organic (carbon based) molecules which are required by the body for use in assisting with enzyme activity or to influence certain physiological functions such as wound healing. Vitamins fall into two categories; those that dissolve in water (Water Soluble Vitamins) and those that do not (Fat Soluble Vitamins).

Vitamin Classification:

Water Soluble	Fat Soluble
B complex	A
B_1- Thiamin	D
B_2- Riboflavin	E
B_3- Niacin	K
B_6- Pyridoxine	
B_{12}-Cobalamin	
Biotin	
Folacin	
Pantothenic Acid	
C	

Although vitamins have diverse and complex functions within the body, the following figure summarizes the major roles that vitamins contribute to physical fitness.

Major Vitamin Functions:

Vitamin	Function
B_1	Energy Release in Mitochondria
B_2	" " " "
B_3(Niacin)	" " " "
B_6	Protein and Amino Acid Metabolism
B_{12}	DNA & RNA Metabolism
Biotin	ATP (energy) Formation
Folacin	DNA & RNA Metabolism
Pantothenic	Energy Release in Mitochondria
C	Collagen synthesis, Cholesterol metabolism synthesis of anti-inflammatory steroids
A	Vision
D	Absorption of Calcium and Phosphorus
E	Prevent O_2 toxicity
K	Blood Clotting

MINERALS are inorganic elements and ions required for a host of body functions. Some minerals are required in relatively large amounts, others in only trace amounts.

Major Minerals	Main Function(s)
Na (sodium)	H_2O balance, nerve function
K (potassium)	H_2O balance, nerve function
P (phosphorus)	bone & tooth structure, coenzyme
Cl (chloride)	acid base balance, H_2O balance
Mg (magnesium)	energy releasing enzymes
S (sulfur)	cartilage, tendon, protein structure
Ca (calcium)	bone & tooth, nerve function, clotting
Trace Minerals	Main Function(s)
Fe (iron)	blood hemoglobin, enzyme function
I (iodine)	thyroid hormone (metabolic rate)
Fl (fluoride)	tooth and bone structure
Zn (zinc)	enzymes
Se (selenium)	enzymes
Cu (copper)	enzymes
Mn (manganese)	enzymes
Cr (chromium)	glucose and energy metabolism

WATER is required to maintain the proper concentration of materials in the body, acts as a solvent, is required for body cooling, aids in joint lubrication and serves in decomposition reactions, for example, the breakdown of complex carbohydrates into simple sugars.

The U.S. Department of Agriculture and the U.S. Department of Health and Human Services have established a set of nutritional guidelines in the form of the food guide pyramid. The food guide pyramid, illustrated below, is designed to provide a visual representation of the recommended standard diet indicating the number of daily servings of each type of food groups. The USDA and USDHHS believe that following the food guide pyramid is a simple way of guaranteeing proper nutrition.

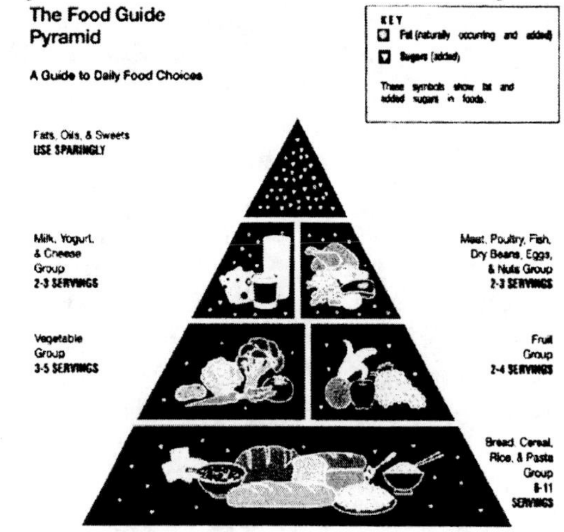

Figure 4.5. The Food Guide Pyramid

Calories

The calorie (spelled with a lower case "c"), is a unit of energy measurement. One calorie denotes the amount of energy, in the form of heat, required to raise the temperature of 1 ml of water by 1 °C. Admittedly, the calorie does not seem to represent all that much energy. In fact, most human activities require, and most food products contain, many thousands of calories. For this reason, when discussing human nutrition and physiology, we generally refer to calories in units of one thousand, a unit called the kilocalorie. Although the proper term for this 1000-calorie unit, the kilocalorie, is commonly used in scientific discussions, many nutritionists, along with the general public, prefer to use the term Calorie (spelled with an upper case "C"). When a slice of bread is said to contain 70 Calories, its energy content is actually 70,000 calories, enough energy to raise the temperature of 1 liter of water (1000 ml) by 70 °C.

An ideal diet would be one in which a person consumes only as many calories as are used in their daily activities. If the intake of calories exceeds the daily usage, the excess food will be converted to and stored as fat as will be discussed later in this chapter. Again, in the ideal diet, approximately 48% of ingested calories should come from complex carbohydrates and naturally occurring sugars. Processed or refined sugars should make up no more than 10% of total carbohydrates. Total carbohydrate intake should therefore account for approximately 58% of the total daily caloric intake. No more than 30% of total calories should come from fat with less than 10% of this being saturated fats. Protein should make up the remaining 12% of total daily calorie intake.

In addition, daily cholesterol intake should be limited to 300 mg/day and sodium intake (mostly table salt) limited to 5 g/day. Cholesterol is a waxy, fat-like molecule carried in the blood by other molecules known as lipoproteins. These lipoprotein carriers come in two forms, *low-density lipoproteins (LDL)* and *high-density lipoproteins (HDL)*.

Excess cholesterol circulating in the blood can contribute to the formation of fatty deposits on the walls of the arteries, narrowing their effective diameter and reducing blood flow. In the coronary arteries of the heart, this can contribute to heart attack. When cholesterol is bound to low density lipoproteins, it tends to remain in circulation within the blood. Cholesterol bound to the high-density lipoprotein is removed from the blood and metabolized by the body's cells.

It is recommended that total blood cholesterol levels be held below 200 mg/dl (milligrams per deciliter). Just as important as total blood cholesterol however, is the ratio of HDL/LDL.

The intake of dietary fiber should be at the level of between 25 to 35 grams per day. Dietary fiber is a form of polysaccharide carbohydrate (complex carbohydrate) which is non-digestible in the human digestive system. Soluble fiber, is soluble in water, rapidly absorbed by the digestive tract, and may help to reduce blood cholesterol levels. Insoluble fiber remains in the digestive tract where it increases stool volume, reduces the amount of time that wastes remain in the large intestine, and may help to prevent against colon cancer.

Nutritional Energy Balance

The nutrients ingested, specifically the carbohydrates, fats and proteins, carry with them material that can be converted into energy. The quantity of this energy is measured in calories and, if not used in driving daily activities, will be stored primarily as fat. The normal intake of nutrients for the average American contains approximately 2400 kCal (kilo calories). Given the recommended ratios for the various nutrient groups, a well balanced diet should contain 6 grams of carbohydrate for each Kg of body weight (2.7 g for each lb), 1.2 g of protein per kg (.55g / lb), and 1.2 g of fat per kg (.55g /lb). Because of the differing energy densities (4 Kcal/g for carbohydrate and protein, 9 Kcal/g for fat), the diet for a normal 130 lb individual (59 Kg) would be as follows.

Table 4.3. Macronutrient Requirements by Weight

Intake by Weight			
Carbohydrate	59 Kg @ 6 g/Kg	=	354 g of carbohydrate
Protein	59 Kg @ 1.2 g/Kg	=	71 g of protein
Fat	59 Kg @ 1.2 g/Kg	=	71 g of fat
Intake by Calories (Kcal)			
Carbohydrate	354 g @ 4 Kcal/g	=	1416 Kcal of carbohydrate
Protein	71 g @ 4 Kcal/g	=	284 Kcal of protein
Fat	71 g @ 9 Kcal/g	=	639 Kcal of fat
Total Calories			2,339 Kcal/day

Weight Management

In order to maintain a stable weight, the amount of calories consumed per day should be roughly equivalent to the amount of calories expended per day. Excess calories consumed, be they proteins, carbohydrates or fats, will be broken down through the metabolic process into the component parts and recombined into various forms of stored energy. Initially, excess calories will be stored in the muscle and liver as glycogen, however, since the body's glycogen storage capacity is limited (about 1,400 kcal worth of stored glycogen), most of the excess calories will be stored as fat (about 100,000 - 130,000 kcal of energy are stored as fat in the normal fit individual). Conversely, if daily calorie intake falls below the level of daily calorie expenditure, the energy deficit will be made up by breaking down energy storage molecules, namely glycogen and fat.

Simply watching calories is not the best way for losing fat and reducing weight. Research has shown that the most effective method of weight reduction is to combine calorie restriction with a program of aerobic and strength training exercise. Aerobic exercise consumes a tremendous amount of energy that, in general, is first supplied by free glucose and stored glycogen and, after about 20 minutes of continuous aerobic exercise, by stored fat. By restricting calorie intake in combination with aerobic exercise, one can compound the effect of quickly depleting glycogen reserves and catabolizing stored fat. Since, pound-for-pound, muscle is a metabolically active tissue and consumes more calories than fat, increasing the body's muscle content through strength training exercise, will increase the resting daily energy requirement and help prevent excess calories from being converted to stored fat. A recent study reported in the journal, Medicine and Science in Sports and Exercise, followed three groups of dieters, one group simply reducing calorie intake, one group engaging in aerobic exercise and calorie reduction and the third group participating in both strength and aerobic exercise with a reduced calorie intake. After a twelve week period, all groups showed similar amounts of weight loss with the group that dieted only losing both body fat and muscle mass; the diet and aerobic exercise group losing fat and increasing oxygen consumption and the diet, aerobic and strength training group losing body fat only and gaining in both oxygen consumption and strength. Only this latter group is poised for long-term weight reduction without any compromise in strength.

Nutrition for Exercise and Athletics

During aerobic activities a working muscle will deplete its store of ATP and creatine phosphate within the first minute of activity. If aerobic activity is continued, the muscle becomes primarily dependent upon a combination of carbohydrate and fat to provide the necessary fuel. As carbohydrate and fat contain differing amounts of energy per unit of weight, and since they are metabolized through slightly different metabolic pathways, the relative amounts of oxygen consumed and carbon dioxide produced during energy release differ as the proportion of the primary energy supply shifts between glucose and fat. This ratio of oxygen:carbon dioxide is known as the ***respiratory exchange ratio (RER)*** with a ratio of .70 indicating fat as the source of energy and a ratio of 1.00 indicating glucose as the source of energy. At rest, the typical RER is approximately .80 indicating that fat is the marginally favored energy supply although a combination of both fat and glucose are being used. As aerobic activity begins and approaches an intensity of 50% VO_{2max}, the RER rises to .85 and to 1.00 as intensity increases to 90% VO_{2max}. This indicates that, for increasing intensities of aerobic activity, the favored fuel source shifts from fat to carbohydrate with carbohydrate being the exclusive fuel source for very high intensity aerobic activities.

Athletes participating in endurance events, those requiring aerobic energy production, perform better on high carbohydrate diets. This is due to two factors. As shown in the graph below, after depleting the muscle glycogen stores, individuals on a high carbohydrate diet will replenish the glycogen stores faster than those on high protein or high fat diets.

Figure 4.6. Diet Effect on Muscle Glycogen Content After One Exercise Session

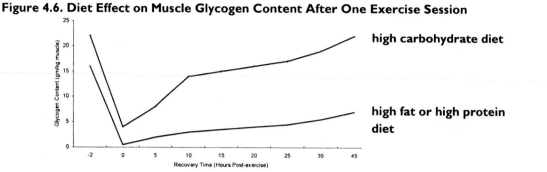

When observed over a period of several days, as in the graph below, it is seen that individuals with a high carbohydrate diet (>70%) will maintain muscle glycogen stores at normal levels even with daily aerobic exercise. Those with a low carbohydrate diet (<40%), will reduce stored glycogen levels by 20%-50% each day under the same exercise conditions.

Figure 4.7. Diet Effect on Muscle Glycogen Content After Multiple Exercise Sessions

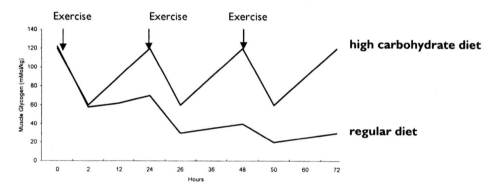

Although, as noted above, glucose supplements can provide a rapidly available source of carbohydrate fuel during endurance or aerobic activities, such simple carbohydrates should be avoided as a major part of the normal or pre-event diet. Complex carbohydrates, as described earlier, should form the bulk of the carbohydrate intake. Reliance on too high an intake of simple carbohydrates like glucose will not promote the long-term storage of carbohydrates but rather, through its stimulation of insulin release, will make carbohydrate reserves less available.

Protein is also important in the diet for the growth and repair of muscle tissue. High protein diets, in general, are not recommended in that they have been shown to be associated with increased risks of cancer, heart disease and osteoporosis. The average American diet contains more than the recommended 12% of calories from protein. If any dietary supplement is considered, it might best be one containing the essential amino acids.

Although often referred to as the culprit for all that is wrong with the American diet, fat does play an essential role in the average diet and an even more significant role in the diet of endurance athletes. Stored muscle glycogen, the primary fuel for intense aerobic activity, can sustain only limited periods of activity, typically 20 – 30 min. Longer-term aerobic activities that exceed this timeframe become increasingly reliant on muscle triglyceride reserves, in other words, stored fat. Low fat diets in which less than 20% of total calories come from fat can compromise this energy storage reservoir and result in premature fatigue. In addition, the absorption of the important fat-soluble vitamins, A, D, E, and K depend on adequate levels of fat in the diet, typically a total fat intake of about 30% of total calories.

Water is of course always an important nutrient but becomes even more so on an increased protein or amino acid diet. During the metabolism of ingested amino acids and proteins, significant amounts of ammonia are released and must be flushed from the blood by the kidneys with a sufficient amount of water.

Fluid Requirements for Exercise and Athletics

As with any machine in our non-perfect world, the energy utilized for muscular contraction is not converted to motion with 100% efficiency. Only about 25% of the available energy contained in carbohydrate and fat molecules is used for muscle contraction; the remaining 75% is lost as waste heat and would greatly increase body temperature if not for our ability to cool off through sweating. Our bodies consist of almost 60% water and this water plays many vital roles which we cannot afford to sacrifice. Unfortunately, sweating results in the loss of large amounts of water from the body, up to 2 liters per hour during strenuous work, which can result in dehydration.

At approximately 1% dehydration we notice the first signs of thirst as our internal systems try to get us to replace this water and, at this point, athletic performance has already become impaired. At 2.5% dehydration research has shown up to a 35% reduction in the capacity for high-intensity, long-duration exercise. At 5% dehydration our nervous system is affected and we begin to notice discomfort

> "I'm not out there sweating for three hours every day just to find out what it feels like to sweat."
> Michael Jordan, Athlete, 1994

and fatigue and may become lethargic or nervous. At a dehydration level of approximately 8%, our sweating decreases as the body desperately tries to conserve water. Our muscle strength decreases as does our ability to perform at peak levels. An 8% dehydration is commonly reached in playing a full set of tennis, a game of football or in long distance running. At 15% dehydration our skin would crack and bleed and we would become delirious; at 20% dehydration we die!

Normal Daily Fluid Balance *(non-exercising)*	
Daily Fluid Intake	**Daily Fluid Loss**
Food and Drink: Respiration:	
2,100 ml/day	800 ml/day
Metabolic Production:	Sweat:
200 ml/day	50 ml/day
	Urine:
	1,300 ml/day
	Feces:
	150 ml/day
Total Intake:	Total Loss:

When dehydration is detected by a region of the brain known as the hypothalamus we become thirsty and seek water, our sweating decreases, and our kidneys reduce urine production. All of this occurs automatically, without conscious thought, as part of the body's automatic internal control system. The thirst mechanism however does not keep pace with our water need, usually lagging behind 3-4%. As receptors in the mouth, esophagus and stomach detect that fluid has been ingested, the thirst reflex decreases even though the actual entry of water into the blood has not yet fully occurred. For this reason, it is necessary to take regular *fluid breaks* during exercise or athletics rather than just relying on thirst alone. It is also recommended that at least one full glass of water (about 300 ml) be consumed about one half hour before the activity begins. Taking water early is important because once activity begins, blood is shifted away from the gastrointestinal system to the muscles. Fluid consumed after this point will be absorbed more slowly.

Many athletes and exercisers seek to replace water with commercially available fluid supplements. The early fluid supplements, containing significant amounts of carbohydrate and electrolytes, actually hurt more than they helped. Fluids which are high in carbohydrate content (generally greater than 2.5 g/dl) can slow the absorption of water into the blood by delaying the emptying of the stomach. One popular fluid supplement has a carbohydrate content of 4 g/dl. Many athletic coaches and trainers do use this supplement but only after diluting it in half.

Providing athletes with a glucose solution to drink during the athletic event (2 - 2.5% glucose) can supplement the glycogen and blood glucose supply and prolong the period of carbohydrate utilization and delay the onset of muscular fatigue. Many of the newer fluid supplements on the market, particularly those that contain a synthetic glucose polymer, have been shown to delay the onset of fatigue by providing a source of glucose, while not significantly interfering with water absorption into the blood. Those who wish to use a commercial fluid supplement should choose carefully.

Replacing fluids after exercise is important for the recovery and repair process that are an important part of the general adaptation syndrome. The consumption of a large quantity of plain water is generally not advised in that its ultimate effect will be to stimulate the urinary excretion of additional amounts of water and important electrolytes. As large volumes of pure water rapidly enter the body the blood becomes diluted, or hypotonic. Receptors in the hypothalamus of the brain detect this hypotonic condition and signal the kidneys to eliminate the extra water and flush away important electrolytes such as sodium and potassium with it. A more gradual absorption of fluid such as that achieved with a moderate electrolyte containing solution is preferred.

Selected Readings:

Anonymous, **Nutrition for Physical Fitness and Athletic Performance in Adults**, *Position of the American Dietetic Association and the Canadian Dietetic Association*, 2000,
http://www.eatright.org/afitperform.html

Clark, N. **The Power of Protein**, *The Physician and Sportsmedicine*, Vol. 24, No. 4, April 1996, http://www.physsportsmed.com/isues/apr_96/protein.htm

Kaslow, S. **Comparison of Fuel Utilization During Walking and Running at the Equivalent Heart Rate Intensities**. *IAHPERD Journal*, Vol. 29, No. 2, Spring 1996, http://www.mum.edu/exss_dept/iahperd/journal/j96s_fuel.html

Sleivert, G., **Training and Competing in the Mystery Zone**, *Sportscience*, September-October 1997, http://www.sportsci.org/news/news9709/sleivert.html

Related Fitness Assessment Activities:

Activity 8. Evaluating Metabolic Rate and Energy Requirement

Chapter 5

Skeletal System

Chapter Contents
- Bone
- The Skeleton
- Articulations
- Musculoskeletal Movements
- Flexibility / Range of Motion
- Effects of Exercise on the Skeletal System
- Selected Readings

Learning Objectives

The material in this chapter will allow you to:
- Understand the structure and function of bone
- Be familiar with the anatomy of the human skeleton
- Understand the mechanism of human movement and joint function
- Understand the factors influencing bone health
- Understand the factors influencing bone disease
- Understand the effects of exercise on the skeletal system

The skeletal system provides a framework for the body within which the organs lie protected and upon which the muscles are anchored. The supporting structures of the skeleton, *bone* and *cartilage*, are joined at regions known as *articulations*, or joints. Holding the bones together are tough, fibrous, connective tissue bands called *ligaments*. Without the assistance of the skeletal system, its bones and joints, muscle contraction could not bring about the coordinated movements we depend on for locomotion, exercise, and athletic skill movements.

Bone

Anatomically, there are two main categories of bone in the skeleton; *long bones* and *flat bones*. As their names imply, long bones are long and slender while flat bones are broad and flat (Fig 5.1). Whether long or flat, all human bones share some common properties. Unlike their structural counterparts in wood-frame buildings, human bone is not solid as are pieces of 2x4" lumber. Rather, bone consists of a hard, dense external casing of *compact bone* within which exists a hollow cavity filled with a branching network of thin bone filaments, or *trabeculae*, referred to as *spongy or cancellous bone*. This arrangement allows bone to have the dual properties of being both strong and light in weight.

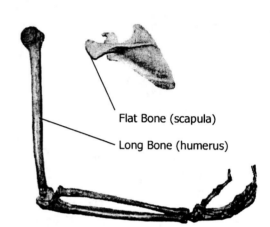

Flat Bone (scapula)

Long Bone (humerus)

Figure 5.1. Bone Categories: Flat and Long

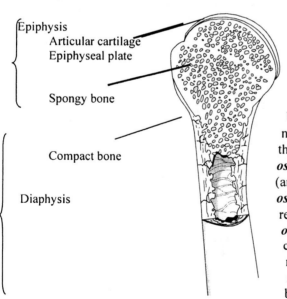

Epiphysis
Articular cartilage
Epiphyseal plate

Spongy bone

Compact bone

Diaphysis

Figure 5.2. Long Bone Structure

Within the spongy bone trabecular network is found the *marrow cavity*, a space occupied by the blood cell producing tissue as well as by arteries, veins, nerves and some storage fat. The bone material itself consists of a protein and carbohydrate containing *matrix* made rigid by the incorporation of mineral salts, most notably calcium. Embedded within the matrix are the bone cells referred to in Chapter 3, the *osteoblasts* which synthesize new bone matrix (and are responsible for bone growth), the *osteoclasts* which degrade bone (and are responsible for bone resporbtion), and the *osteocytes*, mature and generally dormant bone cells. The osteoblasts and osteoclasts, cells responsible for remodeling bone through synthesis and resorption, are referred to as the bone's effector cells. Finally, the bones are surrounded by a nourishing connective tissue wrapping called the *periosteum* from which bone growth (in diameter) can occur.

The long bones, which are typically the weight bearing bones of the body, consist of a cylindrical shaft called the *diaphysis* and two knobby, expanded ends called *epiphyses* (Fig.5.2). The diaphysis is joined to the epiphyses by a zone of cartilage called the *epiphyseal plate*. Except for the articulating, or joint surfaces, the bones are covered with a tissue called periosteum, a tissue rich in blood vessels and nerves. It is from growth within the periosteum that bones increase in diameter, or thickness.

In young individuals, the epiphyseal plate consists of a band of cartilage from which bone growth occurs. In the juvenile and adolescent years, elongation of the diaphysis occurs at the epiphyseal plate, often referred to as the growth plate, resulting in an overall elongation of the bone. Growth hormone from the pituitary gland provides the stimulus for this bone elongation. Such activity is the primary reason for growth during these years. In the late teens or early twenties, the cartilaginous epiphyseal plate is replaced by bone and growth, at least in length, can no longer occur. This calcification is influenced by a hormone from the thyroid gland, thyrocalcitonin.

In the long bones, the ends of the epiphyses, which participate in joints or articulations are covered with a layer of *articular cartilage*, to facilitate the sliding of these surfaces over one another. Flat bones are involved primarily in the protection of underlying organs and are not usually weight bearing. Examples of such flat bones would be the bones of the skull, the ribs, the scapulae (shoulder blades) and the bones of the pelvis.

When viewing the skeleton we often have the tendency to see it as simply a structural framework, something similar to the wood framing of a house or the steel skeleton of a skyscraper. This couldn't be farther from the truth. Bone is a living tissue composed of cells embedded in a matrix containing calcium, potassium, magnesium and other mineral salts. It is the presence of these mineral salts that give bone its rigidity. Softer cartilage lacks these salts. In addition to its role in support and movement, bone also acts as a storage reservoir for these minerals, particularly *calcium storage*. The level of calcium in the blood (a reflection of diet and vitamin

By the Numbers

Human bone has a tensile strength (resistance to bending) of about 17,000 pounds per square inch, comparable to granite (15,000 lbs/in^2). The compressive strength of bone is about 25,000 lbs/in^2, twice as strong as an oak beam and comparable to aluminum and light steel.

intake) is one of the factors influencing bone calcium storage. When calcium is abundant, bone will take calcium from the blood and store it through the action of osteoblast cells. When calcium is deficient bone will give up calcium through the action of osteoclast cells in order to maintain adequate levels of calcium in the blood. It is apparent that sufficient calcium in the diet is necessary for strong bones.

Another factor in bone calcium storage is that of hormones. *Thyrocalcitonin* from the thyroid gland will stimulate bone to take up calcium. *Parathormone* from the parathyroid gland will cause bone to loose calcium. A proper balance between these two hormones is necessary and is normally maintained through the process of negative feedback. These factors are illustrated in figure 5.3. *Estrogen* is a hormone which prevents bone from loosing calcium. Women who have past menopause and women athletes, both with low estrogen levels, are susceptible to loss of bone calcium and the bone weakening disease, *osteoporosis*.

Figure 5.3. Calcium Metabolism

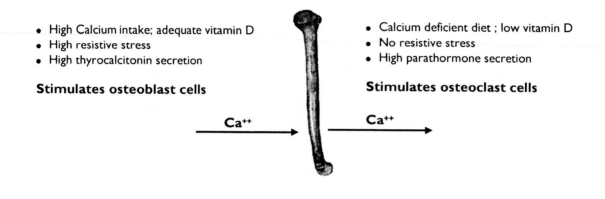

- High Calcium intake; adequate vitamin D
- High resistive stress
- High thyrocalcitonin secretion

Stimulates osteoblast cells

Ca^{++}

- Calcium deficient diet ; low vitamin D
- No resistive stress
- High parathormone secretion

Stimulates osteoclast cells

Ca^{++}

The Skeleton

The human skeleton consists of 206 bones as illustrated in figure 5.4 on the following page. The skeleton can be divided into two parts, the *axial* skeleton and the *appendicular* skeleton. The axial skeleton is that portion of the skeletal system running along the central axis of the body and consisting of the skull, vertebral column and ribs. The appendicular skeleton is comprised of those bones that make up the body appendages, the arms and legs, together with the girdles of bones which connect them to the axial skeleton; the pelvis and pectoral girdles.

Articulations (joints)

An important subset, or subsystem, of the skeletal system is the articular system, the system comprised of the body's joints, or articulations. A joint is technically referred to as an *arthrosis* and the study of joints is known as *arthrology*. The term *articulation* reflects the fact that the bones of the body join in a complimentary fashion or, articulate with each other to form the overall human framework. The articulations are classified according to both structural and functional characteristics. Structural characteristics are determined by the presence or absence of a joint space or capsule as well as the by type of tissue that supports the joint. The functional component, as you might expect, relates to the movements a joint may or may not express.

Fibrous, Cartilaginous and *Synovial* are the three categories that describe the structural components of joints. Fibrous joints lack a joint capsule and the articulations are, instead, supported by fibrous tissue. These fibrous tissues are primarily made up of the protein collagen. The collagen fibers are extremely strong and pliable and are known to resist pulling forces, that is, they cannot be stretched. There are different types of collagen fibers and their characteristics will differ depending on the tissues in which they are.

Figure 5.4. The Human Skeleton

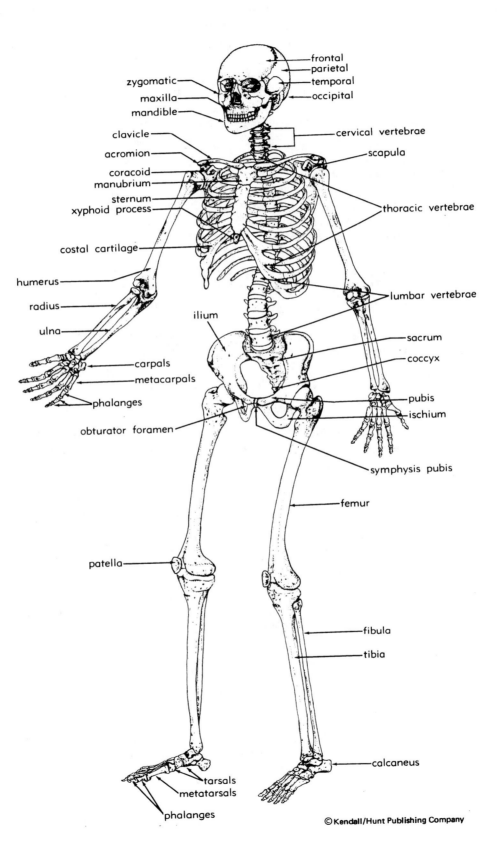

frontal
parietal
temporal
occipital
zygomatic
maxilla
mandible
cervical vertebrae
clavicle
acromion
scapula
coracoid
manubrium
sternum
xyphoid process
thoracic vertebrae
costal cartilage
humerus
radius
lumbar vertebrae
ilium
ulna
sacrum
coccyx
carpals
metacarpals
phalanges
pubis
ischium
obturator foramen
symphysis pubis
femur
patella
fibula
tibia
calcaneus
tarsals
metatarsals
phalanges

© Kendall/Hunt Publishing Company

Like the fibrous joints, the cartilaginous joints lack a joint capsule but the articulations are supported, or held together, by cartilaginous tissue. Cartilage is comprised of both collagen and elastic fibers that can be found in a solid but flexible ground substance. Ground substances are made of organic compounds that keep cells of tissues tightly bound. Chondroitin sulfate is the specific type of ground substance found in cartilage and in which the collagen and elastic fibers are embedded. The elastic fibers found in cartilage are made up of the protein elastin and a carbohydrate-protein (glycoprotein) fibrillin. It is the unique marriage of these substances that enables cartilage to withstand a tremendous amount of stress within reason and still return to its original shape. Because cartilage lacks both nerve and blood supply, nutrients that are responsible for nourishing and promoting healing, are virtually non-existent account for one reason why these types of joints heal poorly.

Synovial joints consist of a joint space or capsule and their articulation is supported by dense irregular connective tissue as well as accessory ligaments in many cases. Dense irregular connective tissue consists of an increased quantity of irregularly organized collagen fibers. The irregular organization of these fibers enables these joints to withstand pulling forces from various angles.

In addition to the structural classifications described above, there are three functional classifications of joints, including *Synarthrosis* joints, which are immovable; *Amphiarthrosis* joints are slightly movable; and *Diarthrosis*, joints which are freely movable.

The bones that help create fibrous joints articulate tightly together, and there is no articular capsule, as a result, fibrous joints produce little to no movement. There are three classification of fibrous joints in the body. *Sutures*, which can be found between the bones of the skull are immovable, or synarthrosis joints. While it is important to keep the bones of the skull tightly fused together in order to protect the brain within, the skull of infants and young children must allow for growth as the brain and skull grow in size. In the developing cranium from infancy to an adult, the joints between the cranial bones are less rigid and spaces are formed between the cranial bones (Fontenelles) which gradually decrease in size with age and eventually fuse to form the sutures. Sutures are considered synarthrosis joints . *Syndesmoses* are fibrous joints characterized as a series of band like ligaments holding the bones together and can be found uniting the tibia and fibula. Because the radius and ulna rotate about each other, this fibrous joint is classified as an amphiarthritic joint. The *Gomphosis* is the last of the fibrous articulations and can be found in the relationship between the teeth and their sockets. Cartilagenous joints also lack a joint cavity produce little to no movement and are therefore synarthrosis.

Cartilagenous joints can be classified into two catagories, *Synchondrosis* and *Symphyses*. Synchondrosis can be seen in the developing osseous tissue between the epiphysis and diaphysis in long bone. Synchondritic joints are short lived as they tend to ossify with maturation. This process of joints becoming ossified is known as *Synostosis*. The process of synostosis can also be seen in some sutures during cranial development. Synchondrosis is classified as synarthrosis because the joints become immovable. Symphyses are joints that can be located in the mid line of the body as seen in the intervertebral discs as well as the pubic symphysis. A symphyses is amphiarthritic in nature lending suppleness and flexibility to the axial skeletal system. Synovial joints are always classified as diarthritic or freely movable. The reason for this lies in physical make up of these joints. Because of their importance to movement and exercise, our focus will be on the synovial joints.

Table 5.1. Joint Classification

Joint Structure & Types	Joint Function	Examples
Fibrous:		
Suture	Synarthrosis	Cranial Bones
Syndesmosis	Amphiarthrosis	Distal Tibiofibular Joint
Gomphosis	Synarthrosis	Teeth and Sockets
Cartilaginous:		
Synchondrosis (Synostosis)	Synarthrosis	Metopic Suture
Epiphyseal Plate		1st Rib and Manubrium
Symphyses	Amphiarthrosis	Intervertebral Discs
		Pubic symphysis
Synovial	Diarthrosis	Planar Joints
		Hinge Joints
		Pivot Joints
		Condyloid Joints
		Saddle Joints
		Ball-and-socket Joints

Synovial Joints and Human Movement

The most important articulations with respect to movement are the *synovial joints* which are classified as diarthroses (freely moveable). The synovial joint involves the ends of two long bones (elbow and knee) or the end of a long bone and the socket of a flat bone (shoulder and hip). The ends of the bones which are in contact are covered by articular cartilage and enclosed within a fluid filled sac, the *synovial membrane* and filled with a lubricating *synovial fluid*, a viscous material having the consistency of raw egg-white. The entire structure is held together with tough, fibrous *ligaments* forming a capsule around the joint.

The articular cartilage, although smooth and solid in its outward appearance, actually has a surface perforated by myriad microscopic pores. In the normal state, the viscous synovial fluid is absorbed into these pores just as a sponge would absorb water. During joint movement, when the articular cartilage of one bone moves against and presses on the articular cartilage of another, the synovial fluid is squeezed out from the pores to lubricate the moving surfaces. As soon as the stress is released from any point, the fluid is once again absorbed.

In some joints, especially those that are subjected to extreme stress, there is an additional pad of fibrocartilage located between the bones and known as an *articular disc* or *meniscus*. The knee would be an example of such a joint. The presence of this additional fibrocartilage insert serves to more effectively distribute the forces placed on the joint across a larger surface area without the need to increase the overall size of the joint.

Figure 5.5. Synovial Joint Structure

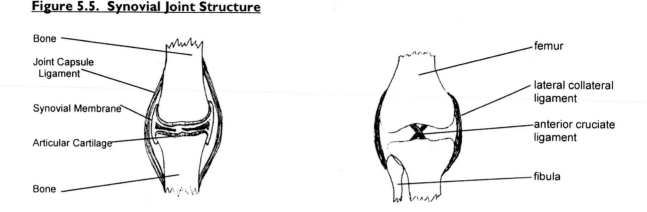

There are several specific types of synovial joints, each characterized by the range and plane of allowable movement and the architecture of the joint's structure. Included among these are **hinge joints**, which resemble the hinged lid on a box in their range of motion. Hinge joints are found at the elbow, knee, and fingers. These joints allow for motion in only one plane (uniaxial). The **ball and socket joint** consists of a rounded, knob-like extension of one bone moving within a cup-shaped depression, or socket of another bone. Examples of ball and socket joints are the shoulder and hip. The ball and socket joint allows for movements in all planes (multiaxial), as well as for rotation and circumduction. The **gliding joint** involves the movement of relatively flat bones sliding over one another as in the wrist, ankle and parts of the vertebrae. These joints allow for a sliding type of motion in two planes (biaxial). The **pivot joint** consists of the cylindrical surface of one bone moving within a ring-like structure of another bone. The pivot joint allows for rotation and is characterized by the joint between the ends of the radius and ulna just below the elbow. The **condyloid joint** is a modification of the ball and socket joint. It consists of an oval-shaped projection of one bone, the condyle, moving within an elliptical cavity of another bone. Movement is provided in many planes (multiaxial) but not rotation. Condyloid joints are found at the base of the fingers (attachment to hand). The last category of synovial joint is the **saddle joint**. The saddle joint involves two bones, each of which has both concave and convex regions on the articulating surface which fit together in a complimentary fashion. The saddle joint provides for movement in several directions (multiaxial) and is exemplified by the attachment of the base of the thumb to the hand.

Ligaments and muscles play an important role both the structure and function of our joints. The shoulder joint is formed by the ball-like head of the humerus fitting into the shallow cup-like socket (glenoid cavity) of the scapula. Because the glenoid cavity of the scapula is shallow the shoulder is capable of unrestricted movement in multiple planes and directions. This, however, renders the joint to be very unstable. Shoulder stability is therefore highly depended on the ligaments and muscles that hold these bones together. These muscles are known as the rotator cuff and play an important role in maintaining the structural integrity of the shoulder joint.

Musculoskeletal Movements

Together, the muscles and skeleton comprise the musculoskeletal system. It is the action of the muscles, pulling on the bones, which is ultimately responsible for movement about the articulations. The following terms describe the types of movement possible in the normal musculoskeletal system:

<u>Flexion</u>: decreasing the angle at an articulation
<u>Extension</u>: increasing the angle at an articulation
<u>Hyperextension</u>: extension past the normal range of motion
<u>Rotation</u>: rotating a bone around its long axis
<u>Circumduction</u>: moving one end of a bone in a circle while keeping the other end stationary
<u>Abduction</u>: moving a body part away from the body midline
<u>Adduction</u>: Moving a body part in towards the body midline
<u>Pronation</u>: turning the hand so the palm faces down
<u>Supination</u>: turning the hand so the palm faces up
<u>Eversion</u>: turning the foot so the sole faces laterally or outward
<u>Inversion</u>: turning the foot so the sole faces medially or inward

Fig. 5.6. Musculoskeletal Movements

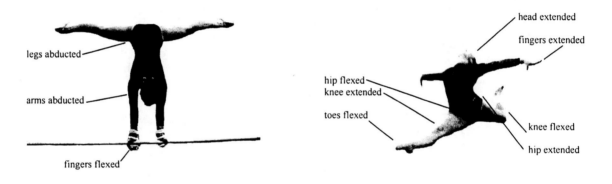

Table 5.2. Examples of Selected Musculoskeletal Movements

Motion	Definition	Example	Muscle Involved
Flexion	Decreases angle at joint	Bicep curl	Bicep brachii
Extension	Increases angle at joint	Tricep extension	Tricep brachii
Abduction	Move bone away from midline	Lateral raise	Deltoid
Adduction	Move bone toward midline	Pectoral Flyes	Pectoralis

Muscles, bones and joints are arranged in such a way as to form lever systems that provide mechanical advantage to human movement. In general, a lever is consists of an object to be moved called the load or resistance (R), the force or effort (E) that is applied to move the load, and a fulcrum (F) or pivot point around which the movement takes place. Levers occur in three different forms, or classes, first, second and third class levers as illustrated below.

74

Figure 5.7. Lever Systems and Musculoskeletal Movement

Figure 5.7. Lever Systems

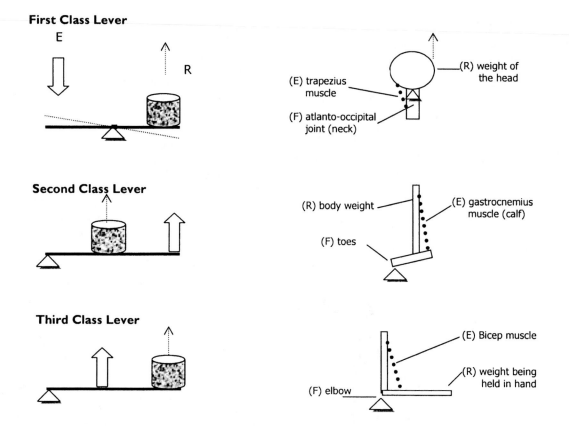

First Class Lever

Second Class Lever

Third Class Lever

The third-class lever is the one most commonly associated with movement of the arms and legs. If we look at the figure above right for the third-class lever we can see that the bicep muscle attachment point is located near the fulcrum (elbow) and not near the resistance (hand). Because the effort (E) exerted by the bicep muscle has to work over a relatively long distance to move the resistance(R), the system works at a mechanical disadvantage. The effort required to move a resistance is the product of the weight of the resistance (R) and the distance (D) it is acting over. We can see the reason for this below.

An object weighing 10 lbs will require 10 lbs of work, or effort, to move it. If our lever system is designed so that the 10 lb. object is located 5 feet away from the fulcrum point (Fig 5.8a, below), the total amount of work required to move it will be 50 ft-lbs. To generate the required 50 ft-lbs of work we would need to press down with an effort of 10 lbs because, distributed along a equivalent distance of 5 feet, 10 lbs would be required to generate the 50 ft-lbs of work (W = F x D).

Work = Force x Distance

Work = 10 lbs of resistance x 5 feet of distance

Work = 50 ft-lbs.

If, as we see in Figure 5.8b, the fulcrum was moved closer to the resistance, the total work required to move it would be only 20 ft-lbs (10 lbs of resistance located 2 feet from the fulcrum = 20 ft-lbs). On the effort side, to generate the required 20 ft-lbs of opposing work, we would need an effort of only 2.5 pounds because the effort point is located 8 feet from the fulcrum (W = F x D ; 20 ft-lbs = 2.5 lbs x 8 feet). In this regard, the lever system provides a large mechanical advantage: it requires only 2.5 lbs of effort to move 10 lbs of resistance.

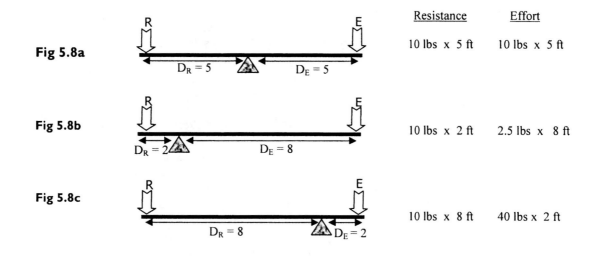

	Resistance	Effort
Fig 5.8a	10 lbs x 5 ft	10 lbs x 5 ft
Fig 5.8b	10 lbs x 2 ft	2.5 lbs x 8 ft
Fig 5.8c	10 lbs x 8 ft	40 lbs x 2 ft

Conversely, if we move the fulcrum point closer to the effort, we create a lever system with a mechanical disadvantage. Here, in Fig. 5c, we see that 40lbs of effort would be required to move just 10 lbs of resistance. The third class lever, as used in the human body, works with this type of mechanical disadvantage. Although seemingly counterproductive, there are several reasons why we are designed this way.

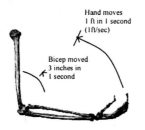

Fig 5.9

In the third class lever as we use it, it is true that a larger effort is required of the muscle to move an object of any given weight. But, this arrangement produces a much greater range of movement at the resistance point than is actually produced by the muscle at the effort point. In addition the speed, or velocity, of the movement at the resistance point is also enhanced, moving at a large multiple of the muscle's actual contraction velocity. As we can see in figure 5.9, a movement of only three inches at the bicep muscle will move the hand through a distance of 12 inches and at a much greater velocity. Therefore, this system has been designed to maximize both range of motion and velocity of motion while sacrificing strength.

Because evolution, for a variety of reasons, has designed us to be compact and streamlined, our bicep muscle does not attach to our radius bone near the hand, which would be mechanically advantageous, but, rather, attaches near the elbow. This requires the muscle to generate significant force to move comparatively light weights.

In reality, each musculoskeletal movement taking place at a single joint is caused by a system comprised of several muscles working together. For purposes of example, let's take a look at the elbow joint. The elbow joint is formed by the junction of the bone of the upper arm, the *humerus*, and the two bones of the forearm, the *radius* and *ulna*. Attached to this joint are the two primary muscles that bring about the movements of the elbow, flexion and extension, the bicep and tricep muscles, respectively (fig. 5.10). Contraction of the bicep muscle causes flexion at the elbow and the bicep is therefore referred to as the *primary mover*, or *agonist*. The tricep muscle, which brings about the action of elbow extension, is referred to as the *antagonist* muscle because of its opposing, or antagonistic, action relative to the bicep. For every movement of the skeleton there is an *antagonistic pair* of muscles. In addition, other muscles may assist the bicep in causing elbow flexion, for example, the *brachialis* and *brachioradial*s muscles, and these would be referred to as second*ary movers* or *assistant movers*.

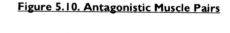

Figure 5.10. Antagonistic Muscle Pairs

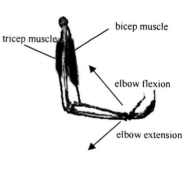

bicep muscle

tricep muscle

elbow flexion

elbow extension

When the bicep contracts or shortens we expect the forearm bones (radius and ulna) and the hand to be pulled up toward the shoulder (Fig 5.10). We do not expect that the contracting bicep muscle would pull the shoulder down toward the hand. This unidirectional movement at the elbow joint is influenced by the action of additional muscles that contract in concert with the bicep and hold the shoulder in place. When the bicep muscle contracts, muscles in the upper back, chest, and shoulder also contract holding the shoulder (actually, the scapula bone) stable so that the bicep has an anchor point against which to work. These muscles are referred to as *stabilizers*. For the bicep muscle acting on the elbow joint, the stabilizers include the *trapezius, pectoralis major*, and *deltoid* muscles.

Movements of the legs, for example the muscle contractions that are responsible for running, jumping, and kicking, rely on muscles of the abdomen and lower back to stabilize the pelvis, against which the leg muscles are anchored. Training the core abdominal and spinal muscles are therefore an important part of training for runners and other track and field athletes for whom these actions are important.

Flexibility

Each joint allows for movement within a specific plane or planes and through specific angles of motion. For example, the elbow joint, the articulation between the humerus bone of the upper arm and the ulna of the forearm allows for extension to 180° (a straight line) and flexion to about 30°. Movement within these normal limits are referred to as the joint's *range of motion*. For every joint there is a normal range of motion that is expected as an indicator of musculoskeletal flexibility. In its simplest interpretation, flexibility is the ability to move the bones of a joint through their normal range of motion. Normal flexibility is an important component of physical fitness. Figure 5.11 illustrates the normal range of motion for the shoulder joint. Although the structure of the joint, the shapes of the articulating ends of the bone, and the health of the articular cartilage all contribute to determining the range of motion, it is the soft tissue structures around and attached to the joint that have the greatest effect.

Table 5.1 lists the factors that help determine flexibility and range of motion. While exercising our joints through their normal range of motion can help prevent their deterioration, not much can be done through exercise to change the physical structure of the joint or to increase the flexibility of the ligaments. The most effective method of improving flexibility is to stretch the muscles though activities that are described in the next chapter.

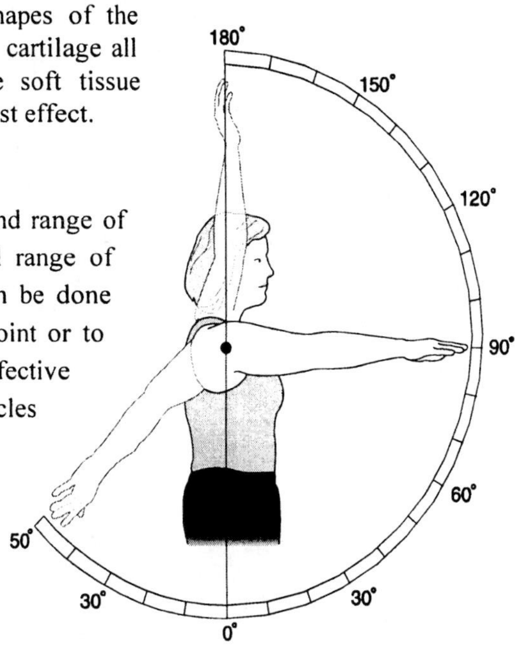

Figure 5.11 Shoulder Joint Range of Motion

Table 5.3 Structural Factors Determining Range of Motion

Structure	Contribution to Limiting Range of Motion
Joint Capusle Ligaments	47 %
Muscles	41 %
Tendons	10 %
Skin	2 %

Each of the structures that make up the various articulations help to determine how freely the joint will move in various directions. The range of free, unrestricted movement of a joint is referred to its *Range of Motion (ROM).* Typical joint movements can either be linear, or rotational. Linear, or translational, movements can be measured in meters or inches. Rotational movements are measured in the degrees of a circle by an instrument known as a goniometer.

The movements allowed by the various types of articulations are, in part, dependent upon the shape of the contact surfaces of the two bones that make up the joint. Typically, the surfaces of the two opposing bones will fit together like a puzzle, having complimentary shapes. In addition to the shapes of the articulating bones, the following factors will also influence a joint's ROM. Synovial joints contain accessory ligaments, typically arranged in pairs, and when one of these ligaments experiences tension or tautness, its ligamentous counterpart will be lax allowing for freedom of movement or "play" within the joint. Muscle tension can contribute to the ligamentous effects on a joint thus assisting in the restriction of movement. In addition, when a muscle is either precontracted or overstretched, the ROM can be affected as well with precontraction limiting ROM and overstretching increasing ROM. Other factors which can affect the ROM include the presence of adhesions or scar tissue which limit extensibility and elasticity, excess adipose or muscle tissue which create physical restrictions, and certain hormones, such as relaxin secreted during the later stages of pregnancy. When joints have been immobilized for a period of time, such as after an injury, synovial fluid may be reduced, ligaments and tendons lose their flexibility, and muscles atrophy, all collectively diminishing ROM.

As we now know, there are several components of a joint that are responsible for creating freedom of movement. Let's explore the role of ligaments. A physical measure of the function of ligaments is the *load displacement curve (Fig 5.12)*, which varies according to the joint studied. In evaluating ROM there are two components of the movement, as seen in the load displacement curve, that are important to understand, these being the *neutral zone* and the *elastic zone*. The neutral zone is usually quite small and is sometimes referred to as the free play of the joint. It is usually found in the first few degrees of motion. The elastic zone reflects the actual movement, or displacement, beginning at the end of the neutral zone through to the end of the ROM.

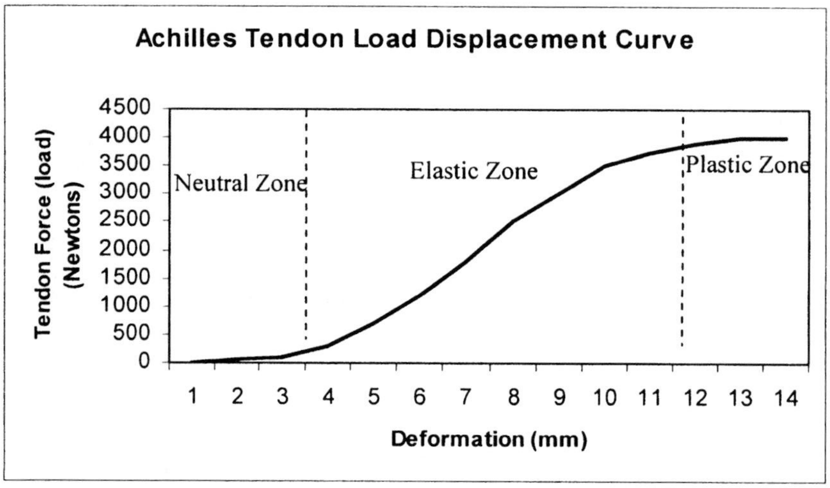

Figure 5.12. Tendon Load Displacement Curve

In order to perform movements during exercise effectively and safely, it is essential that your joint have stability. A joint's stability is measured by the ability of the joint to resist the load placed upon it without compromising its integrity. This is accomplished through the ligaments, muscles, atmospheric pressure, and the osseous tissue (bone).

Healthy ligaments help to keep the bones in proper alignment during normal movements. Muscle and their tendons also assist in stabilizing the alignment of joints. This can be seen by looking at the glenohumeral joint of the shoulder where the glenoid fossa, the socket, of this ball-and-socket joint is very shallow and heavily relies on the supporting structures of ligaments, muscles and tendons for stability. Since the joint capsule is a sealed structure, a vacuum effect is created when the articulating bones are pulled away from each other and the atmospheric pressure applied to the exterior of a joint, exceeding the lowered pressure on the interior of the joint, helps to push the structures back together, stabilizing and supporting the joint.

Recall that all synovial joints are diarthritic or freely moveable. During certain movements, the contact surfaces can move from being optimally aligned to being not optimized. In the optimized position, minimal forces are placed on the joint because the articulating bones are ideally aligned maximizing contact surface area and the joint capsule and ligaments display a healthy tonic state as is the case with the knee joint during leg extension while standing. This position is referred to as a *closed pack position*. Any other position that exists within the joint's range of motion is referred to as an *open packed* or *loose packed position*. In such a position, contact surface area is decreased maximizing the forces experienced by the joint and increasing the tension placed on the joint capsule and ligaments. Additional forces added to joints in the open or loose packed positions, raises the potential for injuries.

Table 5.4. Major Joints of the Human Body

Major Joint	Type of Joint	Action	ROM (Degrees)	Movement Planes
Shoulder	Synovial	Flexion / Extension	90-100 / 40-60	Sagittal
		Abduction / Adduction	90-95 / 0	Frontal
		Internal / External Rotation	70-90 / 70-90	Transverse
		Horizontal Abduction / Adduction	45 / 135	Transverse
		Circumduction		
Elbow	Synovial	Flexion / Extension	145-150 / 0	Sagittal
		Lateral Flexion		Frontal
		Rotation		Transverse
Hip	Synovial	Flexion / Extension	130 / 30	Sagittal
		Abduction / Adduction	35 / 30	Frontal
		Internal / External Rotation	45 / 50	Transverse
		Circumduction		
Knee	Synovial	Flexion / Extension	140 / 0-10	Sagittal
		Internal / External Rotation	30 / 45	Transverse

Effects of Exercise on the Skeletal System

Bone, like most other living tissue, responds to stress by adapting as explained in the General Adaptation Syndrome. Bone cells, specifically the osteoblasts, will deposit new bone matrix when subjected to increased loads and forces, thus thickening and strengthening the bones. They accomplish this by removing calcium from the blood and using it to produce and secrete new, hard, bone matrix. When bone is not subject to stress from load and force, or when blood calcium or vitamin D levels become deficient, bone will atrophy due to resorption of mineralized matrix. This occurs as the osteoclast cells secrete enzymes that digest the bone matrix, returning the calcium to the blood. Bone loss and subsequent bone weakening is common in bedridden patients, in immobilized limbs such as those placed in casts and in astronauts spending prolonged periods in a weightless environment.

The constant action of the osteoclasts and osteoblasts leads to a continual remodeling of the bones that can occur in three distinct modes, the *conservation mode*, the *disuse mode* and the *strengthening mode.* Under normal circumstances, with proper nutrition and moderate physical activity, the ratio of the remodeling activities, synthesis and resorption, are about equal so that the bone remodeling process results in conservation of bone material and strength. That is, the osteoclast-mediated removal of existing bone matrix is balanced by the osteoblast-mediated synthesis of new bone matrix and is referred to as conservation mode remodeling. If physical activity decreases such that the bones are no longer subject to an adequate level of stress, the rate of osteoclast-mediated resorption will exceed the rate of osteoblast-mediated synthesis and bone matrix will be lost, decreasing the density and strength of the bones. This is referred to as disuse mode remodeling.

Subjecting bones to a higher level of physical stress and strain, as is done in many forms of exercise and athletic training, results in a heightened level of osteoblast activity such that the osteoblast-mediated synthesis of new bone matrix exceeds the rate of osteoclast-mediated matrix removal leading to an increased density and strength of the bones. The physical strain applied to a bone during exercise or training activities actually deforms the bones resulting in numerous microscopic fractures or *microdamage*. It is the bone's response to repair this microdamage, acting under the principles of the General Adaptation Syndrome (GAS), that actually results in the bone's strengthening. That the amount of strengthening mode remodeling is proportional to the amount of physical strain applied provides evidence that the body's GAS response will always try to adapt by providing a safety factor against the largest average voluntary stress.

It is believed that under both normal and exercise or training activities, the largest stress placed on our bones comes from our own muscles as they pull against the bones to cause movement against the force of gravity. By forcing our muscles to move greater loads, for example as we do in resistance training exercises, we can enhance the degree of stress and strain and force the muscles into strengthening mode remodeling.

To the extent that exercise and athletic activity increases the stress on bones it is beneficial. In fact, while the acquisition and maintenance of muscular strength is important, the primary reason for the recommendation of regular resistance exercise is for the development and maintenance of strong, healthy bones. This is particularly important for pre-menopausal women in order to stave off the almost inevitable loss of bone density after menopause.

Exercise and athletics can also have detrimental effects on the skeletal system. These involve fractures and dislocations and injury to articular and meniscal cartilages and ligaments. Severe exercise in women, which reduces lean body fat percentages, has been shown to result in a decreased level of estrogen secretion and lead to abnormalities in the menstrual cycle, to sterility and to osteoporosis as described before. Exercising against heavy resistance, such as lifting weights, can cause damage to the epiphyseal plates in young individuals and subsequently retard normal growth. Although as seen above, stress and strain above normal levels can have a beneficial effect on bone, if the strain is too great such that the extent and rate of microdamage formation exceeds the ability of the bone remodeling process, the microfractues can accumulate and result in larger, painful stress fractures. The key, as always, is to exercise to the point of overload but not to the point of excess as we reviewed in the general adaptation syndrome.

The General Adaptation Syndrome and Spaceflight

Since the early days of spaceflight it has become increasingly apparent that one of the most significant physiological difficulties faced by astronauts is the loss of calcium from their bones and the resulting decrease in bone density and bone strength. The data collected has been consistent with Apollo astronauts loosing an average of 0.1% of their bone calcium per week and the American Skylab astronauts loosing up to 50mg of bone calcium per day. The most substantial amount of data were obtained by from the Soviet cosmonaut crews of the Mir space station who remained in space for periods of up to 14 months. These cosmonauts lost an average of 1 percent of their bone mineral density each month, a rate six times greater than the average post-menopausal bone loss typical in osteoporosis.

The reason for this problem is quite simple; it is the general adaptation syndrome working in reverse. While our previous studies on the GAS have all related to improvements, or the building of capacity, in response to overloads of stress, the GAS also predicts that in the reduction, or absence of stress, tissue structures will diminish through the loss of structural and physiologic capacity. Although the reason is apparent, the solution is not and NASA and the international space agencies are working on ways to provide in-space resistance exercises and other therapies to address this problem.

Selected Readings

Beck, B.R. and R. Shoemaker, Osteoporosis: Understanding Key Risk Factors and Therapeutic Options, *The Physician and Sportsmedicine*, Vol. 28, No.2, February 2000, http://www.physsportsmed.com/issues/2000/02_00/beck.htm

Frost, H.M. Muscle, Bone, and the Utah Paradigm: A 1999 Overview. *Medicine and Science in Sports and Exercise*, Vol. 32, No. 5, pp. 911-917, May 2000

Related Fitness Assessment Activities

Activity 9.   Evaluating Flexibility
Activity 10. Kraus-Weber Test of Back Fitness

Chapter 6

Muscle Function

Chapter Contents

- Muscle Function
- Muscle Structure
- Action Potential and Muscle Excitability
- Slow and Fast Muscle
- Natural Talent
- Muscle Strength, Power and Endurance
- Conditioning for Muscular Strength
- Conditioning for Muscular Power
- Conditioning for Muscular Endurance
- Stretching for Warm-up, Cool-down and Flexibility
- Major Muscles of the Body
- Selected Readings

Learning Objectives

The material in this chapter will allow you to:

- Understand the structure and function of skeletal muscles
- Identify and name the major muscles and muscle groups of the body
- Understand the determinants of strength and how to train them
- Understand the determinants of power and how to train them
- Understand the determinants of endurance and how to train them
- Be able to design a program of muscle conditioning for specific purposes

Now that we understand the components of a healthy skeletal system, the framework around which the body is built, and the nature of human movement through lever systems comprised of bones and joints, it is important to realize that movement would not be possible with out the aide of our muscular system. The collaborative functioning of both the muscular and skeletal systems are required to produce human movement and, therefore, we commonly hear reference to the *musculoskeletal* system.

Muscle Function

Aside from its obvious function of producing both fine and gross movements, the muscular system also has other, often overlooked, but equally important functions. Skeletal muscle contractions are commonly associated with gross bodily movements for example; the bones of the forearm moving closer to the humerus during a bicep curl or the range of motion the legs go through during running. While these conscious and voluntary actions account for the more well known examples of muscle contraction, of equal or maybe even greater importance, are the contractions that take place without our conscious awareness. For example, the deep muscles attached to the spine need to constantly contract and adjust in order for the body to maintain proper posture during sitting and standing. In addition, even in conscious movements such as the execution of a bicep curl, the stabilizing muscles of the shoulder contract to support the point of origin and make the bicep curl possible.

The body is made up of series of tubes and pouches that during embryonic development go on to form the organs, glands and blood vessels. In certain locations, the smooth muscles form concentric clamp-like structures called sphincters. In their natural homeostatic state, the sphincter muscles remain contracted to hold the organs' fluids in their proper location and to prevent the fluid from flowing back into the organ once it leaves. Smooth muscles also participate in an important internal function called peristalsis. Peristalsis consists of a rhythmic series of contractions used to push food through the gastrointestinal, or digestive, tract. Smooth muscles that surround the glands of the endocrine system contract to expel hormones when needed. Sphincter muscles in the blood vessels contract and relax to control the flow of blood to various capillary beds throughout the body. Contracted pre-capillary sphincters close off the vessels, diverting the blood away while relaxed sphincters open the vessels allowing blood to flow through.

Muscles are also responsible for helping to maintain a stable body temperature. Human beings are part of a class of animals called homeotherms which are capable of self-regulating their body temperature. The process of generating heat which is a byproduct of muscle contraction is commonly referred to as *thermogenisis*. We are, perhaps, most familiar with this when we shiver to counteract a cold environment and a declining body temperature.

Muscular tissue has four characteristics that make it resilient and able to function in a dynamic fashion. First, muscle has the ability to become excited, the property known as *excitation*, a characteristic also shared with nerve tissue. At rest, muscle tissue maintains a resting membrane potential. This membrane potential is created by the charge difference of the molecules inside the muscle cells relative to the outside of the cells This charge is referred to as the *resting potential*. The resting potential is largely due to a surplus of positively-charged sodium ions (Na^+) outside the cell and a surplus of negatively charged chloride ions

(Cl⁻) inside the cell. At rest, these ions are unable to cross the cell membrane because the normal membrane passageways, the channels, are closed, or blocked by gates. When the muscle cells receive a stimulus signaling them to contract, gated channels located along the cells membrane open. The now open channels allow the ions to flow across the membrane disrupting the resting electrical charge. This change in the electrical charge is referred to as an *action potential*. There are two ways in which the muscles can be stimulated, (1) electrical charges generated within the muscle itself and known as autorythmic charges such as those responsible for the heartbeat of cardiac muscle and, (2) information or stimuli from outside sources such as the chemical signals of nerve or form hormones from the endocrine system or even simple changes in the blood pH (acidity) levels.

Secondly, muscle has the ability to *contract*, or shorten, and therefore create movement once excited. *Extensibility* is the third characteristic and it serves two functions, (1) enabling muscles to contract after being stretched and, (2) enabling muscles to stretch without damage. *Elasticity* is the fourth and final characteristic. And allows a muscle to return to its normal resting state after being stretched.

Skeletal muscles cause movement by pulling against the bones, using them as levers to cause movement about the joints, or articulations, which serve as fulcrum points. There are approximately 430 individual muscles in the human body with about 80 pairs being responsible for most of our major movements. There is a systematic arrangement of muscle, bone and joints in the body that facilitate this movement. For a muscle to cause useful movement, it must attach to at least two different bones connected by a moveable joint. In this arrangement, one bone usually remains stationary while the other moves, hinged at the joint. The muscles are attached to the bones through *tendons*, tough parallel strands of collagen rich connective tissue. The illustrations in Chapter 5 provided examples of the three classes of lever systems and corresponding examples of each within the body. Muscles are usually arranged in antagonistic pairs; the contraction of one muscle has the opposite action from the contraction of the other. Movement about the joint is described by several terms. *Flexion* decreases the angle at the joint while *extension* increases the angle. *Abduction* moves a limb or body part away from the body while *adduction* moves it closer. A look at most body regions will show antagonistic pairs of flexors and extensors or abductors and adductors. Other musculoskeletal movements were described in chapter 4.

A skeletal muscle, for example the biceps, deltoid or rectus abdominus, is composed of numerous cylindrical units called *fascicles*. Each fascicle is composed of numerous cylindrical muscle cells or *fibers*, which are in turn composed of smaller cylindrical subunits called *myofibrils*. Dissection of a myofibril would show it to consist of a membrane bound grouping of thin protein threads or *myofilaments*. There are two types of myofilaments; *actin* and *myosin*, and it is the interaction of actin and myosin which brings about muscle shortening or contraction (Fig 6.1).

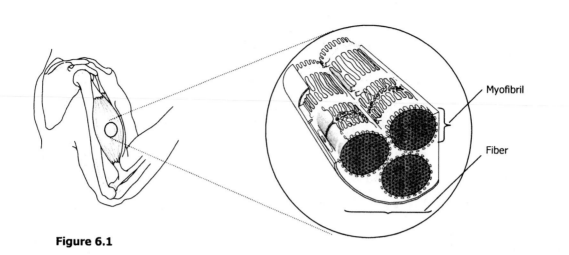

Myofibril

Fiber

Figure 6.1

Myofibrils are made up of many smaller similar units called *myofilaments* or simply, filaments. The filaments are made up of two types, *thick filaments* and *thin filaments*. They do not stretch the entire length of the myofibril instead, the filaments are separated into sections that line up end to end eventually expanding the length of the myofibril. Each section of alternating thick and thin filaments is known as a *sarcomere* and each sarcomere is separated by a dense material called *Z-Lines*.

Attached to both sides of the Z-lines are the thin filaments that protrude in opposite directions into two adjacent sarcomeres. So, there are two separate sides of thin filaments.

Figure 6.2. Sarcomere Units

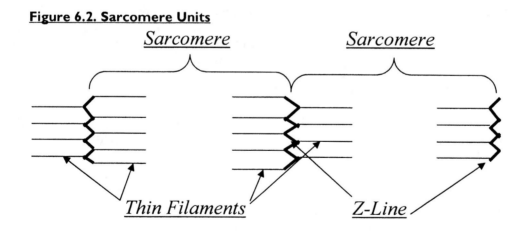

Sarcomere   *Sarcomere*

Thin Filaments   *Z-Line*

Located in the middle of each sarcomere we find the thick filaments overlapping the two ends of the thin filaments. The extent to which they overlap the thin filaments depends on how contracted, stretched or relaxed the muscle is.

Figure 6.3. Myofilament Arrangement in Sarcomeres

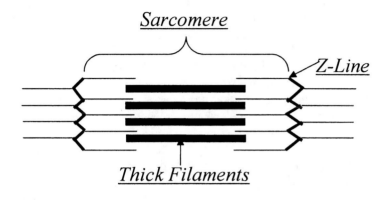

Sarcomere

Z-Line

Thick Filaments

The study of skeletal muscle under the microscope reveals its characteristic striated appearance. These striated appearances are created by the various bands and zones found at various points within the adjacent sarcomeres. The area that stretched the entire length of the thick filament is called the *A band*. It is dark in appearance. The two ends of the A band that overlaps the thin filaments are known as the *Zone of Overlap*. The area that only contains the thin filaments and no thick filaments is the *I band*. This region appears light. The *H zone* is found in the center of the A band and contains only the thick filament. The center of the H zone contains the M line. The M line is where the supporting protein structures are found that help to structurally support the thick filaments.

Figure 6.4. Skeletal Muscle Banding Pattern

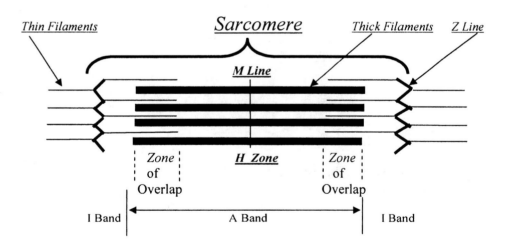

Thin Filaments *Sarcomere* *Thick Filaments* *Z Line*

M Line

Zone of Overlap **H Zone** Zone of Overlap

I Band A Band I Band

Thick and thin filaments are made up of contractile proteins. The thick filaments are made up of the protein *myosin*. Myosin is made up of a few hundred strands that wrap about each other giving rise to its thick appearance. The portion found in the zone of overlap consists of two extensions, known as myosin heads, per myosin molecule. The thick filaments have a hinge where the "heads" project from the thick filament; they also contain two binding sites. One site for binding and splitting ATP and another site for the binding, or grabbing, the actin molecules.

Thin filaments are made up of three separate proteins: actin, troponin and tropomyosin. The protein actin are comprised of two strands of spherical molecules that intertwine with each other. Imagine two pearl necklaces twisted together. On the surface of each actin molecule is a receptor site for the myosin heads. At rest, the receptor sites on the actin molecule are covered by a single strand of the tropomyosin molecule. Also, while at rest, the myosin heads" rest upon the tropomyosin. Attached to the ends of the tropomyosin molecules are the troponin molecules. The troponin molecules have a receptor site for calcium ions.

The contraction of muscle is due to the sliding of the actin filaments in between the myosin filaments. The action is more than just a simple sliding in that it involves the myosin filaments actually pulling the actin filaments by using small *cross-bridges* on the myosin. These cross-bridges act as hands to grasp and pull the actin filament in a manner similar to the hands of the participants in a tug-of-war game. This action requires the presence of ATP as an energy source, and calcium (Ca^{++}) ions which allow the myosin cross-bridges to grasp the actin filaments (Fig 6.5).

In its relaxed state, because of its elastic recoil tendency, skeletal muscle is slightly compressed resulting in a small degree of overlap of the opposing actin filaments on either side of the sarcomere (fig 6.6a). This results in a small degree of interference, reducing the actual number of myosin cross-bridges that can grab and pull each actin filament. As we gently stretch a muscle fiber and pull the actin filaments slightly apart, we increase the number of myosin cross-bridges contacting the actin and, proportionally, increase the strength of the muscle fiber's contraction. We refer to this phenomenon as the *length-tension* relationship. The length-tension relationship shows that a muscle reaches in maximum strength when it has been stretched to between 110% - 115% of its resting length (fig 6.6b).

Figure 6.5. Muscle Contractile Filaments

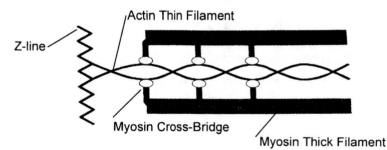

Actin Thin Filament

Z-line

Myosin Cross-Bridge

Myosin Thick Filament

Molecular arrangement of muscle filaments: the actin thin filaments are attached to the Z-lines at one end;

actin thin filaments slide between the myosin thick filaments when pulled by the myosin cross-bridges

Figure 6.6(a). Myofilament Overlap

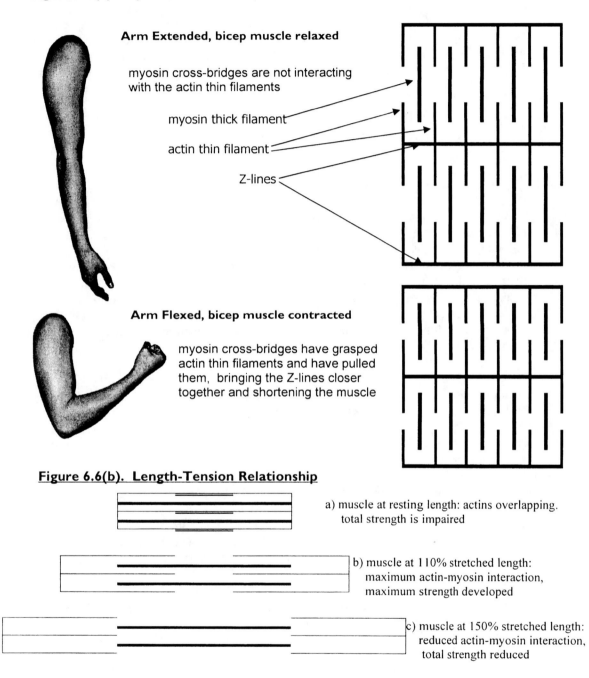

Arm Extended, bicep muscle relaxed

myosin cross-bridges are not interacting
with the actin thin filaments

myosin thick filament

actin thin filament

Z-lines

Arm Flexed, bicep muscle contracted

myosin cross-bridges have grasped
actin thin filaments and have pulled
them, bringing the Z-lines closer
together and shortening the muscle

Figure 6.6(b). Length-Tension Relationship

a) muscle at resting length: actins overlapping.
total strength is impaired

b) muscle at 110% stretched length:
maximum actin-myosin interaction,
maximum strength developed

c) muscle at 150% stretched length:
reduced actin-myosin interaction,
total strength reduced

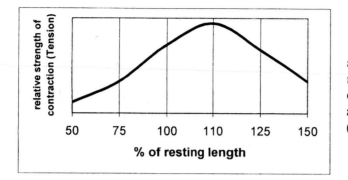

If the muscle is stretched beyond 130-150% of its resting length the actins, being pulled from between the myosin filaments, are no longer capable of making maximum contact and muscle strength rapidly decreases (fig 6.6c).

Action Potential and Muscle Excitation

The muscle cell membrane helps to contain and protect the internal environment of a cell while at the same time selectively allowing certain chemicals to enter or exit. The cell membrane of the muscle cell is known as the *sarcolemma*. The surface of the sarcolemma contains thousands of tiny openings, "holes", that act as an entryway into the cell via tube like structures called ***Transverse Tubules (T-Tubules)***. The T-tubules primary responsibility is to conduct the electric impulse generated from the neuromuscular junction to the inside of the muscle fiber. Inside the muscle cell is the cytoplasm, called *sarcoplasm* in muscle cells. The sarcoplasm contains glycogen, from which ATP can be synthesized, and myoglobin which can both carry and store oxygen.

Surrounding each myofibril is a mesh like network of sacs known as the ***sarcoplasmic reticulum (SR)***. The ends of the SR, known as ***terminal cisterns,*** lie adjacent to the T-tubles. The T-tubules are sandwiched between the terminal cisterns all along the myofibrils. SR acts as a storage facility for calcium. The SR has two specialized features, pumps and gates. At rest, the gates on the SR are closed and the pumps are continually pumping calcium from the sarcoplasm, into the SR.

In order for any action to take place in the body, proper communication needs to occur between the body and the central nerve system (brain and spinal cord -- the processing center of the body) and the central nerve system and body. We will learn about the nervous system in the next chapter. In the musculoskeletal system, this communication occurs at various points along the muscle where a motor nerve interacts with a muscle fiber. These points of interaction are known as neuromuscular junctions. When a muscle is in a relaxed state, The inside of the muscle cell is slightly negative relative to its surrounding. This state is referred to as the resting membrane potential. So, when you decide to do that bicep curl, the end of the motor nerve that communicates with the muscle releases a "communication chemical" known as a neurotransmitter. There are different neurotransmitters for different parts of the body. The neurotransmitter for muscle contraction is called acetocholine (Ach). The Ach attaches to a receptor on the muscle to allow the receptor to open. This is analogous to ringing a door bell, once the person knows it's you, you can enter. When the receptor opens, molecules of sodium (Na+) enter the sarcolemma (muscle cell membrane) making the cell less negative thereby creating an action potential.

The action potential travels along the sarcolemma and when it reaches the T-tubules, the action potentials travels down the T-tubules reaching the inside of the cell. The action potential then opens the gate of the SR where the calcium ions stored. The calcium ions are released faster than they are pumped back into the SR making the sarcoplasm saturated with calcium.

In cells, the organelles are bathed in the cytoplasm. It is no different in the muscle fiber. The sarcoplasm is now saturated with calcium so it finds its way to the troponin molecules and binds to their binding sites. The binding of the calcium ions causes a conformational change on the troponin molecule. This conformational change pulls the tropomyosin away from the actin binding sites thereby exposing them. During this transformation, the myosin heads that were resting on the tropomyosin now attach to the binding sites on the actin molecule creating what is known as a myosin crossbridge.

When these myosin crossbridges are created, the ATP molecule that is associated with the myosin breaks down to ADP + P and the energy released causes the actin molecule to swivel and slide past a section of the thick myosin molecule. Once the actin is finished swiveling, ATP attaches to the crossbridge causing the crossbridge to release and reset to grab the next available binding site on the actin molecule. The action would look like having a few people pulling an anchor out of the water, hand over hand. This process will continue as long as there is enough calcium present to expose the actin binding sites and as long as there is sufficient ATP available.

In summary, muscle contractions cause the Z-lines that the actin molecules attach to approach each other, it is the shortening of the series of sarcomeres that extend the length of the myofibril.

The Ca^{++} is stored in sacs of fatty membrane called *sarcoplasmic reticulum* which are located between and around the myofibrils. The calcium is released when the nervous system stimulates the muscle. The nerve impulse generates an electrical wave that sweeps across the muscle cell membrane. This electrical wave, known as an *action potential*, is transferred to the sarcoplasmic reticulum (SR) where it causes small channels in the SR membrane to open allowing calcium ions to flow out. Unless the nerve continues to stimulate the muscle, the calcium is rapidly pumped back into the SR, ending the contraction. A number of drugs can enhance or mimic this nervous stimulation of the muscle and thereby enhance muscular performance. Among these drugs are caffeine, nicotine, methacholine and carbachol.

Slow and Fast Muscle Fibers

The speed at which muscle responds to nerve stimulation is partly dependent upon the distance the calcium must travel (diffuse) from the sarcoplasmic reticulum where it is stored to the actin and myosin filaments where it acts. In one type of muscle fiber, the sarcoplasmic reticulum is extensive and this distance is greatly reduced. Because the sarcoplasmic reticulum contains much fatty membrane which is normally glistening white in appearance, and because these fibers are rich in sarcoplasmic reticulum, they appear light in color and are called *white muscle fibers*. Because of the small distance the calcium must travel this muscle is capable of very fast response and contraction. White muscle fibers are also referred to as *fast twitch fibers*, or *Type II* fibers. The majority of Type II muscle fibers have more enzymes of the glycogen-lactic acid system for rapid energy production and, biochemically, are referred to as *fast-twitch glycolytic fibers*, or Type IIb fibers. A small subset of fast fibers have the capacity for generating energy aerobically and are referred to as *fast-twitch oxidative*, or Type IIa fibers.

A second type of muscle fiber has a less extensive sarcoplasmic reticulum but more extensive blood vessels and a protein called myoglobin, which, like the hemoglobin of blood is also red in color. These fibers are called *red muscle fibers*, or *Type I* fibers, and are not capable of very rapid contraction. These *slow twitch fibers*, although not rapid in their response are capable of prolonged or sustained contraction and function primarily on aerobic metabolism. In addition, red muscle fibers can utilize fatty acids as an energy source, metabolizing them completely with the aid of oxygen, allowing them to function long after carbohydrate fuels have been exhausted and, biochemically, are referred to as *oxidative fibers*. Further contributing to the slower rate of contractile response is the fact that the process of producing ATP aerobically is a comparatively slow process relative to anaerobic production. The characteristics of the various muscle fiber types are highlighted in Table 6.1.

Each muscle has a mix of red and white (slow and fast) fibers, the precise ratio determined by heredity. Muscles which need to respond quickly and often, but not for prolonged contraction are predominantly composed of white fibers. An example would be the gastrocnemius muscle of the calf which gives a forceful and rapid contraction such as in jumping. Some people are naturally better jumpers because of a genetic predominance of white fibers. The muscles of flight in a bird, located on the chest, would also be white fibers for the quick, short contractions necessary for flight. We know this as the white meat on the breast of fowl such as turkey.

Muscles which must support sustained activity but not necessarily rapid contraction, such as standing, are predominantly red fibers hence the dark meat of drumsticks or legs. Dogs, which are not terribly quick animals but which do have tremendous endurance have muscles in which red fibers predominate whereas cats, which are very quick for short sprint runs but lack the endurance of a dog have muscles which are predominantly white fibers.

Table 6.1. Characteristics of Muscle Fiber Types

Fiber Type	Type I	Type IIa	Type IIb
Classification	Slow Twitch Oxidative	Fast Twitch Oxidative	Fast Twitch Glycolytic
Morphology	Red	White	
Benefit	High endurance, resists fatigue	Strength, quickness, Can use aerobic energy	Highest degree of strength and quickness
Weakness	Slow to react, cannot generate much strength	Limited gains in strength, less endurance than Type I	Fatigues quickly, anerobically fueled only
Example of Use	Distance events, cross-country skiing, marathon	Boxing, gymnastics	Weight lifting, shot put
Trained By	Overdistance, interval training High repetition / low weight	Can be trained for either strength or endurance	Resistance training Low repetition / high weight Best done with rapid contractions

"Natural Talent"?

Athletic training has no effect on changing the relative proportion of red to white fibers although there is evidence that specific training programs can cause inter-conversion of types IIa and IIb. Some individuals seem to have a natural ability or "*talent*" to excel at certain sports or activities. This ability is probably due to their genetic proportions of fiber types. Good sprinters are individuals with a higher proportion of white fibers whereas good marathoners are individuals with a high red fiber percentage. Regardless of training, Carl Lewis, a world-record sprinter, will never become a world-class marathoner and, conversely, marathoner Grete Waitz will never qualify as an Olympic sprinter.

It is not uncommon for muscle biopsies to be performed on athletes to determine their relative fiber percentages. The information gained is of value in directing an individual toward the proper sport, event, or position and in tailoring a training regimen. Table 6.2 shows the percentages of slow and fast fibers in the muscles of athletes from a number of different sports.

Carl Lewis:

A nine-time Olympic champion, Carl Lewis has excelled in track and field events that require the ability to generate and deliver quick, powerful muscle contractions.

Lewis has won Olympic gold medals in the 100 meter and 200 meter sprints, the 4 x 100 meter relay and the long jump. Cool Running has ranked Lewis among the top 3 male runners of the 20th Century.

www.coolrunning.com

Grete Waitz:

Ranked by Cool Running as the #1 Top Woman Runner of the 20th Century, Grete Waitz is a nine-time winner of the New York City Marathon and has set new world records in the event on several occasions.

Beginning her competitive running career at the age of 12, Waitz discovered early on that she did not have much ability competing at short distances.

www.coolrunning.com

Table 6.2. Muscle Fiber Percentages of Selected World Class Athletes

	Slow (Red) Fiber %age	Fast (White) Fiber %age
Marathon Runners	82	18
Distance Swimmers	74	26
Speed Skaters	70	30
Cross-Country Skiers	62	38
Race Walkers	58	42
Middle Distance Runners (800m)	45	55
Weight Lifters	42	58
Shot Putters	38	62
Sprinters / Jumpers	38	62

Muscle Strength, Power and Endurance

Strength:

One important determinant of muscle performance is the strength of the muscular contraction. Muscle strength is, in part, determined by the size of the muscle. All muscle has a contractile force of about 3.0 kg/cm^2 of cross-sectional area. In general, the larger the muscle or the greater the cross-sectional area, the greater the strength. Training to increase muscular strength typically involves an increase in muscle size which occurs primarily through **hypertrophy**, or enlargement of existing muscle fibers - not necessarily the production of new fibers (*hyperplasia*). Hypertrophy of the muscle's contractile elements which lead to gains in strength is referred to as *sarcomere hypertrophy*. Hypertrophy which results in increased muscle mass but not necessarily proportional gains in strength is known as *sarcoplasmic hypertrophy*. Training for sarcoplasmic hypertrophy, which results in larger

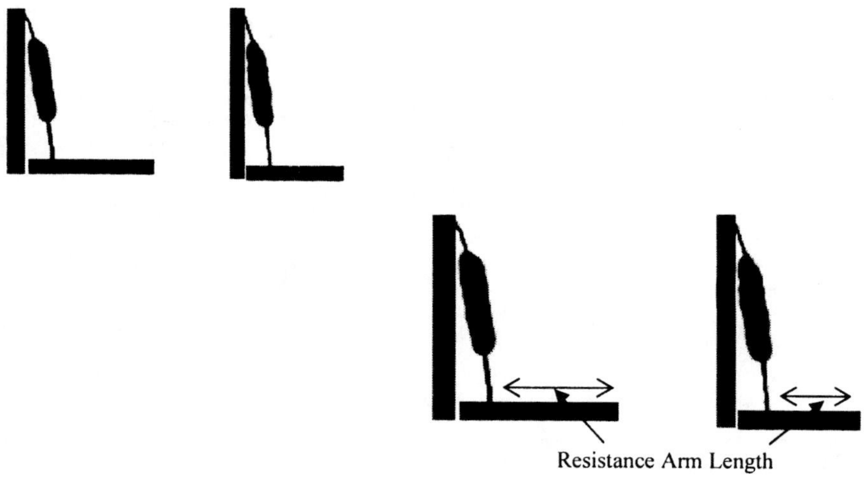

Resistance Arm Length

Fig. 6.7. Mechanical Advantage and Strength Deficit

The maximum amount of weight that a muscle can lift, performing that lift just once, is called the ***one repetition maximum***, or the ***1-RM***. In general, the term *repetition maximum* refers to the number of repetitions of motion that can be performed before fatigue prohibits any further repetitions.

The sarcoplasmic hypertrophy typical of bodybuilders is characterized by increases in size of the non-contractile elements of muscle, namely the sarcoplasm (muscle cell cytoplasm), and energy supply mechanisms.

The second major factor that influences a muscle's strength is the size of the ***motor unit***. A motor unit consists of all the muscle fibers, or cells, connected to a single motor nerve. If a muscle with 1,000 individual fibers receives its stimulus through a nerve with 100 individual nerve fibers, then we can assume that each nerve fiber stimulates approximately 10 muscle fibers. Therefore the size of a single motor unit would be 10 muscle fibers. As the degree of innervation increases, that is, as the motor unit size gets smaller, the potential strength of the muscle will increase. A muscle in which each nerve is shared by only five muscle fibers will be capable of developing greater maximal strength (a lower strength deficit) than a muscle in which each nerve supplies ten individual fibers.

Power:

In addition to strength, the power of a muscle contraction is also important. Power is an indicator of how much work a muscle can perform over a period of time and is measured in kilogram-meters/min (kg-m/min). Because white muscle fibers contract more rapidly than do the red fibers, they are capable of exerting their strength over a smaller interval of time. For this reason, fast-twitch, or white muscle fibers are considered to posses more power than a slow-twitch fiber of equal size and strength.

Endurance:

Endurance is a third parameter of muscle fitness and is a measure of a muscle's ability to perform sustained contraction, ***static endurance***, or to contract repeatedly for a prolonged period of time, ***dynamic endurance***. Static endurance would be demonstrated when a gymnast holds the position of an Iron Cross during competition, in part, with a sustained contraction of the deltoid muscles. Dynamic endurance can be demonstrated by the ability of a marathon runner to repeatedly contract the quadriceps muscles of the legs during a 2.5 hour run. Endurance is a reflection of the muscles efficiency at converting the chemical energy stored in the foods we eat into the mechanical energy of contraction. Because of the increased amount of oxidative enzymes they contain, slow-twitch fibers have a greater endurance than fast-twitch fibers of equivalent size and strength.

Endurance is influenced by the muscles' ability to withstand *fatigue*. Fatigue can be caused by factors within the central nervous system, ***central fatigue***, or within the muscle itself, ***peripheral fatigue***. Central fatigue involves factors such as motivation, pain, and neurotransmitter depletion while peripheral fatigue involves factors at the neuromuscular junction, mitochondria, or within the muscle filaments themselves.

Another factor influencing endurance is the availability of free flowing, oxygen-containing blood to the working muscles. At rest, the blood-carrying arteries and capillaries are open and providing the muscle cells with free access to the oxygen that is required for long-term aerobic ATP production. As muscle begins to contract, the interior blood vessels become squeezed and progressively reduced in diameter, inhibiting blood flow. This inhibition begins when a muscle reaches about 15% of maximum contractile tension and increases until all blood flow is essentially stopped, at about 50% of maximum contractile tension. At this point the muscle becomes reliant on the anaerobic energy supply system.

Conditioning For Muscular Strength

In order for muscles to increase in strength they must be forced to contract under a load. Muscles which contract at or near their maximal load capacity will increase in strength rapidly even if the muscle contracts only a few times per day. This is known as the *overload principle*. It can be said ... "no overload - no hypertrophy" (no pain - no gain). A common way to implement overload training is to use maximum weights in three sets of 4 - 8 repetitions each.

> "Our growing softness, our increasing lack of physical fitness, is a menace to our security."
> John F. Kennedy, President, 1960

If the maximal weight a muscle can lift just once is called the 1-RM, then the maximum amount that can be lifted 4 times would be referred to as the 4-RM. The 4-RM corresponds to approximately 70-80% of the 1-RM value. That is to say, if the maximum amount of weight you can lift with a bicep curl is 100 lbs., and you can do this just once, you should be able to perform that same curl 4 times by using a weight of between 70 – 80 lbs. One hundred pounds would be your 1-RM; 75 lbs. might be your 4-RM. Generally speaking, high-intensity resistance training refers to work with very heavy weights in the 1-RM to 6-RM range. Because of the relatively low number of repetitions, this would more specifically be called *high intensity-low volume training*. Moderate intensity training refers to work with 8-RM to 12-RM weights. Proper rest and adequate protein in the diet is also required to allow the anabolic pathways (muscle protein building) to function properly. This rest would involve one day off between training sessions (usually 3 times per week). Other variations on overload training are described later in this chapter.

In young males with high levels of *testosterone*, a natural male hormone, muscle strength increases through hypertrophy, the synthesis of new muscle protein and the enlargement of existing muscle fibers. In older males and in females, with low testosterone levels, increases in muscle strength with overload training are due in greater part to *neural adaptation*, changes in the relationship between nerve and muscle which results in smaller motor units as described earlier. With neural adaptation there is little increase in muscle size and a relatively low limit to the overall strength increase. Generally, the initial strength gains obtained by anyone beginning a resistance training program are due to neural adaptation alone. These changes can occur quite rapidly and noticeable strength gains can be seen in just a few weeks. Strength gains due to hypertrophy generally take longer, 4-6 weeks minimum, because of the time required to activate genes and synthesize new muscle proteins.

Changes associated with muscle hypertrophy are an increase in the number of contractile actin and myosin filaments, increased amounts of supporting connective tissues, increased numbers of mitochondria, a doubling of stored glycogen, an increase in stored fat and an increase in the enzymes that drive the phosphagen and aerobic systems. It is believed that the increased tension placed on the muscle fibers during resistance exercise result in changes across the cell membrane that trigger the release of growth factor hormones. It is these hormones that most probably initiate the activation of genes within the muscle cell that synthesize new contractile proteins.

Testosterone is a steroid hormone. Steroid molecules are based upon a backbone of cholesterol. Since the effect of testosterone is to stimulate a synthetic reaction or an anabolic pathway, it is generally referred to as an ***anabolic steroid***.

Specificity is another property of strength training. Specificity dictates that only the muscles subjected to overload will increase in size and strength. Although testosterone circulates throughout the body, if you perform curls with the right arm only, it is only the right bicep that will increase in strength.

Overload conditioning can be accomplished through either ***isometric***, ***isotonic*** or ***isokinetic*** exercises. The differences between these three is explained below.

Isometric: An isometric or static contraction is a contraction where the muscle fibers contract without shortening thereby causing no movement about the joint. The term isometric means constant length (*iso*=constant, *metric*=length). An example is pushing against a solid wall (contracting the triceps but not moving the wall) or pulling up against a table bolted to the floor (contracting the biceps but not moving the table). In isometric contractions the muscle develops great tension but does not shorten. Given that the resistance is applied to a non-moving, or static muscle, isometric contractions are referred to as ***static resistance***.

Six seconds of isometric contraction at 75% effort increases strength but only at that particular angle (range of motion) at which the muscle is held during the isometric contraction. This is not an efficient way to build strength throughout the muscles normal range of motion but it will increase muscle mass. It is most beneficial if used to overcome "sticking points" or weaknesses at specific points within the normal range of motion.

Figure 6.8. Strength vs. Joint Angle

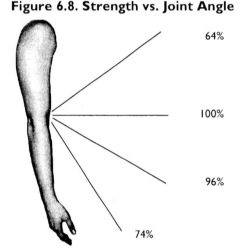

Isotonic: An isotonic contraction is the most familiar form of contraction. It involves the shortening of the muscle due to contraction and therefore causes movement about the joint. The term isotonic means constant tension (*iso*=constant, *tonic*=tension). An example of this type of contraction would be that involved in lifting "free weights" or using a **UNIVERSAL** machine. A problem with isotonic contractions is that the actual amount of work done by the muscle continually changes throughout the range of motion. In curling with free weights for example, there is more actual load in lifting the weight from the knees to the horizontal position than in moving them from the horizontal position to the chest. This is known as ***constant resistance isotonic contraction***. Although the resistance remains constant, the amount of work performed by the muscle changes as the weight is moved through various angles of the joint. This is due to the fact that, because of the arrangement of muscle attachment around the joint, our joints have greater efficiency - or strength - at various angles (Figure 6.8). It is possible to use a device that alters the load over the range of motion by lifting the weights over an eccentric (non uniformly shaped) cam. This more efficient form training is known as ***variable resistance isotonic***

contraction and is accomplished through the use of the NAUTILUS machine. By changing the resistance according to a pre-planned design, the actual work required of the muscle can be maintained at a uniform level throughout the range of motion.

For beginning a weight training program, it is advisable to start at a low intensity and progress gradually. Start upper-body exercises (arms and shoulders) with 30-40% of the 1-RM and lower body exercises (legs and hips) at 50-60% of the 1-RM. When 12 repetitions, with proper form, can comfortably be completed, and when the RPE on the Borg scale approximates a value of 12-13, the weight can be increased by 5% towards the 1-RM value.

When performing isotonic exercise or training it is important to pay attention to and vary the technique during both the contraction (*concentric*) and relaxation (*eccentric*) stages of the movement. During the concentric phase, the muscle is shortening as it produces force. Lowering the weight, the eccentric phase, requires that the muscle produce force as it lengthens. For the most effective training, the contraction phase should be conducted rapidly and smoothly from a position of full stretch. The relaxation phase, where the muscle is returned to the resting position, should be performed slowly, but again smoothly. This phase is often referred to as negative resistance. Eccentric contractions are more effective at building strength than concentric contractions although they do result in more delayed onset muscle soreness after the workout. This would make sense given that strength gains and muscle growth occur in response to the microscopic injury caused by overload training.

Resistance Training with Free Weights versus Machine-Assisted Weights:

Free weight training involves the use of resistance in the form of dumbbells or barbells; weights that are not attached to any device and which are free to move in any direction and for any distance. In machine-assisted training, movement of the resistance is limited in both range and distance. The resistance typically involves weights that are attached to a machine by systems of cables and pulleys (Nautilus and Universal machines), resistance due to air pressure (Keiser machines), resistance from bendable rods or stretchable bands (Bowflex machine), or resistance from the force of gravity (Total Gym machine).

Machines, because they limit the joint range of motion and because the weight, or resistance, is held in place and less likely to fall, are generally considered to be safer than free weight training. In addition, because these machines can isolate movements by restricting the ability of other muscles to assist in each movement, they can better focus on, or isolate, certain muscles giving them a concentrated workout. Finally, because the user is typically restricted in their movements when using resistance machines, there is less likelihood for "cheating", for example, swinging the torso when doing standing bicep curls.

Free weights on the other hand are much less expensive and allow for a greater variety of movements and therefore muscles to be individually trained. Because free weights do not restrict range of motion or distance moved, and because they don't regulate the speed at which the weight can be moved, they are more likely to cause injury, particularly in the beginning exerciser. It is these same factors, however, that make free weights more effective. Because there is no machine-based positioning of the body, any movement accomplished must also utilize the stabilizer and neutralizer muscles. For example, in the Nautilus machine, the elbow is held stationary on a padded platform, isolating the bicep muscle. With a free weight standing dumbbell curl, the shoulder muscles must also be activated during the bicep curl thereby exercising the entire group of muscles involved in to movement. In addition, the speed of contraction can be regulated giving the exerciser the ability to develop power as well as strength.

In general terms, therefore, beginners are better off using machine-assisted resistance training while competitive athletes will be better served by free weights. For those of us in the middle, the choice is ours to make.

Isotonic exercises can of course be accomplished without the aid of any equipment or weights. *Callisthenic exercises* are performed using only body weight and gravity to provide resistance. The common push-up and sit-up are examples of callisthenic exercises.

Isokinetic: Isokinetic contractions are performed with the aid of a machine called a dynamometer which controls the *rate* of muscle shortening by sensing the contractile force and opposing it with an equal force in the opposite direction. The slower contraction rates are the most efficient (60° per second). Isokinetic training is also referred to as *accommodating resistance exercise*.

Table 6.3. Summary of Muscle Contraction Terms

Term	Description
Static Resistance	An isometric contraction developing tension with no change in muscle length
Constant Resistance	An isotonic contraction against a constant load with a change in muscle length
Variable Resistance	An isotonic contraction against a variable load with a change in muscle length
Accommodating Resistance	An isotonic contraction against a resistance that maintains a constant contraction velocity
Concentric Contraction	Muscle tension developed during the contraction (shortening) phase
Eccentric Contraction	Muscle tension developed during the extension (lengthening) phase

Variations of Resistance Training:

Depending on the type of resistance development sought (strength without hypertrophy, power, hypertrophy, endurance, combinations of the above), different patterns of training may be used. The simplest pattern is referred to as simple sets and forms a good starting point for a general resistance training program. In this type of resistance training, an exercise session would consist of three sets of 8-12 repetitions using a weight of approximately 65% - 70% of the 1-RM. Exercises should be selected that involve all of the body's major muscle groups. Training sessions should be repeated on alternate days.

A well-regarded modification of this form of isotonic training is the PRE, or *Progressive Resistance Exercise*. In a PRE training session, muscles are forced to work against increasingly greater loads with each set. In the initial set, the muscle is moved through its entire range of motion in a series of repetitions (usually 10 - 15) using 50% of the 1-RM. In the second set, repetitions would be performed using 75% of the 1-RM and then a final set would be performed using the maximum load.

Taking this one step further is the program of DAPRE or _**Daily Adjustable Progressive Resistance Exercise**_. In DAPRE, four sets of contractions are performed. The first three are identical to those in PRE and would consist of one set of 10 repetitions at 1/2 maximal weight followed by a second set of 6 repetitions at 3/4 maximal weight. The third set would use the maximum weight with as many repetitions performed as possible. The fourth set would then be performed using a weight adjusted on the basis of the maximum number of repetitions which were able to be performed during the third set, the adjustment determined according to the chart below.

# of Repetitions Performed in 3rd Set	Weight To Be Used in the 4th Set
0 - 2	Decrease by 5 - 10 lbs
3 - 4	Decrease by 0 - 5 lbs
5 - 7	Stay as is
8 - 12	Increase by 5 - 10 lbs
13+	Increase by 10 - 15 lbs

Other common variations of resistance training include:

Super Sets
  Multiple circuits consisting of 2-3 exercises, performed continuously, without rest between exercise sets. Rest is taken between circuits.

Training to Failure
  The exercise set is performed with continuous repetitions until a repetition cannot be completed without the help of a spotter.

Forced Repetitions
  The exercise set is performed until failure. Continued repetitions are then completed with the aid of a spotter .

Stripping
  The exercise set is performed to failure. The resistance is decreased and the exercise set is immediately repeated. Continued for three sets.

Twenty-Ones
  The exercise set is performed using only the first ½ of the range-of-motion and repeating seven repetitions. Exercise set is performed again using the second ½ of the range-of-motion. A final set of seven reps is performed using the entire range-of-motion for a total of 21 repetitions.
Super Pump
  The exercise is performed with 15-18 sets of 5-6 reps each

Partial Repetitions (1/4 Reps or Lockouts)
  Limited range of motion contractions performed through only the strongest part of the motion.
  Performed with a spotter or rack upon which the weights may rest. Allows for use of heavier weights and quicker strength gains.

When engaging in a resistance training program, whatever the specific type, there are some generally accepted standards of good practice that should be followed. It is important that we train for balance. Muscles should be developed in antagonistic pairs since both work together to create movement around a single joint. For example, the bicep and tricep muscles should be trained together so that one does not become overly developed while the other does not. If muscles of an antagonistic pair become too far out of balance, injury can occur to the joint. This is most commonly seen as the cause of knee injuries when an overdeveloped quadriceps muscle (knee extension) is improperly balanced by an underdeveloped hamstring muscle (knee flexion). The table below presents the recommended balance to be achieved in various antagonistic muscle pairs.

In addition to training both muscles of an antagonistic pair, attention should also be given to developing the secondary movers, stabilizers, and contralateral (opposite side) muscles as well.

Strength vs. Size

Because of the variability of the *strength deficit* factor, it does not necessarily follow that larger muscles are also stronger muscles, at least with respect to *maximal strength*. In fact, research has shown that progressive resistance exercises utilizing very high loads and very low repetitions result in the maximum strength gains although not in the maximum level of hypertrophy. Individuals interested in maximizing bulk and hypertrophy, competitive body builders for example, are better served performing lifts with lower levels of load at higher repetitions, performing these until the point of failure due to fatigue. While the PRE and DAPRE exercises described earlier are generally recommended for developing overall muscle fitness, those interested in maximizing either strength or size should consider the following training suggestions.

Table 6.4. Training For Strength vs. Training for Size

Maximum Strength	Maximum Size
High maximal strength, low strength deficit	*High absolute strength, high strength deficit*
3 sets of 3 repetitions @ 90% of 1RM 2 sets of 2 repetitions @ 95% of 1RM 2 sets of 2 repetitions @ 97% of 1RM 1 set of 1 repetition @ 100% of 1RM	3 sets of 12 repetitions @ 70% of 1RM
Perform a progression of 8 sets at increasingly higher loads allowing 3 minutes of rest between sets.	*Perform 3 identical sets. At 70% of 1-RM this should approach the point of failure due to fatigue.*

Conditioning for Muscle Power

Conditioning for the development of muscle power, the ability to deliver the muscles' strength in an explosive, or rapid fashion, in accordance with the General Adaptation syndrome requires a specific type of training that forces the muscles to contract rapidly and forcefully under load. With regular resistance training apparatus, training for power will typically consist of performing 5 sets of 7 repetitions at 45% of 1-RM and performing each contraction at maximal velocity. The most efficient training method for maximizing gains in power is *plyometric training*. Plyometric training uses the muscle stretch reflex to produce a stronger, more rapid, explosive contraction. Muscle has a built-in protective mechanism to prevent it from tearing during rapid stretching motions. Given that muscles are grouped in antagonistic pairs, the rapid forceful contraction of one set of muscles (quadriceps for example) will result in a rapid and forceful stretching of the antagonist group (in this case, the hamstrings). If a muscle is stretched too fast and too far, as the hamstrings might be in our example, it will respond with a rapid and powerful reflex contraction meant to oppose the stretch and prevent the muscle from tearing. This phenomenon, which forms the basis for plyometric training, is known as *the reactive neuromuscular response*.

Figure 6.9. Muscle Spindle Fiber

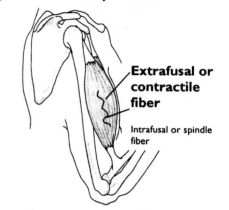

Extrafusal or contractile fiber

Intrafusal or spindle fiber

Within each of our muscles, buried within the center of the contractile fibers, is a small group of non-contractile fibers known as the *intrafusal fibers* or *muscle spindle fibers*. These fibers are actually stretch receptors that detect when a muscle is in danger of tearing. When the spindle fibers detect too rapid and forceful a stretch, they trigger a signal that causes the muscle to rapidly and forcefully contract, opposing the stretch and protecting the muscle.

When a person jumps off a step or box and lands on the ground they are forced rapidly down into a squatting position that causes a rapid and forceful stretching of the hip and leg extensors (the gluteal and quadriceps muscles) as the legs fold to absorb the shock and decelerate the body. This stretch triggers a rapid reflex contraction of these muscles that is faster and stronger than the maximum voluntary contraction. It is therefore called a *supramaximal contraction*. If this natural reflex contraction is induced as a part of an intentional training exercise, and is performed repetitively and with a load applied, the muscles will adapt by increasing their power and coordination for rapid explosive contraction. This is the basis for plyometric training.

Examples of plyometric exercises are *depth jumps* (jumping up and down off an 18" platform or box), *medicine ball twist* (two partners sit back-to back straddling a bench, one partner holding a medicine ball; both partners rotate torsos at the waist on the same side with the first partner handing the medicine ball to the other; both partners turn towards the opposite side and exchange the medicine ball again), *clap push-ups* (perform push-ups as usual but pushing the body up from the floor as fast as possible, force both hands off the ground; as the hands leave the ground clap them rapidly together and put them back in position to catch the body as it returns to the floor), and *throw-down leg lifts* (lying on your back with a partner standing up, straddling your head and facing in the direction of your feet; grab the standing partner's ankles and lift your legs from the waist and without bending the knees; your standing partner will forcefully push your legs back down to the floor; rapidly continue this alternating leg lift and throw down).

For activities requiring explosive power, it is important to remember that absolute strength and power is desirable only if it is developed without large increases in size and bulk. It is not just the absolute power that is important in determining explosive ability so much as it is the power-to-weight ratio. Being a very dense tissue, gains in muscle mass can lead to quite substantial gains in weight which will prove to be counterproductive for individuals seeking improvement in speed, power and agility. It is important that any resistance training be accomplished in a fashion that minimizes muscle hypertrophy.

Conditioning for Muscle Endurance

Conditioning for muscular endurance involves aerobic rather than anabolic activities. This type of training does not attempt to increase muscular strength as a primary objective but rather to increase the efficiency at which muscle can aerobically use fuel as described in the unit on Bioenergetics. Two training regimens are used for this type of conditioning; *overdistance training* and *interval training*.

Overdistance training: Overdistance training relies upon running, swimming, etc., for excessive distances at speeds slower than will be used in the event or competition. It increases several important parameters of the muscle such as increasing the number of mitochondria in each muscle cell (mitochondria are the sites of aerobic energy production), increasing the enzymes which allow muscle to use fat efficiently as an energy source. Muscle will adapt by becoming able to provide energy over these distances. When muscle is activated in any movement, the first fibers to be recruited are the Type I slow twitch fibers. As the speed and force of contraction are increased, more Type II fast twitch fibers are recruited. Overdistance training at relatively low speeds preferentially recruits and develops the slow twitch fibers that are so critical to endurance events.

Interval training: This involves periods of intense training interspersed with periods of rest or low-intensity training. Through interval training the muscles develop a tolerance to lactic acid and therefore are not subject to fatigue so easily. The athlete also learns pace and gets to practice the competitive skill at rates or intensities of actual competition. In addition, the intense activity during the active periods can help to develop increased contraction velocities in the slow twitch fibers. Increases in contraction velocity of up to 20% have been reported.

It is important that a well-devised combination of both overdistance and interval training be used to condition for endurance events.

Unfortunately, you can't have it all. The simultaneous training for both strength and endurance will result in neither reaching the maximum obtained from one type of training alone as illustrated in Figure 6.10.

Figure 6.10. Comparative Strength Gains with Strength vs. Endurance vs. Combination Training

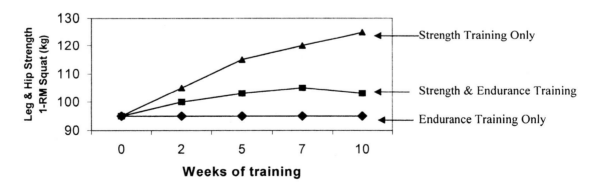

The following table presents a summary overview of the variety of resistance training methods for various outcomes.

	Strength	Hypertrophy	Power	Endurance
Load (% 1-RM)	90	70	85	50
Reps per Set	3	18	3	30
Sets per Session	3	5	3	3
Rest between Sets (min)	4	3	4	1
Speed per Rep (% max)	80	75	95	70
Sessions per Week	3	3	5	7

Damage, Repair and Satellite cells

As we've learned in an earlier chapter, the immediate effect of most exercise activities is to cause physical stress and damage to biological tissues after which the rest and repair process will rebuild the tissues and improve physical capacity. When muscle is damaged in heavy resistance activities several destructive changes are noticed and these include disruption of the extracellular matrix, damage to the sarcolemma, sarcoplasmic reticulum, mitochondria, and myofilaments, loss of microfilament interdigitation, and Z-line streaming.

Eccentric contraction causes some sarcomeres (the weakest ones first) to loose interdigitation as they become stretched past their capacity. Picture this as having the clenched fingers of two intertwined hands being forcibly pulled apart, with the fingers of one hand slipping out of the grasp of the other. The damage progresses from the weakest to the strongest sarcomeres with each successive eccentric contraction. As the eccentric contraction continues, the damage spreads along the myoibrils as adjacent sarcomeres become disrupted. When enough sacromeres become disrupted, the muscle cell membrane (sarcolemma) becomes damaged. Z-line streaming refers to the physical disruption, or breakdown, of the Z-line structures.

The amount of muscle damage that occurs is determined by the length at which the eccentric contraction occurs. The greatest damage occurs at the longest muscle lengths, that is, for example, at the lower portion of the return movement in a bicep curl. The amount of damage is usually greater in Type II muscle fibers than it is in Type I.

The response to exercise induced injuries can be categorized into three stages:

Degenerative Stage: begins within hours of the exercise-induced injury and involves microscopic bleeding, cell injury and death, and an inflammatory response.

Regenerative Stage: begins within 48 hours and is completed in about 5-days depending on how much initial damage occurred

Remodeling Phase: the regenerated or newly formed muscle fibers mature and begin to function as normal muscle.

Myogenic Progentior Cells (MPC's), or *Satellite Cells*, are a population of adult stem cells located within all human muscle fibers. These satellite cells are dormant in normal muscle and will become activated following muscle damage. Once activated, the satellite cells will begin dividing so that they increase in number, move to the site of injury, and fuse with the damaged muscle fibers to repair the injury. In the course of this response, the muscle fibers will increase in width (hypertrophy) and the muscle cells will become stronger. In addition, new sarcomeres are inserted into the muscle fiber and, since the total length of the muscle has not changed, all of the sarcomeres become shorter. This makes the muscle more resistant to subsequent damage from eccentric contractions.

Stretching for Warm-up, Cool-down, and Flexibility

Stretching is important both before and after exercise activities. Stretching the muscles provides a means of enhancing flexibility that helps to protect muscles against injury and increases the range of motion. In the normal aging process, the elastic tissues within tendons and ligaments breaks down leading to a shortening and stiffening of these structures that can limit range of motion and flexibility. A regular program of stretching can delay or prevent some of these age-related changes. Stretching is also important for warming up and cooling down muscle tissue which can also help to prevent injury and increase the efficiency with which muscle utilizes energy. During the repetitive muscle contractions which commonly occur in exercise, muscles have a tendency to tighten or stiffen up. Stretching after exercise will loosen the muscles preventing cramps and soreness.

As described in the unit on Bioenergetics, the contraction of muscle to perform work requires the production and use of ATP, the fuel for muscular contraction. The chemical reactions that are responsible for the generation and use of ATP are all driven by biological catalysts called enzymes, generally, there is one particular enzyme for each of the hundreds of chemical reactions required. Enzymes, which are actually proteins, are temperature sensitive. As body temperature falls below normal (37 ^{0}C, 98.6 ^{0}F), the rate of these enzyme catalyzed reactions slows. As body temperature is raised, the rate of the enzyme catalyzed reactions increases as can be seen in the figure 6.11 below.

Figure 6.11. The Q10 Effect

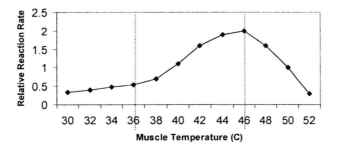

Figure 6.8 illustrates a principle referred to by exercise physiologists as the Q_{10} effect with the example above showing a Q_{10} equal to 2, ($Q_{10} = 2$). What $Q_{10} = 2$ actually means is that for a 10 degree increase in body temperature, the rate of enzyme activity doubles.

Stretching as part of a warm-up prior to exercise increases the blood flow to muscles and actually raises the muscle temperature slightly. This warming of the muscle increases enzyme activity within the muscle cells and makes them more efficient at converting energy into movement.

A proper stretch should be performed slowly and gradually, on muscles that have already been warmed-up, continuing to but not past the point of mild discomfort. Stretching should never be painful for when this point is reached, the muscle can tear. Stretching should also be performed in one continuous motion and the stretch held for 30 seconds. The stretching of each muscle in this way should be performed two to three times. This type of **static stretch** is much safer and much more effective than a bouncing, jerky stretch known as the **ballistic stretch**.

As described earlier, muscles are anchored to the skeleton by connective tissue structures called tendons. Within the tendons are nerve endings which can detect stretch called the *Golgi tendon organs* that are similar in function to the *muscle spindle fibers* discussed earlier. Because they provide information to the brain about the position of muscles and joints they are referred to as *proprioceptors*. When the proprioceptors determine that a muscle has been stretched to a dangerous point, they signal the muscle to contract thereby opposing any further stretching. A stretch taken too far, or a bouncing ballistic stretch can initiate this reflex causing the muscles to contract and negating the stretch. If you try to force the stretch, the muscle or tendon can tear.

In addition to the static stretch noted above, an alternative stretching technique, known as the **PNF stretch**, is used by some. PNF refers to *proprioceptive neuromuscular facilitation* and involves complicated stretching routines requiring the alternate contraction and relaxation of antagonistic muscle pairs. In order to facilitate movement, the nervous system is wired so that when a given is contracted, its antagonist is reflexively, or automatically relaxed. In this way, our muscles are working efficiently with each other rather than against each other. When a Golgi tendon organ detects that a muscle is contracting (interpreted as the tightening of a tendon), it initiates a reflexive relaxation of the antagonist. PNF stretching takes advantage of this phenomenon. Simply put, to enhance the stretch of a muscle, simultaneously contract its antagonist.

Two variations of the PNF stretch are commonly used, the single muscle *contact-relax* stretch and the *contract-relax-agonist contract*. In the *contract-relax* stretch, a targeted muscle is first statically stretched, frequently with the aid of a partner. After a 30-second stretch, the muscle is then isometrically contracted for 3-6 seconds. Following this contraction, the muscle is once again stretched by the partner and can now reach a greater degree of stretch that before the contraction. This sequence can be repeated several times. For the *contract-relax-agonist contract* stretch the first step involves the same type of partner-assisted static stretch as before. Following this stretch, the antagonist muscle is contracted isometrically for 3-6 seconds. Immediately following this contraction, the agonist muscle (the one originally stretched) is stretched again. PNF stretching was developed as a therapy for muscle rehabilitation and is valuable for athletes recovering from injury or for those with limited range-of-motion.

Selected Readings:

Feigenbaum, M.S., **Strength Training: Rationale for Current Guidelines for Adult Fitness Programs**, *The Physician and Sportsmedicine*, Vol. 25, No. 2, February 1997, http://www.physsportsmed.com/issues/1997/02feb/pollock.htm

Shrier, I., **Myths and Truths of Stretching**, *The Physician and Sportsmedicine*, Vol. 28, No. 8, August 2000, http://www.physsportsmed.com/issues/2000/08_00/shrier.htm

Stamford, B. **Cross-Training: Giving Yourself a Whole-Body Workout**. *The Physician and Sportsmedicine*, Vol. 24, No. 9, September 1996, http://www.physsportsmed.com/issues/sep_96/cross.htm

Related Fitness Assessment Activities:

Activity 11. Evaluating Muscular strength

Activity 12. Determining Muscle Cross-Sectional Strength

Activity 13. Evaluating Muscle Power

Activity 14. Evaluating Muscular Endurance

Activity 15. Evaluating Core Musculature Fitness

Chapter 7

Muscle Anatomy

Chapter Contents
- Muscle Structure
- Major Muscles of the Human Body
- Muscle Fiber Arrangement
- Revisiting Muscles, Joints, and Levers
- Posture
- Selected Readings

Learning Objectives

The material in this chapter will allow you to:

- Understand the gross anatomic structure of human muscles
- Understand the fiber arrangement within muscles
- Identify and name the major muscles and muscle groups of the body
- Understand the role of bone, muscle, and joints in normal posture

---

110

Muscle Structure

Muscle comprises almost 50% of the total weight of the human body with 40% of this being *skeletal* muscle and the remaining 10% being *smooth* and *cardiac* muscle. Cardiac muscle is, as its name implies, the muscle of the heart. Smooth muscle is the muscle that is found in the internal organs (stomach, intestines, uterus, etc.), blood vessels and glands. Skeletal muscle is the muscle anchored to the bones of the skeleton and is the muscle responsible for movement and athletic activities as well as contributing to the body's appearance. Skeletal and cardiac muscles are referred to as *striated* muscles because they appear striped when viewed under the microscope. Smooth muscle, lacking these striations, appears smooth.

Let's begin with an exploration of the major muscles of the human body.

MAJOR MUSCLES OF THE BODY

Muscles that move the upper extremities (shoulders and arms)

Trapezius: Large triangular muscle of the upper back which originates on the vertebrae of the upper back and inserts onto the shoulder. When contracted, the action is to pull shoulder and arm back.

Rhomboideus: (major and minor): Small muscles running between the vertebral column and the scapula (shoulder blade). When contracted, their action is to pull the shoulder blades towards the middle of the back, rotating the shoulders rearward (retraction).

By the Numbers
There are over 600 skeletal muscles in the human body.

Serratus anterior: Located on the sides of the chest, this muscle originates on the ribs in front and inserts onto the scapula. When contracted, its action is to pull the shoulders forward (protraction).

Pectoralis major: A large, fan shaped muscle on the front surface of the upper chest. It originates from the center of the chest and inserts onto the humerus (upper arm). Its action is to pull the arm forward and across the chest.

Pectoralis minor: A small muscle located under the Pectoralis major. It originates from the ribs on the front of the chest and inserts onto the shoulder (scapula). When contracted, its action is to pull the shoulder forward and down.

Latissimus dorsi: A large triangular muscle, originating from the midline of the lower back, rising and curving around the sides and inserting onto the humerus (upper arm). Its action is to pull the arm back as in a rowing motion.

Deltoid: A triangular muscle covering the shoulder joint. Its origin is on the shoulder and it inserts onto the humerus. Its action is to adduct the arm.

Biceps brachii: Located on the front of the upper arm, the biceps originates on the scapula (shoulder) and inserts onto the radius (forearm). Its action is to flex the forearm. The biceps brachii are used when performing curls.

Triceps brachii: Located on the back of the upper arm, the triceps originates on the scapula (shoulder) and humerus (upper arm) and inserts onto the ulna (forearm). Its action is to extend the forearm. The triceps are used in performing push-ups and when pressing free-weights overhead.

Rotator Cuff Muscles: The rotator cuff refers to a group of four small muscles which originate on the shoulder blade (scapula) and insert onto the humerus (upper arm). The individual muscles are the *Supraspinatus*, *Infraspinatus*, *Teres Minor* and *Subscapularis*. These muscles function to stabilize the shoulder joint and to rotate the arm.

Muscles of the abdomen:

Rectus abdominus: A large muscle running parallel to and along the midline of the anterior abdomen. It originates from the pelvis and inserts onto the sternum and ribs. Its action is to flex the torso. This is the major muscle used in doing sit-ups.

External (and internal) obliques: Muscles running between the pelvis and ribs at an angle to the midline of the body. Their actions are to tense the abdominal wall or bend the torso towards one side.

Muscles that Move the Lower Extremities (hips and legs):

Gluteus maximus: The major muscle of the buttocks originating from the sides and back of the upper pelvis and inserts onto the femur (large bone of the thigh). The action of the gluteus maximus is to extend the leg at the hip (pull back as if to get ready for a kick), and to rotate the hip laterally (towards the outside).

Gluteus medius (and minimus): Located mostly under the Gluteus maximus, the Gluteus medius originates on the lateral crest of the hip and inserts onto the femur. Its action is to abduct the leg at the hip (lift out towards the side) and to rotate the hip medially (towards the inside). A third muscle, the Gluteus minimus, has the same attachments and action as the Gluteus medius.

Adductors femoris: A group of several muscles originating on the lower front surface of the pelvis and inserting onto the middle or rear surface of the femur. Their actions are to adduct (pull back to the midline) the leg.

Quadriceps femoris: The Quadriceps refers to a group of four muscles located on the front surface of the thigh. The muscles included are the *Rectus femoris*, *Vastus lateralis*, *Vastus medialis* and *Vastus intermedius*. The quadriceps group has two different actions. The rectus femoris muscle serves as a hip flexor (raising the thigh up towards the abdomen) and the three vastus muscles serve as foreleg, or knee, extensors.

Hamstrings: The Hamstrings refer to a group of three muscles (Biceps femoris, Semitendinosis and Semimembranosis) located on the rear of the thigh. The Hamstrings originate on or near the head of the femur and part of the pelvis and insert onto the tibia, the larger of the bones of the lower leg. The action of the Hamstrings is to flex the leg (bend at the knee) or extend the thigh (pull thigh rearward).

Gastrocnemius: The large, prominent muscle of the calf. The gastrocnemius originates from the sides of the femur near the knee and inserts, via the Achilles tendon, onto the heel of the foot. Its action is to assist in flexion of the leg at the knee and to extend the foot (toes pointed down).

Tibialis anterior: The muscle running along the front surface of the shin over the tibia. The tibialis anterior originates on the femur near the outside of the knee and inserts onto the foot near the big toe. Its action is to flex the foot (toes pointed up).

113

Figure 7.1. Human Muscular Anatomy: Anterior View

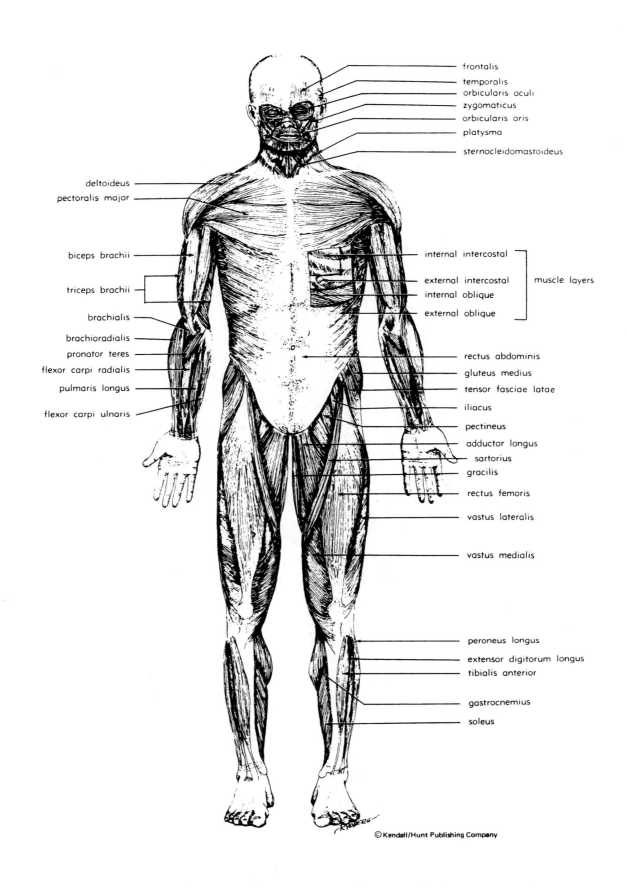

frontalis
temporalis
orbicularis oculi
zygomaticus
orbicularis oris
platysma
sternocleidomastoideus

deltoideus
pectoralis major

biceps brachii

triceps brachii

brachialis
brachioradialis
pronator teres
flexor carpi radialis
pulmaris longus
flexor carpi ulnaris

internal intercostal
external intercostal
internal oblique
external oblique

muscle layers

rectus abdominis
gluteus medius
tensor fasciae latae
iliacus
pectineus
adductor longus
sartorius
gracilis
rectus femoris
vastus lateralis

vastus medialis

peroneus longus
extensor digitorum longus
tibialis anterior

gastrocnemius

soleus

© Kendall/Hunt Publishing Company

114

Figure 7.2. Human Muscular Anatomy: Posterior View

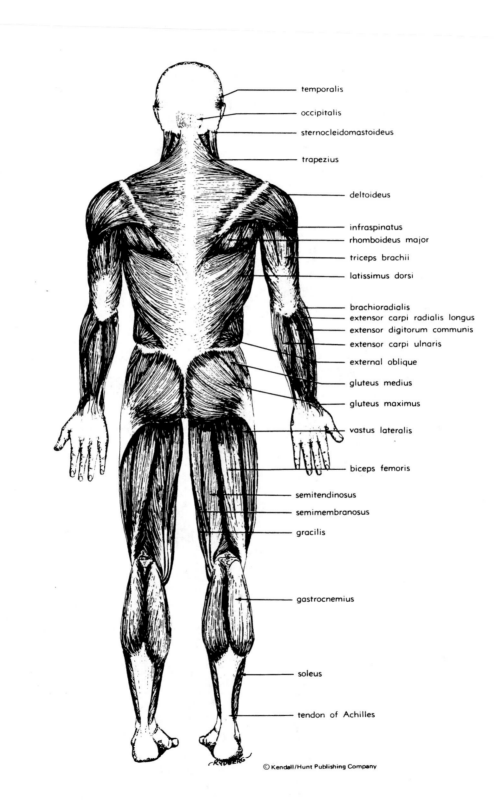

- temporalis
- occipitalis
- sternocleidomastoideus
- trapezius
- deltoideus
- infraspinatus
- rhomboideus major
- triceps brachii
- latissimus dorsi
- brachioradialis
- extensor carpi radialis longus
- extensor digitorum communis
- extensor carpi ulnaris
- external oblique
- gluteus medius
- gluteus maximus
- vastus lateralis
- biceps femoris
- semitendinosus
- semimembranosus
- gracilis
- gastrocnemius
- soleus
- tendon of Achilles

Muscle Fiber Arrangement

As we've seen earlier, anatomic muscles are comprised of cylindrical units, or bundles of fibers, called fascicles. Each fascicle in turn, is composed of numerous bundles of cylindrical muscle cells or fibers which run parallel with each other with the fascicles. The arrangement of these fascicles and fibers within the muscle can assume one of two types of patterns, a *parallel* pattern or a *pennate* pattern.

In the parallel arrangement, the muscle fascicles and fibers all run side-by-side parallel to the long axis of the muscle. There are five different parallel arrangements, depending on the overall gross shape of the muscle: ***Flat, Fusiform, Strap, Radiate*** and ***Circular***. Flat muscles tend to be thin and wide, like a bed sheet but obviously much smaller. They originate from broad tendons. An example can be found in the oblique muscles of the abdomen. In Fusiform muscles, the fibers originate from a narrow tendon, become wide in the middle or belly of the muscle, and then narrow once again as they join to the opposite tendon. The bicep muscle presents a classic example of the fusiform arrangement. Strap muscles are long and symmetrical throughout their length and appear similar in shape to the strap of a belt, hence the name. An example the strap muscle arrangement is the sartorius muscle of the thigh. Radiate muscles are a cross between flat and fusiform muscles. They begin from a broad tendon and converge to a central tendon. Radiate muscle are usually triangular in shape. The pectoralis major and trapezius muscles are examples of the radiate muscle pattern. Circular muscles are actually strap muscles that are arranged in an orbital, or circular, pattern. They form sphincters around openings in the body. Some examples are the orbicularis oculi around the eye and the orbicularis oris surrounding the mouth.

In the pinnate arrangement, the muscle fascicles and fibers run diagonally to the central tendon. The fibers can run along one side of the central tendon termed ***unipennate***. We find this type of arrangement in the biceps femoris. The fibers may also run on two sides of a central tendon and are referred to as ***bipennate*** muscles. We can find this type of arrangement in the gastrocnemius and rectus femoris. Lastly, there is the ***multipennate*** arrangement of muscle fibers. These types of fibers attach from many angles to a central tendon and can be found in the deltoid muscle or the gluteus maximus.

Figure 7.3. Muscle Fiber Arrangement

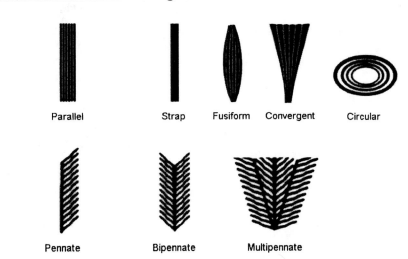

In general, the pennate muscles contain more fascicles which run along a central tendon compared to the parallel arrangements which contain fewer fascicles originating from a tendon and converging into one. As a result, pennate muscles tend to have a larger cross sectional area therefore they can exert more force in a shorter period of time over a shorter distance thereby creating more power and strength compared to parallel muscle. Pennate muscles sacrifice range of motion for force. Parallel muscles run the length of the tendon and as a result they sacrifice strength and power in favor of greater range of motion. Here is a rule of thumb, longer muscle fibers equal greater Range Of Motion while increased total cross sectional area equals greater power.

Revisiting Joint and Lever Systems

As we've studied in the previous chapter, human musculoskeletal movements are created by the interaction of bones, joints, and muscles arranged in lever systems. In a common example, we can look at the humerus, radius and ulna as they join at the elbow and can understand the creation of a third class lever system by action of the bicep muscle. The bicep, the main muscle involved in the flexion of the elbow, would be referred to as the primary mover. Table 7.1 below lists several of the major joint systems of the body and indicates the primary movers for a variety of actions, or movements of which each joint is capable.

Table 7.1.

Joint	Movement	Primary Movers
Scapulothoracic:	Fixation	Serratus Anterior, Pectoralis Minor Trapezius, Levator Scapulae, Rhomboids,
	Upward Rotation	Trapezius
	Downward Rotation	Rhomboids, Pectoralis Minor, Levator Scapulae
	Elevation	Rhomboids, Levator Scapulae, Trapezius
	Depression	Pectoralis Minor, Trapezius
	Protraction	Serratus Anterior, Pectoralis Minor
	Retraction	Rhomboids, Trapezius
Glenohumeral:	Flexion	Anterior Deltoid, Pectoralis Major
	Extension	Latissimus Dorsi, Teres Major, Pectoralis Major
	Abduction	Middle Deltoid, Superspinatus
	Adduction	Latissimus Dorsi, Teres Major, Pectoralis Major
	Internal Rotation	Latissimus Dorsi, Teres Major, Subscapularis, Pectoralis Major, Anterior Deltoid
	External Rotation	Supraspinatus, Infraspinatus, Teres Minor, Posterior Deltoid
	Horizontal Abduction	
	Horizontal Adduction	
Elbow:	Flexion	Biceps Brachii, Brachialis, Brachioradialis
	Extension	Triceps Brachii, Anconeus
Radioulnar:	Pronation	Pronator Quadratus, Pronator Teres
	Supination	Biceps Brachii, Supinator
Wrist:	Flexion	Flexor Carpi Radialis, Flexor Carpi Ulnaris, Palmaris Longus, Flexordigitorum superficialis
	Extension	Extensor Carpi Radialis Longus, brevis, ulnaris, Extensor Digitorm Longus
	Ulna Deviation (*Abduction*)	Extensor Carpi Radialis Longus and brevis, Flexor Carpi Radialis
	Radial Deviation (*Adduction*)	Flexor and Extensor Carpi Ulnaris

Core Muscles

Much is currently made of "core" training programs and the importance of the "core" in a variety of athletic events. The term "core" is generally used to reference the area of the body that falls between the bottom of the sternum and the knees and involves the muscles of the abdomen, lower back, and hips. These core muscles function to help maintain an upright posture, support the internal abdominal organs, and stabilize the pelvis and torso during dynamic movements. As we've come to understand with respect to musculoskeletal movements and lever systems, a stable point of origin is required to maximize strength and power in human movements. A strong core, through its stabilization of the pelvis, is therefore essential for the generation of quick and powerful leg movements.

Included among the core muscles are the *rectus abdominus, external and internal obliques, transverse abdominus, erector spinae, multifidus, gluteus maximus, latissimus dorsi, hamstrings,* and *quadriceps*.

Posture

Our body's skeletal system is analogous to the framing of a house. When a home's framing is strong and sturdy, it creates a safe environment in which we can live. The same is true for with our body; when our skeletal system is healthy and functioning optimally, it gives us a solid framework to protect us, support our internal organs, and allow for movement. When purchasing a home, it is important to understand that while the outside may be attractive and clean, the framing underneath may be seriously flawed. The same is also true with us. In fact, many sport and exercise enthusiasts are so concerned with the observable finished product, the superficial muscles as viewed through the skin that they ignore the critically important internal framework.

When posture, the natural alignment of the musculoskeletal system, is in proper alignment, minimal stress is placed on the ligaments, allowing the articulations to function optimally within their physiologic range of motion. This allows the tendons and muscle to operate more effectively and efficiently and to conserve energy. Good posture maintains the integrity of the spinal column, allows for safer movements throughout the day, improves self confidence and enhances daily activities. When there are even minor misalignments within our posture, both the novice and experienced exercise professional run the risk developing a host of musculoskeletal injuries because of the dynamic interaction that exists between the skeletal, muscular and articular systems.

Before beginning any exercise or athletic program, individuals as well as coaches and trainers should be acutely aware of importance of proper posture, the dynamic interactions, and the potential risk that exist when the skeletal system has deviated from its norm. As we explore postural integrity, the astute student should also begin to think about exercises to avoid in minimizing risk while at the same time adding exercises that will help to correct the faulty posture.

Posture, also known as the attitude, of the body should not only be observed from the seated or the standing position but careful attention should also be given to the body's attitude during motions such as running, walking and exercising. The dynamic body can give us information that the static body cannot, such as what part of the gait is being affected during walking or running, which leads us to the next logical question, why? Once we investigate why, we can begin correcting the underlying cause.

Let's investigate! The body is three dimensional so when it becomes misaligned the structure(s) can misalign with respect to superior, inferior, anterior, posterior, lateral translation, and rotational components. To complicate matters even further, postural distortions usually occur in one or more of these combinations. However, we can gain a majority of what we need to know from only three primary positions, *Anterior to Posterior* and *Posterior to Anterior* as well as the Lateral view. You may be familiar with the term **Center of Gravity (COG)**. COG is a point where all forces acting on a body are concentrated. It is the point where gravity acts. In a static standing position the center of gravity is typically focused at the second sacral tubercle (S2). To properly observe posture, have the individual wear minimal clothing in order to observe all of your anatomical land marks, also have them remove their shoes to inspect their feet. The client should assume a normal relaxed standing posture, preferably in front of a body alignment grid. If a grid is not available, there are computerized posture systems on the market that utilize digital cameras to aid in the analysis. The trainer or your partner should stand back far enough to observe the whole body. The trainer should walk around the body while the client remains still to observe the posture from the anterior, lateral and posterior angles. Such an analysis will be conducted as part of lab Activity 16.

While observing from the anterior and posterior positions, an imaginary vertical line known as the Line of Gravity (LOG) should be drawn sagitally passing through the direct center of the vertebrae separating the left and right sides of the body equally. The LOG indicates the forces acting upon the joint structures. During the analysis process the following structures should be observed for balance and symmetry: Head and Neck, Vertebral Column, Glenohumeral Joint, Scapula, Elbows and Wrists, Pelvic Girdle and Hips, Knees and Feet.

Head and Neck: Does the head tilt up or down, does it tilt to the left or right, does the head rotate or laterally translate to the right or the left? Observe the muscles of the *sternocleidomastoid (SCM)* and the upper aspect of the *trapezius* for balance and symmetry. The lower neck and upper back is a transitional region so check if there is any rounding of the shoulders or upper back.

Vertebral Column: Observe the spinal column for any evidence of possible scoliosis (lateral curvature of the spine). This can be done by palpating the spinous processes of the vertebrae, observing uneven scapulas, or uneven distances of the arms from the torso. The cause could be congenital meaning it developed during embryonic development such as improperly formed vertebrae. Or, it could be acquired because of the stresses improperly applied to a developing body.

Glenohumeral Joint: Is on shoulder higher than the other, do the shoulders rounded forward? The glenohumeral joint are surrounded by anterior, posterior and medial deltoid muscles as well as the muscles that make up the rotator cuff muscles. If the delicate balance between these muscles is disrupted, the structure will be altered. The reason rounded shoulders is common place is because the anterior deltoids as well as the *pectoralis major* are strong and shortened and the medial, posterior deltoids and the rotator cuff muscles are elongated and weaker.

Scapula: The scapulas are often affected when the glenohumeral joints are affected because they collectively help make up the pectoral girdle. The scapulas too often find themselves protracted because the shoulders are commonly rounded and because the middle aspect of the traps and the rhomboids are either weak or long.

Elbows and Wrists: In the normal relaxed postural position, the palms of the hands should face the body. When the shoulders become rounded and the scapulas protract for reasons previously discussed, the glenohumeral joint becomes internally rotated. When the glenohumeral joint internally rotates, the entire upper extremity misaligns and we begin to see the dorsal aspect of the hand.

Pelvic Girdle and Hips: The anatomical landmark for the pelvic girdle is the anterior superior aspect of the iliac crest. When the posture is in proper alignment, these points should be level bilaterally. When they are not level, they will alter the lower extremity because the articulation of the femur in the acetabulum will be altered. This can have deleterious effects on the hips, knees and ankles.

Knees: If the knees are not in their proper alignment they can present as "knock knees" or "bowl legs" also referred to as genu valgum and genu varum respectively. This is important when designing exercise programs because of the potential increase in stress placed on these joints.

Feet: When observing posture, be sure to examine the feet for three arches. There are two longitudinal arches one on the medial aspect of the foot and one on the lateral aspect of the foot, and there is a transverse arch that can be found between the medial and lateral longitudinal arches. The longitudinal arches span from the heal (calcaneus) to the distal aspect of the metatarsals, the articulations between the ball of the foot and the toes. When the structures of the feet are in there proper alignment, the medial arch will present as the highest of the three arches and prevent the medial aspect of the foot and the ball of the foot from striking the ground. The purpose of the arches are to dissipate mechanical loads placed on the body. When the bones of the feet are properly aligned and the integrity of the arches are maintained, the feet transfer approximately 60% of the body's to the heels and 40% to the ball of the feet.

One common postural distortion involving the lower extremities in known as ***Pronation Distortion Syndrome*** and it involves the loss of the medial longitudinal arch in conjunction with genu valgus presentation of the knees and internal rotation of the thighs. This syndrome is commonly seen during squatting, lunges, jumping, and walking up stairs. You may also notice that people who have this syndrome will have trouble keeping their heels on the ground while squatting. The tight or strong muscles involved with pronation distortion syndrome are: *peroneals, gastrocnemius, soleus, iliiotibial band, hamstrings, the adductors and iliopsoas*. The elongated or weak muscles include: *posterior tibialis, anterior tibialis, vastus medialis, gluteus medias and maximus*.

While observing the anterior and posterior aspect for proper alignment presents us with a tremendous amount of information, without continuing to observe the lateral aspect of the postural picture, the puzzle will be incomplete. While some of the structures being observed are the same, the two vantage points give us unique information. A properly aligned posture observed from the lateral view should present as follows. The imaginary vertical LOG should pass through the following points: The middle portion of the ear, mid shoulder, middle aspect of the greater trochanter, mid aspect of the lateral knee and approximately 2cm. in front of the ankle.

Head and Neck: Unfortunately, a majority of the population today present with a forward head posture caused by chronic flexion of the cervical spine.

Vertebrae: From the lateral view, the spinal column should exhibit a smooth anterior curve in the cervical spine known as lordosis; a smooth posterior curve in the dorsal/thoracic region known as kyphosis; and another smooth anterior curve in the lumbar region again referred to as lordosis. Because of the interconnectedness of the entire body, a kinetic chain of events can cause the exaggeration or diminishment of these curves. This is especially true in the spine. When the head protrudes forward from the shoulders due to chronic flexion of the cervical spine the normal lordotic curve diminishes and can become hypolorditic and eventually over time a kyphotic curve. When the head approximates a forward head posture, a couple of sinereos involving muscles occurs causing a hyperkyphotic curve in the thoracic region. This type of pattern when found is commonly referred to as *Upper-Crossed Syndrome*. People with this type of patterning may experience challenges with overhead movements, pushing and pulling as well as actively stabilizing the cervical spine. This pattern is commonly found in people who sit for extended periods of time or perform repetitive unidimensional movements. People with upper-crossed syndrome can exhibit excessively strong, short precontracted or tight upper abdominal, anterior deltoid, pectoralis major, levator scapulae, teres major, upper trapezius, subscapularis, latissimus dorsi, scalenes, rectus capitus and the sternocleidomastoid (SCM) muscles. other muscles in the region such as the rhomboid, middle and lower trapezius, serratus anterior, posterior deltoid teres minor infra spinatus longus coli and capitus muscles may be weak or too stretched.

As the kinetic chain of events plays out and we approach the lumbar spine, one of two situations can present themselves based on the musculature surrounding the lumbar spine and lower extremities. One situation is referred to as the *Lower-Crossed Syndrome* and the other is known as a *Sway Back Posture*.

With the lower-crossed syndrome, the pelvic girdle tilts forward exaggerating the normal lordotic curve. When this posture is present, it is not uncommon for individuals to experience lower back pain and or anterior knee pain. with lower-crossed syndrome can exhibit excessively strong, short precontracted or tight iliopsoas, rectus femoris, tensor fascia latae, the adductors, erector spinae, quadratus lumborum, gastrocnemius and soleus muscles. other muscles in the region such as the gluteus maximus, hamstrings, gluteus medius, transverse abdominus, multifidus, internal oblique and the anterior and posterior tibialis may be weak or too stretched. This pattern is also found in individuals who sit for prolonged periods.

A sway back posture causes the pelvis to tilt up causing a loss of lordosis or a flattening of the lumbar curve. The muscles that present with a shortening or tightness are the lower rectus abdominus, hamstrings, gluteus maximus, thoracic extensors, cervical flexors. The opposing muscles that may get weak or elongate are the thoracic-lumbar fascia, quadratus lumborum, erector spinae, tensor fasciae latae, ilio psoas (hip flexors) and rectus femoris.

Glenohumeral Joint: See glenohumeral and vertebrae section above.

Pelvic Girdle and Hips: See vertebrae section above.

Elbow and Wrists: As the shoulders round forward, the glenohumeral joint internally rotates causing the elbows and wrists to translate in front of the LOG. Here we find the elbows and wrist anterior to the ribs. The proper postural position will find the elbows and wrist at the sides of the body.

Chapter

8

Nervous System

Chapter Contents

- Nerve Cells
- Nerve Transmission
- Nervous System Organization
- Simple Reflex
- Coordinated Movement
- Exercise and the Nervous System

Learning Objectives

The material in this chapter will allow you to:

- Understand the anatomical and functional organization of the nervous system
- Understand the way in which information is coded and transmitted within the nervous system
- Understand the mechanism and examples of simple reflex pathways
- Understand the mechanism and examples of coordinated athletic movements
- Understand the effects of exercise on the nervous system

The Nervous System

The ability to sense the position of our limbs, to detect the levels of oxygen, carbon dioxide, and lactic acid in the blood and to coordinate and integrate the action of our muscles all depend upon the structures and functions of the nervous system. As with all organ systems, the nervous system is composed of organ-level structures that include the brain - the nervous system's central processor, the peripheral nerves and spinal cord - conduits for information movement, and various sensors and receptors that feed information about our body's environment and activities through the nerve fibers and into the processing and decision-making units.

Nerve Cells

Each of these structural units of the nervous system, brain, nerves, spinal cord and receptors, are composed of collections of cells that include both supportive connective tissue cells called *glia,* and information signaling cells called ***neurons***.

Figure 7.1. The Neuron

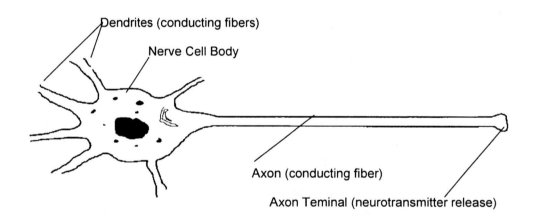

Neurons are cells that are capable of transmitting information in the form of electro-chemical pulses, similar in some ways to the conduction of information through a copper wire as pulses of electricity or through a fiber-optic cable as pulses of light. Because of the special properties of the neurons' membrane, they are capable of carrying these information-transmitting electro-chemical impulses along their length and passing them on to other neurons, sometimes in long chains and sometimes in highly branching networks. In this way, information can be transmitted throughout the body in very complex patterns. Chains of these neurons, linked end-to-end and aggregated in bundles make up our nerve fibers. Other neurons, because of the structure of their membranes, are capable of initiating impulses in response to specific sensations. These neurons make up the sensors and receptors of the body.

Nerve Transmission

The nerve cell membrane is constructed in such a way as to separate the electrically charged ions of sodium (Na⁺), potassium (K⁺) and chloride (Cl⁻) in specific proportions that make the inside of the cell negative relative to the outside. The amount of this charge measures approximately 70 mV (millivolts) when the cell is at rest and not conducting any information and is referred to as the neuron's *resting potential*. When stimulated, the membrane becomes temporarily permeable to these ions as membrane channels open and close causing the cell to reverse its charge with a small section of the interior of the cell becoming briefly positive and then immediately resetting back to its negative 70 mV resting charge as the ions are pumped back across the membrane to their original, resting concentrations. This brief positive charge, the *action potential*, is propelled along the nerves axon as a single pulse of information. The number of pulses generated per second and the sequence in which the pulses are generated and propelled allows the nerve to code the information as a series of positive and negative pulses, similar to the binary code of computer information, a series of 0 and 1 pulses (off and on transistor settings). Thus, information is transmitted along the neuron in the form of electrical pulses.

When the electrical pulse reaches the end of one neuron, it is chemically transmitted to the next neuron by molecules called neurotransmitters, released from the end of sending neuron and triggering an action potential in the membrane of the receiving neuron. In this way the information can be passed from one neuron to the next as an electro-chemical signal; electrical within a single neuron and chemical between the neurons.

Figure 7.2. Nerve Transmission

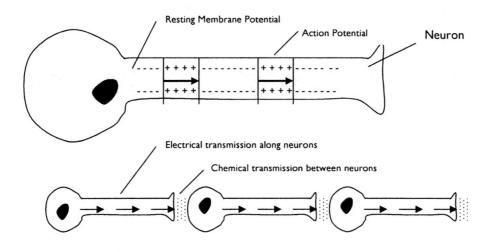

Nervous System Organization

The structures and functional responsibilities of the nervous system are classified into two component parts, the *central nervous system* and the *peripheral nervous system* with each of these components consisting of several subsystems as illustrated in Figure 7.3.

Figure 7.3. Structural Organization of the Nervous System

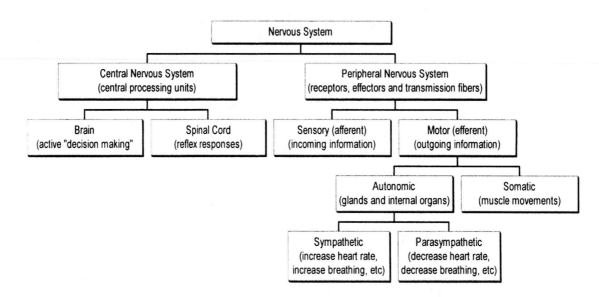

The central nervous system, consisting of the brain and spinal cord, serves as the main information-processing and decision-making unit of the nervous system and is encased within the protective bony shell of the skull and vertebral column, respectively. The peripheral nervous system consists of the various sensors and receptors (heat, cold and pain receptors in the skin; taste and smell receptors in the mouth and nose; visual receptors in the eyes, etc.), the nerve fiber bundles that carry sensory information from the receptors and into the central nervous system and also carry motor information from the central nervous system out to the *effectors*, the muscles and glands that are under nervous system control. Motor information destined for control of muscles and movement is classified as *somatic output* while that destined for regulation of the homeostatic functions (heart, respiration, temperature control, digestion, etc.) are classified as *autonomic or visceral output*.

> **By the Numbers**
> There are over 100 billion neurons and 2 trillion glial cells in the human nervous system. Human nerve cells carry information at a speed of 120 meters/sec.

Simple Reflex

With the nervous system constantly monitoring our immediate environment and the condition of the body we are continually adjusting the body in response to changing situations, often as automatic reflexes accomplished with no conscious effort. In these circumstances, *simple reflex* responses are generated within the spinal cord, relayed back out by motor nerve fibers, and result in some specific response to the initial signal from the sensor. Examples of such simple reflexes can be found in our response to stepping on a tack or burning our finger on a hot stove and are known as the *flexor withdrawal reflex*. In these circumstances, sensory information is generated within pain receptors in the skin and carried into the spinal cord. Once inside the spinal cord, the information is relayed through interneurons to somatic motor neurons and a message is sent rapidly out to the muscles of the leg or arm which, in these examples, rapidly withdraw our foot from the tack or our hand from the stove. In this specific reflex, illustrated in Figure 7.4, the motor output always leads directly to a flexor muscle, not to an extensor, and the reflex is therefore known as the flexor withdrawal reflex. Going back to our examples you will note that we always withdraw our hand from the hot stove by contracting the bicep muscle, a flexor, never by contracting the tricep. When we step on a tack we reflexively withdraw the foot by contracting the hamstring muscles, flexors, never by contracting the quadriceps. This is simply the way our nervous system is "hardwired". Although the response is automatic and accomplished without conscious effort, the brain is typically "notified" of the condition and response by other interneurons in the spinal cord.

Figure 7.4. Simple Reflex Pathway

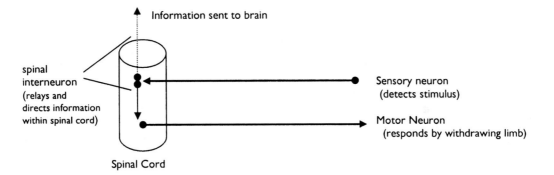

Coordinated Movements

The Central Nervous System is also responsible for coordinating more complicated and intricate responses. In performing an athletic activity, a springboard dive or a golf swing for example, many sensory inputs are involved and the coordinated activity of many muscles is required, unlike the simple situation of responding to a hot stove. In diving for example, information is received from visual receptors in the eyes, determining distance from the water), vestibular (balance and position) receptors in the inner ear, determining position as you jump on the board or tumble through the air, and pressure receptors on the soles of the feet, detecting whether you are standing on your feet, pressing hard against the board as you push off in for a jump, or airborne with no pressure sensation at all. All of this information is brought into the spinal cord by sensory neurons, rises up through the spinal cord and enters the brain, and reaches the brain's outer surface, the *cerebral cortex*.

Performing the actual dive requires pushing off from the board by contraction of the quadriceps and gastrocnemius muscles, flexing into the tuck position by contraction of the abdominal muscles and extending the arms and forming a wedge with the hands to enter the water by coordinated contraction of multiple muscles in the pectoral girdle and arms. The information controlling the timing, sequence, duration and strength of each of these movements travels from the cerebral cortex, down through the spinal cord and out to the muscles through the somatic motor neurons. The receipt and processing of all of these sensory inputs, the coordinated response to move all of the muscles in proper sequence, and the continual feedback-directed adjustment is controlled by intricate collections of neurons in the higher brain center regions of the cerebrum and cerebellum.

In part, the ability to perform such coordinated movements depends upon a sensory function known as *proprioception*. Proprioception refers to the body's ability to have sensory awareness of the position of each of the joints (*static proprioception*) as well as the direction, speed, and force of actual movements (*dynamic proprioception*). Static proprioception plays an important role in our maintaining normal posture while dynamic proprioception is required for the high speed, coordinated activities of sport and exercise. Proprioception depends upon a complex network of receptors, or sensors, distributed throughout the musculoskeletal system. Among the receptors participating in proprioception are the muscle spindle fibers within each skeletal muscle, the Golgi tendon organs, ligament mechanorecptors in the joint capsules and cutaneous receptors in the skin. Also contributing to our ability to perform complex, coordinated movements are the visual and vestibular systems.

The *vestibular system* consists of a set of sensors located within the middle ear that include the *semicircular canals*, the *utricle*, and the *saccule*. The semicircular canals are responsible for detecting motion and the utricle and saccule for detecting static, three-dimensional position of the body in space. All consist of fluid-filled bony chambers in which floats a gelatin-like body. Embedded within this gelatin are fine hair-like projections of receptor cells (called hair cells). The action of gravity pulling on the gelatin material in the utricle and saccule, or of motion and inertia acting in the semicircular canals, allows for the sensation of movement (Fig 7.5).

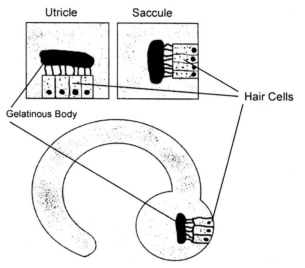

Figure 7.5. Sense Organs

Exercise and the Nervous System

The Role of Repetitive Practice

By repeating the precise sequence of activities that occur during coordinated actions such as diving or driving a golf ball, through hours and hours of practice, the brain becomes accustomed to receiving the necessary information, to plotting the necessary actions, and to signaling the muscles in the precise sequence, duration and strength required for each activity. Over time the neurons involved will develop permanent connections, enhance their ability to signal one another rapidly, and develop neural pathways that will make the action almost automatic. This is a predictable response of the general adaptation syndrome. It is important that the proper technique is used during training so that faulty movements do not become automatic.

The nervous system, through its continual monitoring of the body's internal conditions, is also responsible for the adjustment of heart rate and respiratory rate during exercise and for activating the sweat glands to control body temperature.

Endorphins and "Runner's High"

Morphine and opium-like compounds exert their pain reducing (anesthetic) and mood altering effects by binding to receptors on the nerve cell membrane within specific regions of the brain and modifying the generation and transmission of action potentials. Researchers studying the effect of these drugs were interested in the reason why human brain cells would have naturally occurring receptors for these drugs which were not naturally found in the body. Their research uncovered the presence of opium-like molecules in the brain, called endorphins that were produced during times of stress and trauma and acted upon these brain cell receptors to reduce pain and fear and to generate a feeling of calm and peace. These same endorphins are produced during vigorous exercise and are, in part, responsible for similar feelings among people engaged in vigorous exercise for long periods of time. Just as people can develop addictions to morphine and opium, we can also become addicted to exercise. In fact, serious runners who, because of injury or other circumstances must stop running for prolonged periods, exhibit all of the classical symptoms of withdrawal.

128

Selected Readings

Vassiliki, L, G. Panayiota. **Basic Concepts of the Nervous System Anatomy and Physiology.**
Wirescript Online Magazine.
http://www.wirescript.com/cgibin/HyperNews/get.cgi/lv9901.html

Related Fitness Assessment Activities

Activity 17. Assessing Proprioception
Activity 18. Assessing Response Time

Chapter

Respiratory System

9

Chapter Contents
- The Need for Gas Exchange
- Respiratory Anatomy
- Regulation of Respiration
- Effects of Exercise on the Respiratory System
- Selected Readings

Learning Objectives
The material in this chapter will allow you to:
- Understand the structures and function of the human respiratory system
- Understand how gasses are transported within the body
- Understand the concept of VO_{2max} and its use as a performance measure
- Understand the effects of exercise on the respiratory system

The Need for Gas Exchange

Shared in common with all aerobically powered organisms, we require a steady supply of oxygen to help harness the power contained in the foods we consume as fuel. As our activity level goes up during exercise or athletic competition, our body's demand for energy, and therefore for more oxygen, rises. The inability to provide our working muscles with a sufficient supply of oxygen is one of the primary limiting factors in aerobic athletic performance.

The respiratory system provides for the exchange of gasses between the environment and the interior of the body. The cells within the body, especially the cells of muscle, require oxygen (O_2) to allow for the metabolic reactions which provide energy for work, growth and repair. These metabolic reactions produce carbon dioxide (CO_2) gas as a waste and this must be eliminated from the body. As one engages in physical activities such as exercise and athletics, cells become more active, the metabolic rate increases and the demand for gas exchange becomes greater.

The capacity of an individual's respiratory system to exchange gases between the atmosphere and the blood and the capacity of the cardiovascular system to transport the gasses between the lungs and the tissues are the major limiting factors in athletic performance. A measure of the ability to provide and utilize oxygen under maximal aerobic performance is the $VO_2\ max$, or the maximal O_2 consumption, typically measured as the ml of O_2 consumed per minute, for each kilogram of body mass (ml/min/kg). In fact, one common measure used to describe overall fitness is, quite simply, the $VO_2\ max$. The $VO_2\ max$ provides a measure of more than just respiratory system performance since a variety of other factors also contribute to how efficiently the working body utilizes oxygen. Included among these other factors are, (1) the effectiveness of the blood in carrying oxygen, (2) the capacity of the cardiovascular system to distribute the oxygen-rich blood to the working muscles and, (3) the ability of the muscles to efficiently use the oxygen to release energy for contraction. Under normal conditions, the average individual uses approximately 3.5 ml of oxygen per minute, per kilogram of body weight. In well-trained, elite athletes, these systems can combine to obtain, deliver, and use over 80 ml of oxygen per minute, per kilogram of body weight as illustrated in Table 8.1

Table 8.1 – World Class Athlete $VO_2\ max$ Levels	$VO_2\ max$ (ml/min/kg)	
	Male	Female
Long-distance running	70 – 80	60 – 75
Swimming	60 – 70	50 – 60
Gymnastics	50 – 60	35 – 45
Running Sprints	45 – 55	35 – 45

Respiratory System Anatomy

The respiratory system consists of the nasal cavity and related structures, a series of air passageways, the lungs and the muscles responsible for the respiratory movements. The *nasal cavity* is a hollow space behind the nose through which the inhaled air passes and in which it is warmed, moistened and filtered. The nasal cavity is lined with an epithelium (a layer of cells) which secretes mucus and which has a brush-like surface of cilia. The mucus traps inhaled dirt and bacteria which are swept away by the cilia towards the throat where they are swallowed and destroyed by digestion. The air then passes into the *trachea*, or windpipe, then into the smaller *bronchi*, *bronchioles* and finally, into the *alveolar air sacs* of the lung. The air in the alveolus is separated from the blood within the lung capillaries by a membrane only two cell layers thick. It is across this membrane that the gasses are exchanged. There are approximately 700 million alveoli in our two lungs accounting for an alveolus-capillary exchange area about equal in size to a full doubles tennis court.

Figure 8.1. The Human Respiratory System.

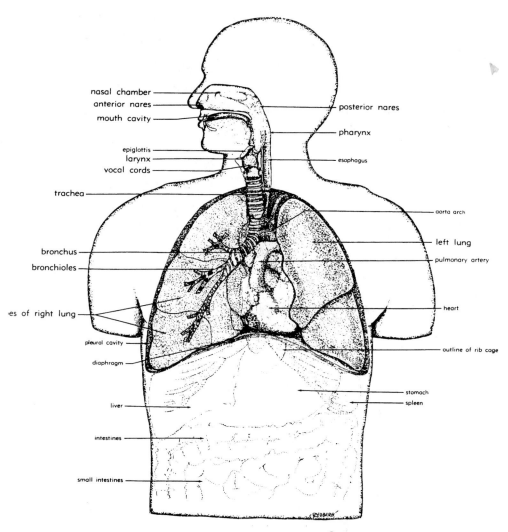

© Kendall/Hunt Publishing Company

Air is drawn into the lungs by the negative pressure created when the *thorax* (chest cavity) expands. This expansion is due to the contraction of the certain respiratory muscles; the *diaphragm* which separates the thorax and abdominal cavities, the *external intercostal* muscles located between the ribs, and to a smaller extent, the *trapezius* muscles of the back and shoulder. Air is expelled from the lungs when the thorax returns to its normal size by relaxation of the above muscles along with contraction of the *internal intercostal* muscles. These respiratory movements are regulated by the nervous system in response to blood CO_2 and acid levels.

Figure 8.2. Respiratory Airflow

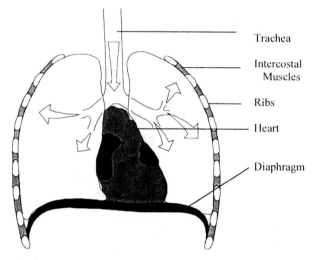

Trachea

Intercostal Muscles

Ribs

Heart

Diaphragm

When the demand for gas exchange increases, as it does during exercise or athletic competition, the nervous system adjusts the rate and depth of respiration. At rest, the muscles responsible for respiration consume approximately 3% of the body's total energy requirement. Under conditions of maximal exercise, the respiratory system may require as much as 30% or more of the body's total energy demand   Under normal resting conditions, the *respiratory rate* is 12 - 18 respirations/min and the *tidal volume*, the volume of air inhaled in a single respiratory cycle, is about 500 ml. The total volume of air passed through the respiratory system in one minute, the *Minute Ventilatory Volume* or M.V.V., is the product of these two.

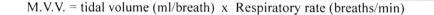

M.V.V. = tidal volume (ml/breath) x Respiratory rate (breaths/min)

Figure 8.3. Skeletal Mechanics of Respiration

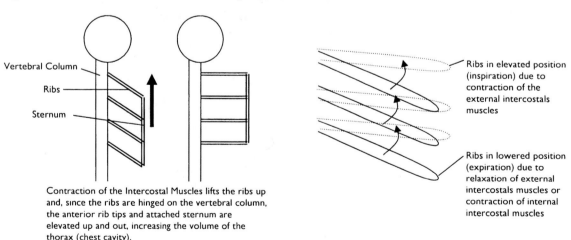

Vertebral Column

Ribs

Sternum

Contraction of the Intercostal Muscles lifts the ribs up and, since the ribs are hinged on the vertebral column, the anterior rib tips and attached sternum are elevated up and out, increasing the volume of the thorax (chest cavity).

Ribs in elevated position (inspiration) due to contraction of the external intercostals muscles

Ribs in lowered position (expiration) due to relaxation of external intercostals muscles or contraction of internal intercostal muscles

Regulation of Respiration

Located within the walls of certain major blood vessels of the body are nervous system sensors, the ***chemoreceptors***, which are constantly measuring the levels of oxygen, carbon dioxide, and pH of the circulating blood. As exercise activities increase, oxygen levels decrease, carbon dioxide levels rise, and the pH becomes more acidic. These changes are detected by the arterial chemoreceptors which send a signal to the respiratory control center in the brainstem (the stalk at the base of the brain) indicating the need to increase the rate and depth of breathing. The activated respiratory control center sends out a signal through the nerves stimulating the intercostal and diaphragm muscles to increase the pace of their activities as indicated in Figure 8.4.

Figure 8.4. Nervous System Control of Respiration

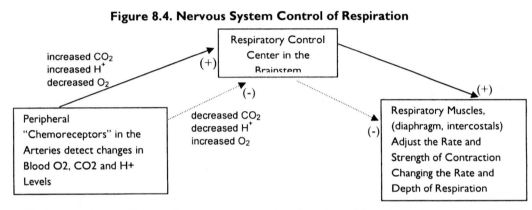

Under normal conditions, the respiratory system is not working at maximum capacity. The excess capacity of the respiratory system which can be tapped during exercise consists of a reserve volume of air which can be inhaled over and above the normal tidal volume, the ***inspiratory reserve volume***, and a reserve capacity of the respiratory system to exhale air in excess of that inhaled, the ***expiratory reserve volume***.

To better appreciate these respiratory values do the following: breathe in and out normally. The volume of air you pass through your lungs in each respiratory cycle equals your tidal volume. Again, breathe in and out normally. Stop after a normal inspiration. Now forcibly inhale more air on top of the normal tidal inspiration. The volume of air you just inhaled represents your inspiratory reserve volume. Once again, breathe normally. Stop after a normal tidal expiration. Now forcibly exhale as much air from your lungs as possible. This volume of air represents your expiratory reserve volume. The sum of the tidal volume, inspiratory and expiratory reserve volumes represents the maximal volume of air which can pass through the respiratory system and is called the ***vital capacity***. The vital capacity is a measure of the "fitness" of the lungs and respiratory muscles. These volumes can all be measured with an instrument called a respirometer or spirometer and, if graphed, would appear as in Figure 8.5.

A normal individual should be able to exhale 83% of the vital capacity in one second, a parameter known as the ***forced expiratory volume - one second***, or, $FEV_{1.0}$. This measurement is an indication of the condition of the respiratory passageways through which the air passes on its way to and from the lungs.

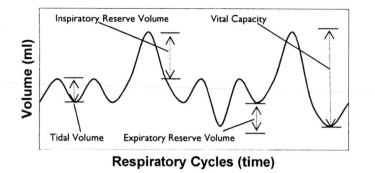

Respiratory Cycles (time)

Figure 8.5. Respiratory Cycle Volumes

The respiratory movements bring air into the lungs which then diffuses into the blood across the alveolar wall. Within the blood, oxygen is carried to the tissues by *hemoglobin*, a protein in the red blood cells.

Hemoglobin is a very interesting protein from which the body demands two very different tasks. While circulating through the lungs, hemoglobin must have a high affinity for oxygen so that it can absorb and carry as much oxygen as possible. When hemoglobin circulates through the capillaries in muscle and other active tissues however, it must readily give up its absorbed oxygen. In these tissues, hemoglobin must have a low affinity for oxygen. One protein with two very different functions. The hemoglobin molecule responds to a number of factors which influence its oxygen affinity. Under conditions of high oxygen concentration (pulmonary capillaries), hemoglobin has a high affinity for oxygen, picking up as much as it can. Under conditions of low oxygen concentration (active muscle capillaries), the shape of the hemoglobin molecule changes, in essence, closing the oxygen binding sites. The oxygen is released and is made available to the active tissues. The oxygen-hemoglobin dissociation curve below shows this phenomenon.

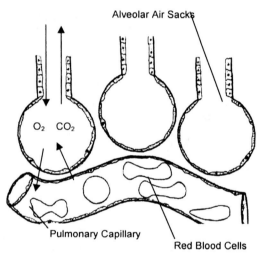

Figure 8.6. Pulmonary Diffusion

As illustrated by the dotted line on the oxygen-hemoglobin dissociation curve, a shift of the curve to the right will lower the affinity of hemoglobin for oxygen and release more oxygen to the tissues. Increasing body temperatures and decreasing body pH will shift the oxygen-hemoglobin dissociation curve to the right.

Figure 8.7. Oxygen-Hemoglobin Dissociation Curve

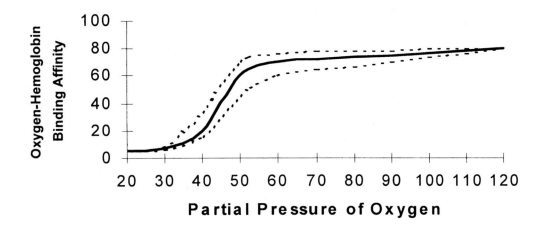

Carbon dioxide, the waste product of active tissues, is carried to the lungs for exhalation within the fluid portion of the blood by chemically combining with water to form *bicarbonate* ion and acid. Blood laden with carbon dioxide is more acidic than normal blood and this acidity is one the stimuli for increased respiratory activity. Changes in blood pH, which are a reflection of blood CO_2 content, are detected by sensors located in blood vessels of the body.

Effects of Exercise on the Respiratory System

Exercise, especially aerobic or endurance activities, has a number of beneficial effects on the respiratory system. Most prominent among these is an increase in the strength of the respiratory muscles. The diaphragm and intercostal muscles, like most muscles, respond to overload by adaptation, that is, they hypertrophy and develop the ability to better cope with that stress in the future. A strengthening of the respiratory muscles allows us to better use the air handling capacity of our lungs and respiratory passages. These changes all work towards increasing the VO_2 max, the ability of the body to deliver vital oxygen to the working cells and tissues.

In addition, the diffusion rate of gasses across the respiratory membranes increases as the walls of the alveoli become more permeable to oxygen and carbon dioxide. An increased blood supply within the lungs also develops. Together, both of these changes allow more of the inhaled oxygen to be picked up by the blood and carried to the working muscles. Table 8.2 shows the effect of maximal exercise on the respiratory function of a normal, physically fit individual. During maximal exercise respiratory rate typically increases a little over three times normal, tidal volume increases five-fold, the total volume of air processed by the respiratory system (ventilation) increases over twenty times, and the amount of oxygen actually taken up into the blood increases almost 15 times. In the well-trained elite endurance athlete, respiratory function and efficiency increases even more so, indicative of the training-induced adaptive improvement as described above.

TABLE 8.2. Comparative Respiratory Capacities

	Normal Individual	Normal Individual at Maximal Exercise	Elite Athlete at Maximal Exercise
Tidal Volume (L/min)	0.5	2.5	3.5
Vital Capacity (L)	5.8	6.0	6.2
Ventilation (L/min)	6	125	190
Breaths/min	12	40	50
O_2 Uptake (ml/kg/min)	3.5	50	70

Although the respiratory system is capable of detecting and responding to increased demands such as those associated with exercise and athletic participation, its capabilities are limited. As an individual's activity level rises from resting towards their maximal aerobic workload ($VO_{2\ max}$) the respiratory system's capacity to respond and keep pace works fine until a level is reached equal to about 70% of the $VO_{2\ max}$. As the activity level progresses past this point, the respiratory system becomes increasingly unable to keep pace with the demand and the working muscles are no longer provided with an adequate supply of oxygen to generate energy (ATP) aerobically. This point is referred to as the ***anaerobic threshold***. Once the anaerobic threshold has been passed, the body must rely on anaerobically generated ATP to support muscle activity. This results in the generation of increasing levels of lactic acid which can begin to impair performance.

As with all exercise-related gains in physical fitness, the improvement in VO_2max will be lost if exercise is discontinued. Thankfully, as illustrated in Figure 8.8 below, it is easier to maintain the improvement than it was to originally gain it. The graph illustrates a typical gain in VO_2max of 25% (from about 40 to 50 mlO2/kg/min) during an 8-week training period. While ending all subsequent exercise results in an immediate and rapid loss of all gains, exercising only twice per week allows the improvement in VO_2max to be maintained.

Figure 8.8. Effects of Training and Detraining on VO_{2max}

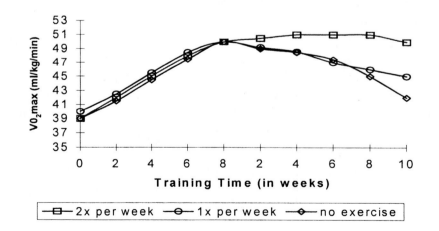

The increased rate and depth of respiration during exercise can cause problems as well, especially if exercise occurs in an area with airborne pollutants. Health safety standards for air pollutants were designed to protect people at normal activity levels from exposure to harmful levels. When exercising, the volume of air brought into the respiratory system increases so much that harmful levels of pollutants can be inhaled even at acceptable safety standards. Also, as activity levels increase, the tendency to breathe through the mouth develops circumventing the filtering apparatus within the nasal cavity.

A report in the journal *Physician and Sports Medicine* describes how 17 members of the Yale University track team were treated for respiratory difficulties after practicing on a new indoor track. It seems the floor was recently refinished using toluene and ethyl acetate. Although the levels of the pollutants were measured to be below OSHA standards, the athletes were exposed in 30 minutes to what the average worker received in 8 hours.

Similar hazards can be encountered when running near traffic inhaling high levels of lead, carbon monoxide and asbestos. Health spas, ornately decorated with carpets, furniture and wall coverings can pose a problem because of high levels of formaldehyde and other organic gasses given off by the foam paddings, varnishes and glues. It is not necessarily the most well-appointed health club, one with nice carpets and furniture, that provides the best work out environment.

Selected Readings:

Mink, B.D., **Exercise and Chronic Obstructive Pulmonary Disease: Modest Fitness Gains Pay Big Dividends**, *The Physician and Sportsmedicine, Vol. 25, No. 11, Nov. 1997,* http://www.physsportsmed.com/issues/1997/11nov/mink.htm

Related Fitness Assessment Activities:

Activity 19. Evaluating Respiratory Fitness

Chapter

10

Cardiovascular System

Chapter Contents

- The Network for Internal Transport
- Cardiac Anatomy
- Cardiac Physiology
- Blood Flow
- Blood
- Exercise and the Cardiovascular System
- Selected Readings

Learning Objectives

The material in this chapter will allow you to:

- Understand the need for a constantly functioning circulatory system
- Understand the structure and function of the heart
- Understand the dynamics and regulation of blood flow
- Understand the effects of exercise on the cardiovascular system
- Understand the concept of and be able to determine an individual's exercise benefit zone

The Network for Internal Transport

In order to do their work the muscles and other tissues of the body require large amounts of oxygen and nutrient carrying blood, especially during periods of strenuous activities such as exercise. Without a constant supply of fuel, and a constant supply of oxygen to "burn" that fuel, these energy-requiring activities could not be sustained. Wastes produced by the body's cells during such activity must be carried away for subsequent removal by the excretory systems of the body. The task of transporting nutrients, wastes and gasses is accomplished by the cardiovascular system, comprised of the heart, blood vessels and the blood. Blood, the vehicle that transports these materials, travels through a highway-like network of blood vessels, propelled by under pressure generated by the heart.

The circulation of blood begins at the heart and passes through the *arteries*, vessels conducting blood away from the heart, to reach the various parts of the body. The arteries branch into smaller *arterioles*, vessels distributing blood to small areas of tissue, and finally branch into smaller diameter *capillaries*. The capillaries are able to reach every cell of the body and provide them with the nourishment and oxygen they require while also removing the wastes produced by the cells. These are the vessels through which the actual exchange of materials occurs between the blood and the tissues. After passing through the tissues, the capillaries rejoin to form *venules* (analogous to the arterioles) and the venules join to form the larger *veins* which return the blood to the heart (Figure 9.1).

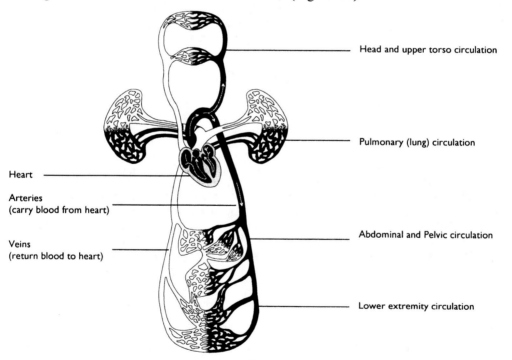

Figure 9.1. Cardiovascular System Overview

Cardiac Anatomy

The heart is a muscular, four-chambered pump with an internal system of one-way valves, an electrical generating system, and an electrical conducting system. The contraction of the cardiac muscle within the heart's walls provides the force for pumping the blood and is initiated by self-generated electrical impulses that must be rhythmic and coordinated in order for the heart to function properly.

The heart has four chambers, two *atria* and two *ventricles*, and is divided in right and left halves so as to actually be two separate but connected pumps, each made up of a first and second stage. Blood returning to the heart carries carbon dioxide, a waste product of metabolism and is received by the upper right chamber of the heart, the right atrium. Muscles in the wall of the atrium contract and squeeze the blood through a one-way valve, the tricuspid valve, into the right ventricle, a large muscular pumping chamber (Figure 9.2a). The muscles in the wall of the ventricle contract to propel the blood through the *pulmonary arteries* to the lungs where the waste carbon dioxide is exchanged for fresh oxygen. The blood then returns through the *pulmonary veins* to the upper left receiving chamber of the heart, the left atrium. Again, the atrial muscles contract forcing blood from the left atrium through the bicuspid valve into the large, muscular pumping chamber, the left ventricle. Contraction of the left ventricle forces blood out through the *aorta,* or aortic artery, and to the tissues of the body, completing the cycle (Figure 9.2b). The tricuspid and bicuspid valves, located between the atria and ventricles, are referred to as the *A-V valves* (atrioventricular). Another ser of valves, located between the ventricles and the arteries they feed, are referred to as the *semilunar valves*.

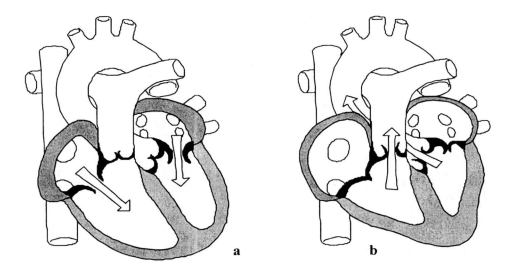

a   b

Figure 9.2. Cardiac Circulation: (a) The contracting atria propel blood through the A-V valves and into the pumping chambers of the ventricles. (b) Contraction of the ventricles

Cardiac Physiology

The ultimate role of the heart is to pump blood into the arteries for distribution throughout the body. The amount of blood pumped by the heart in one minute is known as the *cardiac output* and is usually about 5,000 milliliters/min (about 1¼ gallon). Cardiac output, the volume of blood pumped by the heart per minute, is determined by the volume of blood pumped with each beat, or *stroke volume*, and the number of beats per minute, or *heart rate*. As shown in the equation below cardiac output is seen to be the product of heart rate and stroke volume. Multiplied together, they give the amount of blood pumped by the heart each minute. The following figure provides an example of this relationship.

$$C.O. = H.R. \times S.V.$$

$$4900 \text{ ml/min} = 70 \text{ beats/min} \times 70 \text{ ml/beat}$$

During exercise, because of the increased levels of activity, the muscles greatly increase their demand for oxygen, nutrients and waste removal. To supply the muscles with this increased demand, the cardiac output of the heart must also increase and this is accomplished in several ways. Simply increasing the heart rate for example, from 70 to 80 beats per minute, will increase the cardiac output from 4900 to 5600 ml/min as can be predicted from the equation as illustrated below.

$$5600 \text{ ml/min} = 80 \text{ beats/min} \times 70 \text{ ml/beat}$$

We are all aware that our heart rate increases during exercise. A good aerobic workout requires that the heart rate increase from resting levels (usually between 60 and 80 bpm) to anywhere between 60% and 85% of maximum capacity (usually 130 - 180 bpm). The heart, like any muscle, responds to increased stress in accordance with the general adaptation syndrome. Obtaining the cardiovascular benefits of aerobic exercise requires achieving an exercise heart rate within this range and, for this reason, this range is referred to as the *exercise benefit zone*. Figure 9.3 below shows the age-adjusted exercise benefit zone.

By the Numbers

The human heart beats, on average, 70 times per minute, 100,000 times per day, 36,500,000 times each year and 2.5 billion times over a 70 year life. It pumps approximately 1 gallon per minute, 1,400 gallons per day 525,000 gallons per year and 37 million gallons over a 70 year life.

The exercise benefit zone provides a way of determining just how hard your heart needs to work to achieve the overload that will result in positive, long-term adaptation.

Figure 9.3. Exercise Benefit Zone

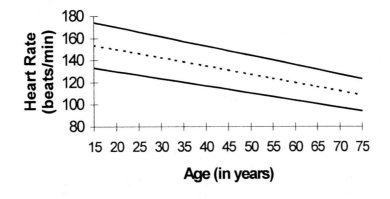

In the most simplified calculation, ***maximum heart rate*** can be estimated by subtracting your current age from 220 (220 – age). Taking 60% of this value will give you an estimate of the lower limit of the exercise benefit zone; taking 85% will give you the upper limit. For example, the exercise benefit zone for a 20 year old is calculated as follows:

$$MHR = 220 - 20$$
$$MHR = 200 \text{ bpm}$$

Lower limit of EBZ = 200 x .60	**Upper limit of EBZ = 200 x .85**
Lower limit of EBZ = 140 bpm	**Upper limit of EBZ = 170 bpm**

This simple formula has been refined and, in its more sophisticated form, is known as the ***Karvonen formula***. This modification takes into account the subject's normal resting heart rate, an indicator of existing cardiac fitness, as well as the subject's age. Calculating the exercise benefit zone according to the Karvonen formula is shown below.

Resting Heart Rate (RHR) = heart rate (pulse rate) at rest
Maximum Heart Rate (MHR) = 220 - age
Heart Rate Reserve (HRR) = MHR – RHR

Lower end of Exercise Benefit Zone = (HRR x .6) + RHR
Upper end of Exercise Benefit Zone = (HRR x .85) + RHR

Aside from increasing the heart rate which most of us are already aware of, increasing the stroke volume can also increase cardiac output. Stroke volume is itself the product of two factors; the strength of cardiac contraction (*contractility*) and the amount of blood in the ventricles. Due to the nature of the heart muscle itself, the strength of contraction increases when body temperature increases or when blood pH decreases. A decrease in blood pH is due to an increased acidity of the blood. During exercise, because of increased muscular activity and elevated metabolic rate, the body temperature increases (we know this because we sweat in an attempt to cool off), and the blood pH decreases. Even without an increase in heart rate, exercise would result in an increased cardiac output due to changes in stroke volume alone. With both factors, H.R and S.V., being affected, the output of the heart increases greatly.

As would be expected, the heart is only able to pump out as much blood as is returned to it through the veins. During muscular activity, the contraction of skeletal muscle exerts a force against the veins which increases blood flow back to the heart. This increase in *venous return* during activity provides the ventricles with more blood and allows the heart to increase its stroke volume and therefore, increase cardiac output even if heart rate was not to increase. Exercise and athletic activities, placing substantial demands upon the cardiovascular system in order to supply the working muscles with nutrients, oxygen and waste removal, can result in tremendous adjustment in the normal rates of cardiovascular function. Table 9.1 illustrates some of these changes in both the normal individual and the elite athlete.

Table 9.1. Comparative Cardiac Values: Rest vs. Exercise

	At Rest	Normal Individual Maximal Exercise	Elite Athlete Maximal Exercise
Heart Rate (b.p.m.)	70	190	190
Stroke Volume (ml/beat)	70	140	180
Cardiac Output (ml/min.)	5,000	25,000	35,000
Systolic Blood Pressure (mm/Hg)	120	200	200
Diastolic Blood Pressure (mm/Hg)	80	85	70

Blood Flow

The blood which is pumped by the heart is distributed throughout the body by the vascular system. The arteries are the vessels which carry blood away from the heart, the capillaries allow for the exchange of nutrients, wastes and gasses between the blood and the tissues and the veins return blood back to the heart. During periods of rest or inactivity, when the demands of the muscles are minimal, blood flow to the musculature is reduced. In fact, most regions and organs of the body have the capacity to self-regulate the amount of blood flow they receive. The regulation of blood flow to a particular body region or organ is accomplished by changing the size, or diameter, of the arteries leading to it by varying the level of contraction of smooth muscle cells in the blood vessels' walls. If the diameter of the artery is increased (*vasodilation*), blood flow increases. If the diameter of the artery is decreased (*vasoconstriction*), the blood flow decreases. Figure 9.4 illustrates the structures in the blood vessel that are responsible for allowing this regulation.

Figure 9.4. Blood Vessel Structure

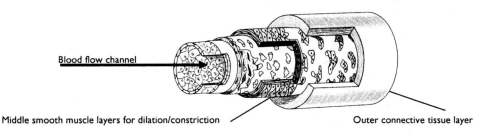

Blood flow channel

Middle smooth muscle layers for dilation/constriction

Outer connective tissue layer

We can see illustrated in the set of equations below, the relationship between the rate of blood flow in a vessel and the factors which effect it.

$$\text{Blood Flow} = \frac{\text{P1} - \text{P2}}{\text{R}} \qquad \text{equation I}$$

$$\text{where} \qquad \text{R} = \frac{\text{l n}}{\text{r}^4} \qquad \text{equation 2}$$

The equation isn't really as frightening as it seems. Equation 1 shows that the rate of blood flow is equal to pressure gradient in the vessel, that is, the difference in pressure at the two ends of the vessel (P_1 - P_2), divided by the resistance to blood flow (R).

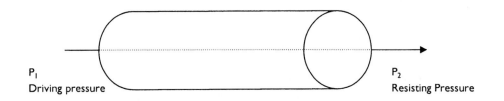

P_1
Driving pressure

P_2
Resisting Pressure

If the pressure at one end of the vessel (P_1) is greater than the pressure at the other end (P_2), then blood will flow in the direction from P_1 to P_2. The greater the pressure difference, the faster the blood will flow. If P_2 were greater than P_1, then blood would flow in the opposite direction. Equation 1 also shows that the speed, and therefore the amount of blood flow, is reduced by the increasing the resistance (R) in the blood vessel.

Equation 2 shows the factors which effect the resistance. The resistance is determined as the product of the vessel length (l) times the blood viscosity, or thickness (n), divided by the radius of the vessel raised to the fourth power. Quite simply, since the length of the blood

146

vessel is constant and the thickness of the blood changes only minimally, the primary way to change resistance is to change the radius, or size of the blood vessel. This we have seen to be controlled by vasoconstriction and vasodilation.

Since the volume of blood in the body is relatively constant, if we increase the blood flow to one particular area, for example the intestinal tract, we will decrease the volume of blood available to flow through other regions, for example, the muscles. It is this phenomenon which dictates that people shouldn't exercise strenuously or swim for example, after eating a large meal. Conversely, one shouldn't eat large meals immediately after exercising. Table 9.2 shows the shift of blood flow during different states of activity. To supply the increased demand of the exercising muscles, heart and skin for blood, vessels in these tissues dilate and vastly increase the blood flow. Blood is shunted away from the kidneys, digestive organs and connective tissues as blood vessels in these organs constrict. A steady blood flow is maintained to the brain at all times.

By the Numbers
It takes approximately 30 seconds for blood to flow from the heart, through the body (systemic circulation) and return through the heart. The blood passes through approximately 60,000 miles of capillaries.

Table 9.2. Regional Blood Flow Shifts During Exercise

Tissue	Blood Flow (Resting) ml / minute	Blood Flow (Moderate Exercise) ml / minute
Skeletal Muscle	750	8,000
Heart Muscle	150	550
Skin	450	1,700
Brain	650	650
Digestive Organs	1,350	600
Kidneys	1,000	550
Bone / Connective Tissue	650	450
Total Cardiac Output	5,000	12,500

Blood

In one sense, the purpose of the cardiovascular system is to move blood throughout the body. The propulsive force provided by the heart and the ability of the arteries and veins to direct and regulate blood flow ensure that blood will be delivered to and from the appropriate tissues and organs at the appropriate times. Carried within the blood are nutrients to feed our muscles and brain, waste materials being transported for disposal, hormones traveling from the glands where they are produced to the cells and tissues they must regulate and life sustaining oxygen and the cellular waste product carbon dioxide.

By the Numbers
The average woman has about 4,500,000 red blood cells in each ml of blood (about 20 drops). The average man has 5,000,000. The red blood cells which live for only 120 days are replaced at the rate of 2.5 million new red blood cells each second, or approximately 200 billion per day.

Blood is comprised of fluid, cellular structures, and dissolved and suspended molecules. The fluid, called blood *plasma*, is a mixture of water, various salts and minerals, and proteins. Among these proteins are the disease-fighting antibodies which, along with the white blood cells, comprise an important part of the immune system. The white blood cells, or *leucocytes*, account for only a small fraction of the cellular structures within the blood. *Platelets*, small cellular remnants of larger bone marrow cells, along with the plasma protein fibrin, help facilitate the clotting response which helps seal torn blood vessels resulting from injury. Far and away the most numerous of the blood cells elements are the *erythrocytes* or red blood cells. Mature circulating erythrocytes are nothing more than membrane-bound sacs of the oxygen-carrying protein *hemoglobin*. If allowed to stand for a period of time, or if expedited by spinning in a high-gravity centrifuge, the cellular elements of blood will settle out to the bottom of the container leaving the clear, pale yellow plasma above. Typically, red blood cells will account for between 40%-45% of the total volume of a blood sample, a clinical measure known as the *hematocrit*.

Figure 9.5. Blood and Blood Elements

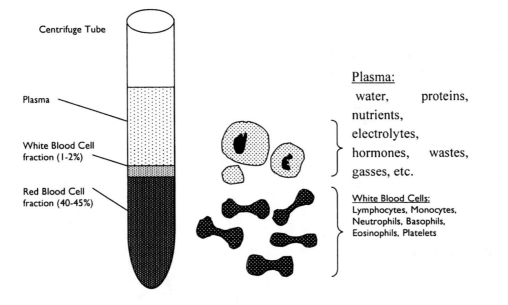

Exercise and the Cardiovascular System

The benefits to the cardiovascular system derived from exercise and athletics were once believed to be primarily restricted to activities which are aerobic in nature. It was thought that very little benefit was gained from activities such as weight training, archery and other activities relying only on the phosphagen and glycogen-lactic acid systems. Recent research articles in journals such as *Circulation* and *Hypertension*, publications of The American Heart Association, and demonstrated that weight training exercise has measurably beneficial effects on blood cholesterol and triglyceride levels, blood pressure, body fat percentage, and glucose metabolism, all important contributors to cardiovascular health. Both the American Heart Association and the American College of Sports Medicine now recommend that resistance training be incorporated as part of the regular exercise activities for all Americans.

For exercise to actually benefit the heart and circulation, the heart rate must re raised from resting levels to anywhere between 65% and 85% of maximal heart rate. This specific range of heart activity is known as the exercise benefit zone. This level of activity must be maintained for at least 20 minutes and should be performed at least three times each week.

The heart, like any muscle, responds to overload by producing more contractile proteins, a process known as hypertrophy. The hypertrophied heart of an athlete, with its stronger musculature, is capable of pumping more blood with each beat and thus requires fewer beats to maintain normal circulation. This is the reason for the athlete having a lower heart rate. While the typical resting heart rate of a normal individual may range from 72-80 beats per minute (BPM), the resting heart rate of the aerobically-trained Tour de-France athlete, Lance Armstrong, is only 30 bpm.

A heart placed under overload develops a system of collateral blood vessels which provide the heart muscle with a greater blood flow. There is additional evidence that the diameter of the blood vessels feeding the heart muscle also increases. It is in these ways that exercise benefits the heart.

A good exercise program will also benefit the cardiovascular system by lowering serum (blood borne) triglycerides (fats) and harmful LDL cholesterol while raising the amount of beneficial HDL cholesterol. In addition, the adhesiveness or "stickiness" of platelets, the blood clotting elements, is reduced. These factors taken together, help prevent conditions which narrow the blood vessels such as arteriosclerosis and atherosclerosis. They reduce the chance of blood clot formation and lower the risk of heart attack and stroke.

Selected Readings:

Cox, M.H., **Exercise for Coronary Artery Disease: A Cornerstone of Comprehensive Treatment**, *The Physician and Sportsmedicine*, Vol. 25, No. 12, December 1997, http://www.physsportsmed.com/issues/1997/12dec/cox.htm

Related Activities:

Activity 20. Evaluating Cardiovascular Fitness

Activity 21. Evaluating Cardiovascular Disease Risk

Chapter  11

Special Considerations

Chapter Contents
- Issues for Women
- Issues for Seniors
- Issues for Children
- Selected Readings

Learning Objectives

The material in this chapter will allow you to:
- Understand how the anatomical and physiological differences between the genders impacts exercise and athletic performance
- Understand the benefits and risks of exercise for women
- Understand the age-related changes that occur within the human body and their implication on health and athletic performance
- Understand the benefits and risks of exercise for seniors
- Understand the implications of childhood and adolescent development on exercise
- Understand the benefits and risks of exercise for children

Issues for Women

Nature has endowed us with a variety of subtle differences that make each of us unique and in many ways, slightly different from each other. The effects of exercise on the female body differ in many ways from those on the male. The predominant reason for this is found in the anatomical and physiological difference between males and females.

Anatomical and Physiological Considerations

Many of the anatomical, physiological and behavioral differences between men and women can be directly attributed to differences in the types, ratios, and sequencing throughout life of hormone production and release. Hormones, messenger molecules produced within certain tissues and glands of the body, exert a wide range of effects influencing such things as bone and connective tissue growth, muscle mass, metabolic rate and mental attitude. Perhaps most prominent among the hormones responsible for the gender-associated differences are testosterone, estrogen, and progesterone, three steroid-based hormone molecules. These hormones are classified as steroids because they are based upon a backbone molecule derived from cholesterol, a type of fat classified as a sterol. Subtle variations to the sterol backbone result in differences between these hormones. Testosterone is produced in large amounts by the testes and in smaller amounts by the adrenal glands. Men therefore have greater amounts than do women although women do have measurable amounts of circulating testosterone. Estrogen and progesterone are produced in large amounts by the ovaries and in smaller amounts by the adrenal glands. Women therefore have higher levels of circulating estrogen and progesterone although there are measurable amounts in men as well.

Due to the higher levels of naturally circulating anabolic steroid hormone testosterone, the male develops a larger, more heavily boned skeleton and a stronger musculature than the female. The tendons and ligaments of males tend to be tougher and more resistant to damage than in females. In the female, the circulating steroid hormone estrogen leads to the deposition of a relatively thick layer of subcutaneous (under the skin) fat. The table below highlights some of the differences in bodily composition between males and females.

Table 10.1 . Body Composition as % of Total Body Weight

	Female	Male
Bone Mass	12%	15%
Muscle Mass	36%	45%
Total Body Fat	26%	15%

Anatomically, women have narrower shoulders and wider hips than do males (a lower *androgyny index*). With the need for our feet to be under our center-of-gravity, the wider hips result in the need for a greater angling inward of the femur (thigh) and a greater angle of attachment to the knee of the quadriceps muscle group. This angle, known as the Q-angle, at which the quadriceps muscle group pulls on the knee joint typically ranges from 0-12% (Fig 10.1). Given the size and strength of the quadriceps muscle group, Q-angles of greater than 12% can put serious strain on the knee joint. The wider pelvis also results in a greater side-to-side motion during running, which, together with the angled attachment of the quadriceps, places added torque on the knee during running. With smaller ligaments and tendons, there is greater mobility about the knee joint and this may increase the susceptibility to knee damage. Research has shown that the risk of injury varies throughout the menstrual cycle with a greater percentage of ACL injuries occurring during the ovulatory phase (days 10 – 14) of the cycle. The lower bone density of the female also increases the risk of developing stress fractures from repeated contact with a hard running surface or during high impact aerobic exercise.

The shorter stature and wider hips of the female provides for a lower center of gravity and therefore, more stability than in the male. Although this has several obvious positive aspects it can limit the jumping ability of the female athlete.

As stated above, females have a comparatively narrower shoulder width than males. Most women also have an exaggerated degree of hyperextension of the elbow and an outward angling of the forearm. These factors contribute to a less than maximally efficient angle of muscle attachment for weight bearing activities which may be further compounded by the reduced muscle mass.

Figure 10.1. Pelvic and Lower Extremity Skeletons; Female & Male

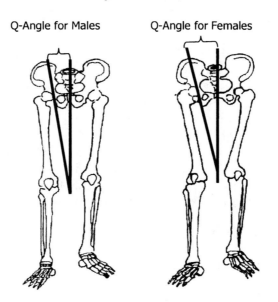

Q-Angle for Males   Q-Angle for Females

Due to the estrogen-induced deposition of subcutaneous fat, a woman's body fat averages 26% of total body weight whereas a male averages 15%. Circulating testosterone in the male results in an average muscle mass of 45% of total body weight while in the female muscle mass averages 36%. Testosterone also stimulates the formation of red blood cells providing males with 15% more oxygen carrying hemoglobin than females and 6% more red blood cells. Due to regular losses through menstruation, females also have a tendency towards iron deficiency.

Another consequence of lower testosterone levels is the smaller muscle mass and reduction in strength in the female. Generally speaking, a female has 50% of the upper body strength (shoulders, chest and arms) of the male, 78% of the forearm strength, 83% of the trunk strength and 106% of the hip strength per lean body mass. There is no difference with respect to the ratio of slow:fast muscle fibers, however the mean fiber diameter is smaller in females, and muscular strength is directly related to fiber diameter.

Because of the generally smaller body size, the female heart is smaller than that of the male with a smaller stroke volume and lower cardiac output. To compensate for this the average heart rate for a female is 5 - 8 beats faster than for a male. The female possesses a smaller thorax and less lung tissue than the male resulting in a smaller vital capacity and lower total lung capacity.

Metabolism and Energy Supply

Several recent studies have provided evidence that the metabolic pathways fueling exercise and athletic activities differ between men and women. Studies on the respiratory exchange ration (RER), an indirect measure of the relative ratio of carbohydrate versus fat oxidation, indicates that women tend to use proportionally less carbohydrate and more fat in fueling long-term aerobic activities than do men. At comparable levels of aerobic intensity, women have a lower RER and show significantly less depletion of muscle glycogen stores than men. Because of this, and as confirmed through other studies, the technique of carbohydrate loading is less effective for women and does not result in any substantial delay in time-to-exhaustion.

Menstruation, Fertility and Exercise

Strenuous exercise can reduce the lean fat percentage in the female athlete that often results in lowering of circulating estrogen levels. This can induce noticeable suppression of the menstrual cycle, amenorrhea, and may result in transient infertility. In addition, the deficiency in estrogen levels can result in loss of bone calcium leading to osteoporosis. Some studies have shown that a minimum body fat percentage of 17% is required for the onset of menstruation and 22% for the maintenance of normal menstruation. Exercise and athletic activity may cause amenorrhea by decreasing body fat below this minimum and subsequently interfering with the hypothalamus (a region within the brain) and pituitary gland.

While exercise and athletics can influence the menstrual cycle, there is apparently little significant effect of menstruation on athletic ability, and there is no reason to curtail exercise and athletic activities during menstruation.

Exercise in Pregnancy

Pregnancy is a normal, healthy condition and, as such, should not be considered a reason to refrain from exercise activities. A woman in good physical condition who, prior to pregnancy participated in a regular exercise program, should be able to continue exercising with some moderation. In fact, pregnancy may be a good time for a non-exerciser to carefully begin a moderate exercise program. A well planned, executed and monitored exercise program during pregnancy can help maintain posture and reduce low back pain, control weight gain, lessen stress, anxiety and depression, increase energy, and speed the post-partum recovery period.

The American College of Obstetricians and Gynecologists recommends the following guidelines for exercise during pregnancy.

Limit strenuous exercise to no more than 15 minutes at a time. The pulse rate should be kept below 140 beats per minute and body temperature should not be allowed to rise above 101 °F. Both pulse and temperature should be taken both before and immediately after exercise. Be sure to warm-up and cool-down gradually.

Avoid high impact activities that involve abrupt movements and resistance exercises with heavy weights. Recommended aerobic activities involve low-intensity and low-impact workouts of 20-30 minutes in duration, three times per week. Swimming, stationary bicycling and low-impact aerobics classes are typical examples. Recommended resistance exercises include light-resistance at 12-15 repetitions, three times per week.

Avoid exaggerated extension of the joints. Progesterone released during pregnancy will soften tendons and ligaments making these structures easier to tear. Slow, gentle, static stretching, after warming-up, and held for 10 – 30 seconds is ideal.

Be sure to take adequate fluid before, during and after exercise.

Check with your physician before beginning, or when continuing with an exercise program during pregnancy. There are conditions which could result in complications and these include high blood pressure, toxemia, persistent bleeding, and incompetent cervix.

Injuries

Because of the anatomical and physiological differences noted above, the risk of certain types of injuries is greater in females. As discussed earlier, women are more prone to knee injuries than are men; in fact, the incidence of injury to the anterior cruciate ligament is four to eight times higher in women than in men. Among the more common complaints are those of breast soreness usually caused by excessive movement of the breast tissue. This movement may result in straining of the internal connective tissue or abrasions of the skin and nipple from contact with clothing or apparatus. Usually, proper breast support during exercise and athletics will prevent this.

Women are more prone to injury from participation in contact sports, especially if undertaken with males. This is primarily due to the smaller body size, lower body density, lower ratio of fat to muscle and lower bone density.

A condition referred to as the *Female Athlete Triad*, or Female Triad, includes the combined presence of a menstrual disorder (amenorrhea, dismenorrhea), an eating disorder (anorexia, bulimia), and osteoporosis. The symptoms reflect both physical and psychological components often driven by a misguided perception of body image. Because the effects of bone loss may become irreversible, parents and coaches of young women engaged in competitive sports should pay particular attention to signs of this condition.

As indicated in Chapter 1, the benefits of exercise and athletic participation far outweigh the risks for most individuals. Given this knowledge, it is unfortunate that so many women are not taking advantage by exercising. The 1996 *Surgeon General's Report on Physical Activity* indicated that almost one-third of all women over the age of 45 did not participate in regular physical activity.

Issues for Seniors

Aging, in its most simple definition, is the progressive deterioration in the structures and functions of a mature organism that occurs over time. In our current understanding of the aging process, it is believed that this results from a combination of genetically programmed changes and the inevitable wear-and-tear accumulation of damage that comes through the process of living. These age-related changes progress along a continuum, many of them beginning in the latter half of the teenage years and progressing through to the debilitating changes of senescence. Among the earliest changes we typically note are the decreasing acuity of our vision and hearing, decreases in our joint mobility, and visible changes in our skin. The latter stages of the aging process are often characterized by loss of muscle mass and strength, loss of bone mass, cardiovascular diseases and loss of mental acuity. Age-related changes in the skeletal system include osteoporosis, a weakening of bone due to loss of bone minerals and matrix, and osteoarthritis, the degeneration of the articular cartilage. Osteoporosis afflicts approximately on third of all women over the age of 60 and, on average, all women will lose between 35%-50% of their bone mineral content by age 90. Between the ages of 30 and 80, men will lose 60% of their muscular strength. Between the ages of 25 and 50, muscle mass decreases, on average, by 4% per decade and after the age of 50, by 10% per decade. Ligament strength decreases by 50% between the ages of 20 and 80. Our aerobic capacity, which peaks at about age 20, declines by approximately 1% per year. Table 10.2 highlights some of these and other age-related changes within our various physiological systems.

Table 10.2. Physical Changes Between Age 30 and 70	
Cardiac Output	⇩ 30%
Vital Capacity	⇩ 10-40%
Basal Metabolic Rate	⇩ 8-12%
Muscle Mass	⇩ 25-30%
Grip Strength	⇩ 25-30%
Flexibility	⇩ 20-30%
Bone Mass (E)	⇩ 25-30%
Bone Mass	⇩ 15-20%
Blood Pressure (systolic)	⇧ 10-40%
Blood Pressure (diastolic)	⇧ 5-10 %
Nerve Fiber Conduction Velocity	⇩ 10-15%
From: Smith, EL, and C. Gilligan. *The Physician and Sportsmedicine*, Vol 11:92 (August 1983)	

Although there is probably little we can do to ever stop the aging process, there is a growing body of scientific evidence that, through a program of regular life-long exercise, we can both delay the onset of many of these age-related deficits and reduce their debilitating effects when they do occur. In two separate studies reported in the *Journal of Applied Physiology*, it was shown that (1) engaging in a regular program of endurance exercise can increase VO_{2max} by 30% over a period of 6 months in 60-70 year old individuals and, (2) that a 9-12 month program of walking, for just 45 minutes per day 4 days per week, increased the aerobic capacity of seniors by 24%. A report in the *Journal of the American Medical Association* demonstrated that an 8-week program of high-intensity exercise performed by frail nursing home residents age 86-96, increased muscle mass by 9% and strength by 74%. This same exercise program increased walking speed by 50% in half of the exercising participants. Finally, and perhaps most notably, a recent study reported in the *Journal of the*

American Medical Association demonstrated that there was a 43% reduction in the risk of death from multiple causes among vigorous exercisers and a 29% reduction among occasional exercisers.

The American College of Sports Medicine released its Position Stand on Exercise and Physical Activity for Older Adults in 1998. In its extensive review of nearly 250 recent scientific and clinical studies, the ACSM concluded that, "Participation in a regular exercise program is an effective intervention/modality to reduce/prevent a number of functional declines associated with aging." A well designed and practices exercise program has documented benefits on the improvement of cardiovascular health, muscle mass and strength, bone density, flexibility, postural stability and balance, the preservation of mental function, a reduction in depression and an increase in life expectancy. These reports confirm two very important principles, (1) that exercise provides life-long and life-prolonging benefits and, (2) that it is never too late to begin an exercise program.

> **"If I'd known I was gonna live this long, I'd have taken better care of myself."**
> Eubie Blake, Musician, on his 100th Birthday

Injuries

Because of the anatomical and physiological changes associated with the aging process, senior citizens engaging in exercise or athletic activities have a greater tendency towards certain injuries. As the protein molecules within collagen and elastin fibers of the connective tissues become more cross-linked with age their suppleness and flexibility decrease causing them to become brittle. This results in an increased risk of the tendons and ligaments to tear under stresses that would not normally have been problematic in earlier years. Coupled with changes in bone structure, namely the increased resorption of bone matrix, the connection between tendons and bone and between ligaments and bone weakens, increasing the chance of complete separation (avulsion) of these structures from the bone. The aging process also results in changes in the chemical nature of the proteoglycan molecules making up the matrix of cartilage. As we age, the water content of our cartilage becomes increasingly reduced, lessening the ability of the cartilage to absorb stresses without damage and increasing the risk of injury to the articular cartilage and menisci. The general dehydration of our system coupled with changes in the skin, reduces the ability of older athletes to dissipate heat through evaporative sweating increasing the risk of heat-related injuries. Finally, because of the almost inevitable age-related changes in the cardiovascular system, the risk of cardiovascular incidents, such as angina attacks and heart attacks, is increased.

Issues for Children:

While it is easy for us to acknowledge the increasing sedentary state of many senior citizens and the resultant incidence of physical and physiological degeneration, it seems counterintuitive to believe that our younger citizens are in a similar state of hypokinetic unfitness. Our mental image young children and adolescents is of physically active people in near constant motion. Unfortunately, the reality is that approximately 50% of all young adults in America between the ages of 12 – 21 are not vigorously active on a regular basis and almost 15% are not physically active at all. Organized participation in school-based physical education classes had dropped to 25% in 1995 from 42% just four years earlier. Although a 1996 report by the Surgeon General and U.S. Centers for Disease Control recommended that all students in grades K-12 participate in school-based physical education classes on a daily basis, a national survey showed that most high school students take physical education for only one of their four high school years and that 42 of the 50 states allow students to forego physical education classes completely. A 1999 survey of 13,000 teenagers showed that only 1/3 were physically active 5 or more times per week and that they watched, on average, between 14 and 20 hrs of television per week.

In the decade between 1981 and 1991 the percentage of children classified as overweight increased by 20%. In the following seven years, from 1991 to 1998, the incidence of obesity increased an additional 12% to 18% across all age groups, races and educational levels. Epidemiological studies have shown that children who are overweight have increased risk for developing hypertension, hyperlipidemia, diabetes, respiratory problems, musculoskeletal problems and suffer from lowered self-esteem. Forty-percent of overweight children and 70% of overweight adolescents go on to become overweight adults. Bad habits developed during childhood tend to follow us for life.

Although it is common knowledge that participation in a regular exercise program is beneficial to most, if not all, adults, young children and adolescents also have much to gain from a well designed and regular exercise program. The Surgeon General's Report on Physical Activity and Health encourages all people over 2 years of age to participate in at least 30 minutes of moderate physical activity per day. The Council for Physical Education of the National Association for Sport and Physical Education goes further recommending at least 30-60 minutes per day. The National Association for Sport and Physical Education (NASPE) recommends at least 150 min of school-based physical education per week at elementary level, and 225 min/week at middle and high school levels. The American Heart Association recommends 30 minutes of moderate-intensity exercise per day for children five years of age and older.

The benefits of regular exercise in children and adolescents is well documented. In a longitudinal study of 40 pre-pubertal boys it was shown that those who participated in at least 30 minutes of resistance exercises per day for at least three days per week had a bone mineral density in their lumbar spinal vertebrae almost twice that of a control group that did not similarly exercise. A similar study in 81prepubertal girls showed similar results. Other studies have shown that 12 week exercise program of stationary cycling for 30 minutes per session, three times per week will lower total cholesterol and improve the LDL/HDL ratios in prepubertal children, and that regular aerobic exercise will lower children's blood pressure and reduce incidents of emotional stress.

Starting the habit of regular physical exercise early in life has been shown to produce long-term benefits that carry well into adulthood. A longitudinal study that followed a group of 147 men and women showed that those who received daily physical education during school in the 1970's were more likely to be physically active as adults and less likely to smoke. In another study, it was shown that children who had an enhanced physical education program, that is one that involved at least five hours of physical education activities per week, had greater functional lung capacities than a comparative group of students that participated in only standard physical education classes.

The decline in physical activity with age, in children as well in adults, seems to be consistent across cultures and even across species. In humans, the decline in physical activity is most rapid between the ages of 13 and 18, declining somewhat more rapidly in males than in females. The decline, although constant throughout life after the age of 12, is much more rapid in adolescence than it is throughout adulthood and may be related to social factors such as increasing demands of work and family responsibilities. In an attempt to address this concern, the United States Congress passed a bill in December 2000 providing up to $400 million over a five-year period to support the development of physical education programs in grades K-12. The Physical Education for Progress Act, or PEP, states that, "Every student in our Nation's schools, from kindergarten through grade 12, should have the opportunity to participate in quality physical education. It is the unique role of quality physical education programs to develop the health-related fitness, physical competence, and cognitive understanding about physical activity for all students so that the students can adopt healthy and physically active lifestyles."

Injuries

Because the development of many of the body's structural and physiological systems is not completed prior to the end of adolescence, exercise and athletic activities can pose a special set of risks to the young athlete. The relatively slow development of the complex human nervous system results in young children having significantly less neuromuscular coordination than a late adolescent or adult, thus, there is an increased risk of injury in activities that require a high degree of coordination. Because bone growth is generally not completed until the late adolescent years, children tend to have skeletons that are more yielding to the deforming stresses that might cause fractures in mature individuals and are somewhat less prone to fractures. However, because the bone lengthening process requires that the epiphyseal plates of long bones be uncalcified, these bone structures, commonly referred to as the growth plates, are susceptible to injury if subject to repetitive high loads and may lead to growth abnormalities.

Selected Readings:

Arendt, E, **Common Musculoskeletal Injuries in Women**, *The Physician and Sportsmedicine*, Vo. 24, No. 7, July 1996, http://www.physsportsmed.com/issues/jul_96/arendt.htm

Ganley, T., C. Sherman. **Exercise and Children's Health**. *The Physician and Sportsmedicine*, Vol. 28, No. 2, February 2000. http://www.physsportsmed.com/issues/2000/02_00/ganley.htm

Mazzeo, R.S. et al., **ACSM Position Stand on Exercise and Physical Activity for Older Adults**. *Medicine and Science in Sports & Exercise*, Vol. 30, No. 6, pp. 992-1008, 1998.

Shephard, R.J., **Aging and Exercise**. *Encyclopedia of Sports Medicine and Science*, 1998. http://www.sportsci.org/encyc/agingex/agingex.html

Smith, A.D., **The Fit Woman of the 21st Century: Making Lifelong Exercise the Norm**, *The Physician and Sportsmedicine*, Vol. 26, No. 8, August 1998, http://www.physsportsmed.com/issues/1998/08aug/smith.htm

Smith, A.D., **The Female Athlete Triad: Causes, Diagnosis, and Treatment**, *The Physician and Sportsmedicine*, Vol. 24, No. 7, July 1996, http://www.physsportsmed.com/issues/jul_96/smith.htm

Chapter  12

Drugs and Ergogenics

Chapter Contents
- Performance Enhancement
- Stimulants
- Painkillers
- Performance Enhancers
- Equipment
- Selected Readings

Learning Objectives

The material in this chapter will allow you to:
- Understand the use and abuse of pharmalogic agents in exercise and athletics
- Understand the use and abuse of nutritional supplements in exercise and athletics
- Understand the use and abuse of physical assistive devices in exercise and athletics

Performance Enhancement

Improvements in general physical fitness and in sport-specific performance are generally dependent upon the interaction of training, diet, genetics and lifestyle. Because the effects of these interactions take time and have limits, and because of the desire for more immediate gratification and a greater competitive edge, fitness enthusiasts and athletes have sought ways to enhance their performance gains through the use of *egrogenics*. Ergonenics refers to the administration of drugs or other agents, or the use of assistive devices, for the purpose of improving athletic performance. Most ergogenic aids can be categorized into one of the following broad categories: *pharmacological* (drugs and hormones, both natural and synthetic), *nutritional* (food supplements or diet manipulations such as sports drinks, amino acid supplements, creatine, and carbohydrate loading), *physiological* (oxygen breathing, blood doping), *physical* (weight belts, running suits, nasal dilating strips, running shoes), and *psychological* (visualization techniques, hypnosis). Drugs, supplements, and assistive devices of various forms have long been used by athletes, some for very legitimate purposes, others with less than honorable intent. Ergogenic aids with which you might be most familiar are include the use of anabolic steroids for the enhancement of muscle development, cortisone-based anti-inflammatory drugs, protein or carbohydrate-rich nutritional sports bars, weight-lifting belts for back support, and full-length swim suits recently used in the Olympics to reduce frictional water drag. As can be seen from this brief list, ergogenic aids can be legal or illegal in athletic competition, helpful or harmful to long-term health, and of documented or questionable utility in actually enhancing performance.

Drugs can be used in athletics for either therapeutic or ergogenic purposes. Therapeutic use implies the administration of drugs primarily for treating injuries. Taking two or more ergogenic aids together is known as *stacking*, gradually increasing the doses of ergogenic aids over time is known as *cycling* and interspersing periods of high level ergogenic cycles with periods of smaller doses is known as *bridging*.

The following is a summary of some of the more common ergogenic aids.

Stimulants

Caffeine: A strong stimulant of the central nervous system which also acts as a vasodilator and diuretic. Caffeine will raise metabolism by 10-20% by causing the release of adrenaline which stimulates glycogen breakdown and stored glucose release. Caffeine can decrease reaction time (quicken reactions) and delay the onset of fatigue, but at a price. Cardiac arrhythmias (abnormal beating) can develop and dehydration can be increased. Caffeine is also a *lipolytic* agent facilitating the breakdown of stored fat and releasing free fatty acids into the bloodstream. Because of its lipolytic action, caffeine can increase the ability to use fat as an energy source and to spare the use of muscle glycogen. Caffeine is a member of the class of compounds known as *methylxanthines* that also includes *theophylline* and *theobromide*.

Caffeine can be detected in the urine and high levels are banned by the International Olympic Committee and the NCAA (generally in excess of the equivalent of 5 cups of coffee).

Amphetamines: Commonly called uppers, pep pills, speed, bennies and dexies, amphetamines act as central nervous system stimulants. Amphetamines are provided as *Benzedrine, Dexedrine* and *Desoxyn.* Although it is assumed that amphetamines will delay the onset of fatigue, increase aggressiveness and diminish the perception of pain, there is little evidence that supports the use of amphetamines in enhancing athletic performance. The dangers of amphetamine use include cardiac arrhythmias, poor judgement, paranoia and confusion.

Clenbuterol: Clenbuterol is a central nervous system stimulant that has added anabolic effects resulting in the increase of protein synthesis and muscle mass and decreasing body fat. Clenbuterol also increases the are of glycogen release from the liver and free fatty acids from adipose tissues. Clenbuterol use has been associated with the onset of headaches, anxiety, insomnia, anorexia, rapid heart rate, heart attack and stroke.

Painkillers

DMSO: DMSO (dimethyl sulfoxide) is a common industrial solvent which is readily absorbed through the skin. It had been thought that DMSO, applied as a liquid or gel, would help speed the healing of muscle and skeletal injuries. There is no concrete evidence that this is so. The adverse effects of DMSO include, skin rash, nausea, headaches, and impaired vision.

Demerol, darvon, codeine: The drugs are classified as narcotic analgesics, or painkillers. While their use does enable injured athletes to continue participating in activities, they do so by blocking the normal warning signals of bodily injury. In addition, these drugs cloud mental performance and are addictive.

Aspirin, Acetominophen, Ibuprofin: These drugs are non-narcotic analgesics and are used as painkillers. Although generally non-addictive, the use of painkillers to allow continuation of athletic activities can lead to serious bodily injury. Taken in large amounts, or regularly over long periods of time, these drugs can be dangerous.

Ethyl Chloride: A topically applied liquid (or spray) which causes a localized loss of sensation at the site of administration. It gives the perception of "freezing" the area. Flouri-Methane is another such substance.

Xylocaine: A local anesthetic which removes the perception of pain at the site of injection. It is similar to the anesthetics used by dentists.

Corticosteroids: Corticosteroids include the steroid based hormones normally released by the cortex of the adrenal gland along with a number of synthetic analogs. Corticosteroids are normally used for their anti-inflammatory capacity and are administered to reduce the pain and swelling associated with joint injuries. Corticosteroids are typically administered by injection (into joints).

Performance Enhancers

Protein Supplements: Many athletes, particularly those interested in muscle development, feel a need to increase their daily protein intake. Some do this through dietary changes such as eating steaks or drinking raw eggs. Others rely on commercial protein supplements like Amino Fuel, Body Builder and Pro Muscle. Neither of these methods are usually required or generally recommended. Dietary protein intake normally supplies the body with all of the necessary amino acids for building muscle and other protein based tissues within the body. Of critical importance with respect to dietary intake are the essential amino acids; those which can not be manufactured by the body. A normal, balanced diet usually provides the necessary amino acids for protein synthesis, even for those concentrating on building muscle mass. Recall that the primary requirement for building and strengthening muscle is resistance exercise. There is little direct evidence supporting the need for amino acid or protein supplements. In fact, an overabundance of these nutrients can lead to a lowering of blood pH (acidosis) and dehydration.

Carbohydrate Supplements: Carbohydrate provides the primary energy supply for athletic activities. Readily available stores of carbohydrate may be depleted during endurance activities. Carbohydrate supplements, usually in liquid form, can provide a short-term source of carbohydrate fuel. Carbohydrates ingested and not used by the body may be stored as glycogen (a carbohydrate polymer) or fat.

Anabolic Steroids: Most often taken as a synthetic hormone, anabolic steroids stimulate the biochemical pathway which builds protein. Anabolic steroids are available, by prescription, under such trade names as Anadrol, Anavar, Dianabol, Durabolin, Maxibolin and Winstrol. Anabolic steroids do enhance muscle growth and lead to increases in strength by stimulating the protein synthetic pathways although they contribute nothing to muscle endurance. Serious, adverse side effects however include hair loss, liver disease, bleeding, high blood pressure, acne, testicular atrophy, personality change and possible heart disease. Long term use of anabolic steroids can suppress the immune system and increase the number and severity of infectious diseases. In adolescents who have not yet finished bone elongation, the use of anabolic steroids may stunt growth. Anabolic steroid use is banned by both the NCAA and IOC. Androstenedione is a testosterone precursor and will lead to increased testosterone levels about one hour after ingestion.

Growth Hormone: Growth hormone is naturally secreted by the pituitary gland. Its major effects are to increase general cellular growth and to influence carbohydrate metabolism. While some studies have shown that taking growth hormone supplements will stimulate muscle development leading to an increase in lean body mass and will aid in the utilization of glucose as an energy source, others have shown it to have no effect on either increasing strength or muscle mass or decreasing muscle breakdown. Both the NCAA and IOC have banned the use of GH.

Creatine: Creatine is an amino acid that, when used as a dietary supplement, has been shown to help the body store energy. In the chapter on Bioenergetics it was explained how the molecule creatine-phosphate provides a back-up storage of high-energy phosphates that can be used to replenish ATP within the muscle when powering short-term activities. Creatine supplementation has been examined in several research studies and was shown to improve performance in high-intensity, short-term activities. Twenty grams per day for a period of six days was shown to result in noticeable improvement. There is also some indication that creatine supplement can strengthen and build muscle as well, probably through it effect on enhancing the energy available for strength training. To date, no adverse effects of creatine supplements have been demonstrated.

Blood Doping: Aerobic capacity is in part determined by the ability of the blood to carry oxygen from the lungs to the working muscles. The oxygen carrying capacity of the blood is a function of the amount of hemoglobin present. Since hemoglobin is carried in the red blood cells, increasing the number of red blood cells will increase the hemoglobin content and aerobic capacity. Blood doping involves the removal of a quantity of blood from an individual and storing it briefly under refrigeration. After several weeks, the body will have replenished its normal number of red blood cells. Prior to competition, red cells from the refrigerated supply are injected into the athletes' vascular system, temporarily increasing the total number of red blood cells and hemoglobin content. Blood doping is also referred to as *blood packing* and *blood boosting*. Blood doping was developed by the U.S. Navy at the end of World War II in an attempt to allow bomber pilots to fly at higher altitudes and avoid enemy antiaircraft fire. While blood doping is effective (the 1972 Olympic gold medallist in the 5,000 and 10,000 meter races engaged in blood doping) it can have serious side effects. The increased red blood cell number increases the viscosity (thickness) of the blood creating a greater workload for the heart and potentially restricting flow through small blood vessels. Blood doping is banned by the NCAA, the US Olympic Committee and the International Olympic Committee.

rEPO (recombinant Erythropoietin): Erythropoietin is a natural hormone produced by the kidneys in response to blood oxygen concentration that stimulates the bone marrow to increase the production of red blood cells. rEPO is a synthetic human erythropoietin made by hamster ovary cells in culture that have been genetically engineered to contain the human erythropoietin gene. Injections of rEPO will begin to increase red blood cell numbers in about 5-6 days and can produce effects similar to blood doping.

L-Carnitine: One of the essential amino acids, carnitine plays a role in carrying free fatty acids (FFA) into the mitochondria where they are used for ATP synthesis. It is believed that L-carnitine supplementation may help cells to efficiently use FFA as an energy source. Research however has not confirmed any such effect.

Choline: The choline molecule is precursor in the synthesis of the neurotransmitter acetylcholine which may become depleted during prolonged exercise. Although there is no conclusive evidence, some believe that a diet rich in choline (fish, liver, eggs) can help increase endurance.

Glycerol: A byproduct of fat metabolism, the glycerol molecule helps the body to retain water and has been shown through numerous studies to increase athletic performance for endurance activities in hot weather. Glycerol is available as a pure supplement or as part of several commercially available hydration drinks.

Phosphate: The phosphate molecule acts as a chemical buffer to maintain pH within the body fluids and muscle during conditions that typically produce excess acidity. Active muscles relying on anaerobic metabolism produce lactic acid that can lower the local pH and bring about fatigue and decreased muscle performance. Phosphate has also been shown to increase creatine phosphate stores in muscle and 2,3 diphosphoglycreate (DPG) in the tissues that enhances oxygen release from hemoglobin. Phosphate, taken a doses of .3g/kg body weight in the form of sodium phosphate solutions, has been shown to enhance endurance and to raise the anaerobic threshold.

Equipment

Weight Belts: Weight belts are 4"-6" wide belts made of stiff leather or vinyl that are used in heavy lifting. Their purpose is to provide added support to the lumbar region of the spine during heavy or prolonged lifting and they do this by helping to increase the pressure within the body (Intra Abdominal Pressure – IAP) by as much as 10% - 40%. The increased IAP is proposed to help to share and distribute the compressive load that lifting heavy weights would normally exert on the vertebrae and discs of the lower, lumbar spine. Not only does this help to protect the vertebrae and discs but also it has been shown to increase by 5% -15% the weight that can be lifted. A recent study by the National Institute for Occupational Safety and Health has determined that weight belts do not lower the incidence of lifting-related back injuries. Further, the elevated IAP can lead to rapid rises in blood pressure that may be harmful to certain individuals.

Full-Length Swim Suits and Running Suits: The 2000 Summer Olympics brought us images of the first wide-spread and officially-sanctioned use of full-length body suits for swimmers and runners. Competitive bicycle, bobsled and luge racers have used similar suits for years. As imperceptible as they may seem, the minute but numerous hairs on our skin create friction and drag in the fluids (liquids and gasses) that flow over our body's surfaces. While originally evolved for purposes of thermal insulation and sensory perception, this inherited characteristic of our mammalian ancestors reduces our efficiency as we attempt to move rapidly through air or water. Although the benefits are not great, in events such as these every thousandth of a second counts.

Breathe-Right Nasal Strips®: In watching almost any NFL professional football game you are likely to see the athletes wearing a bandage-like adhesive strip across the bridge of their nose. These devises, marketed as the Breathe-Right Nasal Strips consist of an adhesive strip in which is embedded a flexible but elastic metal strip that, when folded, attempts to spring back to its original flat form. When the adhesive band containing the metal strip is folded across the bridge of the nose, its attempt to straighten out actually pulls open the nasal passageways (the nostrils within the nose) and external nares (the nostril openings at the tip of the nose). It is believed that this will increase the air flow rate into and out of the nose allowing for more efficient respiration.

Running Shoe Technology

The evolution of the simple sneaker into today's variety of athletic shoe technology has given us an ever increasing selection of shoes specialized for basketball, tennis, running and cross-training. The development of new shoe technology and design, which follows research into human movement analysis and material science, provides an example of the progress in ergogenic science. The purpose of a good running shoe is to provide for the cushioning of impact forces and the facilitation of proper alignment of joints during the running motions, all while minimizing the actual weight of the shoe. A shoe with insufficient cushioning can stress joints, injuring the articular cartilage and hastening the development of stress fractures in the bones. Too much cushioning however can reduce the ability of the shoe to stabilize the joints and can lead to alignment-related injuries such as Achilles tendonitis. Increasing the rigidity and stability of the shoe can make it too inflexible and add to its weight. The development of new, lightweight materials and an increasing understanding of the mechanics of human running have lead to the current generation of shoes with wide and well-cushioned heels to accommodate heel-strike forces, upward-curled toe regions to facilitate toe-spring and push-off, dual-density midsoles to minimize foot-roll and pronation, and lightweight nylon replacing canvas and leather upper portions. One thing to be sure of is that next year's running shoes will show continued change.

Selected Readings:

Armsey, T.D. and G.A. Green. **Nutrition Supplements: Science vs. Hype**, *The Physician and Sportsmedicine*, Vol. 25, No. 6, June 1997, http://www.physsportsmed.com/issues/1997/06jun/armsey.htm

Eichner, E.R., **Ergogenic Aids: What Athletes Are Using and Why?**, *The Physician and Sportsmedicine*, Vol. 25, No. 4, April 1997, http://www.physsportsmed.com/issues/1997/04apr/eichner.htm

Kuipers, H., **Anabolic Steroids: Side Effects**, *Encyclopedia of Sports Medicine and Science*. March 1998. http://www.sportsci.org/encyc/agingex.html

Williams, M.H. (Ed)., **Nutritional Ergogenics and Sports Performance**. *The President's Council on Physical Fitness and Sports Research Digest*, Series 3, No. 2, June 1998, http://www.indiana.edu/~preschal/digests/june98/digestsjune98.htm

Wright, K. **Watching Your Steps**, *Scientific American*, September 2000, http://www.sciam.com/specialissues/0900sports/0900wright.html

Chapter 13

Sport and Exercise Injuries

Chapter Contents
- Pain
- Inflammation
- Treating Exercise and Athletic Injuries
- Preventing Injuries
- Common Injuries
- Selected Readings

Learning Objectives
The material in this chapter will allow you to:
- Understand the causes and mechanism of the inflammatory response
- Understand the need and mechanism for immediate treatment and for long-term treatment of exercise and athletic injuries
- Understand how proper conditioning, technique and equipment can lower the risk of injury
- To know and understand the most common exercise and athletic injuries and their treatment

Pain

Participation in sport and exercise activities, while providing significant health benefits, is not without some risk of injury. Tens of thousands of individuals are injured each year in exercise and sport related accidents. Seventy-five percent of all these injuries stem from nine very common activities: basketball, dance, figure skating, football, gymnastics, running, soccer, skiing and tennis.

Pain is the fundamental signal of an injury. Local damage to a tissue injures or irritates nerve endings in the immediate area which, in turn, send messages to the brain indicating an injury. The brain interprets this signal and produces the conscious sensation of pain. Pain is a message from the brain indicating, to you, that something is wrong. It is nature's way of discouraging you from using the injured area. It is important to heed this message. The pain may begin immediately or may appear several hours after sustaining the injury.

Inflammation

Inflammation is the most usual local response to an injury. When a tissue is injured, tiny blood vessels often break causing bleeding into the tissue. *Mast cells*, located near the blood vessels in the injured tissue, release the chemicals *histamine* and *heparin*. Histamine causes the blood vessels to expand, or dilate, allowing more blood to flow to the injured area. It also causes the junctions between the cells of the capillary walls to loosen, allowing fluid and disease fighting white blood cells to flow from the blood into the tissues. Heparin, a chemical that inhibits blood clotting, also serves to allow fluid to flow into the injured tissue helping to flush out debris and dilute any toxins.

Figure 12.1. Inflammatory Response

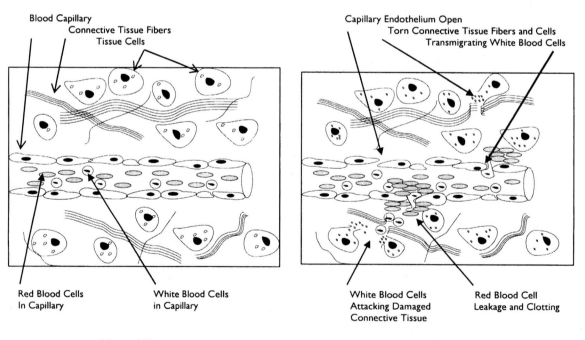

Normal Tissue

Inflamed Tissue

This accumulation of warm, red blood and of fluid within the injured tissue is responsible for the swelling, redness and warmth that are typically noted at the injury site. The pressure developed within the injured tissue by the accumulation of fluid, presses on nerve endings and contributes to the sensation of pain at the injury site.

Although we typically associate inflammation and the pain it causes as the unwelcome side effect of a sports-related injury, the process is actually one which helps to limit further damage and to begin the healing process.

The Acute Inflammatory Phase (0 - 7 days)

Shortly after the initial injury, damaged cells in the immediate region begin to die and release their lysosomal digestive enzymes into the surrounding tissue. In response to the injury and cell death, blood vessels in the region dilate bringing increased blood flow to the area of injury resulting in localized redness (*rubor*) and warmth (*calor*). This increased blood flow, known clinically as *hyperaemia*, can be as great as ten times the normal amount. Capillary walls, which are usually sealed fairly tightly between the endothelial cells lining them, become leaky and increase their permeability allowing the leakage of blood plasma fluid and proteins as well as the outwards migration of white blood cells into the damaged tissue. The flooding of the injury site with this fluid results in the characteristic swelling (*tumor*). This protein rich exudates contains *antibodies* that can help fight local infection, *fibrin* to help form blood clots to seal broken blood vessels, and *neutrophils*, a type of white blood cell that scavenges and eliminates dead and dying material from the injury site. The combination of all of these activities creates great pressure within the injured tissue activating sensitive nerve endings and causing localized pain. This acute inflammatory phase lasts from 1to 7 days.

The Proliferative Phase (7 - 21 days)

Approximately one week after injury, most of the damaged tissue has been removed and growth and regeneration is beginning. During the proliferative phase, connective tissue cells called fibroblasts proliferate and begin synthesizing new connective tissue fibers and matrix. The predominant fiber that is initially produced is Type-3 collagen, a somewhat weak and brittle arrangement of the more dense and tougher Type-1 collagen that was originally found in the tissue. The matrix, or gelatin-like supporting material, is synthesized and, in its early form, has a very high water content. Capillaries also begin to proliferate, replacing those that were damaged or have degenerated, and reestablishing a healthy blood supply to the area. The proliferative phase continues for about two weeks.

The Maturation and Remodeling Phase (3 - 12 months)

During the maturation phase, water is resorbed from the connective tissue matrix and the collagen fibers aggregate and align along the planes of stress into the stronger Type-1 configuration.

Treating Exercise and Athletic Injuries
Immediate Treatment

For most athletic injuries, immediate treatment should follow the *RICE,* or *PRICES principle*: RICE and PRICES are mnemonics, RICE standing for, *R*est, *I*ce, *C*ompression and *E*levation. In short, Rest means to stop exercising or using the damaged tissue. Continued activity can lead to further damage and long-lasting complications. Ice means to apply ice to the injured area to minimize swelling, bleeding and edema. Ice will cause the blood vessels to constrict minimizing blood flow into the area. Compression implies manually pressing or wrapping an elastic bandage around the injured area. This will help force accumulated fluid out of the injured tissue and reduce further swelling by compressing blood vessels. Elevation means to raise the injured area above the level of the heart. This will also reduce local blood flow and minimize swelling. PRICES includes the addition of the initial step, *P*, for *P*rotection, and the final step, *S*, for *Support* or stabilization.

PRICES

P – Protect the area from further injury

R – Rest the injured area to allow the healing process to begin

I – Ice the injury, apply cold, to reduce pain, bleeding, and swelling

C – Compress the injured area, for example with an Ace bandage, to control swelling

E – Elevate the injured area to further reduce bleeding and swelling

S – Support and stabilize the injured area, for example with a splint, sling, brace or cast

Usually, if the injury is not severe, significant healing will take place after about 48 hours. If the pain and swelling have subsided, you may begin moderate activities using the injured area. After this light activity, again apply the RICE or PRICES regimen. Activities can be gradually increased as long as they can be done without pain.

It is important not to remain inactive for too long following an injury. Within 24 hours of an injury and the subsequent inactivity, you will begin losing strength in the inactive muscles. Flexibility and range of motion within the joints will also be lost during periods of inactivity. If the injury keeps you from performing aerobic activities, cardiorespiratory endurance will also begin to suffer. As a general rule, it requires three days of rehabilitation training to make up for the losses from each day of inactivity.

Long-Term Rehabilitation

Perhaps more importantly, the resumption of gradual activities such as mild stretching and light resistance are critical during the proliferative phase. To ensure that Type-1 collagen forms along the desired lines or planes of maximum stress, the healing tissue must be subject to that stress although in very moderate amounts. Prolonged immobilization will result in a more randomly oriented collagen replacement and a less effective recovery. Failure to pay attention to this will result in the random orientation of replacement collagen and the resultant loss of both strength and flexibility in the rehabilitated structures.

Proprioceptive Rehabilitation

Damage to muscle, tendons, and ligaments that occurs in exercise and athletic injuries may also frequently result in impaired proprioception. As was presented in Chapter 7, the body contains a complex proprioception system in which receptors continuously update the central nervous system as to the position and motion of each of the body's joints. The nervous system then uses this information to continually adjust signals to the muscles so as to maintain a stable posture or control the body's movements. Injuries that effect muscle and tendon may damage the muscle spindle fibers and Golgi tendon organs that provide proprioceptive input while damage to the ligaments of the joint capsules may interfere with their sensory signals. Damage to these receptors may be due to either direct trauma (tearing or crushing) or to the high internal pressures that develop during the swelling phase of the inflammatory response. Proprioceptive damage can result in deficiencies in performance once healing has been completed.

The early application of RICE can help to prevent the swelling-related pressure damage. Specific skill-related exercises begun during the rehabilitation process can help to "retrain" and restore normal proprioceptive function and eliminate performance declines.

The best advice is to pay attention to, and follow the signals from your body. The timing and intensity of reestablishing training should be based upon the ability to tolerate activity without significant discomfort.

Preventing Injuries

Injury prevention should be the goal of everyone participating in exercise or athletic activities. While it will not be possible to avoid all injuries, paying proper attention to each of the following four items can go a long way towards reducing the chance of being injured:

Proper Conditioning
Proper Technique
Proper Equipment
Avoidance of Overtraining and Overuse

Exercise and athletic activity by their very nature place stress on body structures and systems. The single most frequently identified risk factor for exercise and athletic injuries is the amount of exercise itself. Accounting for all other variables, the risk of injury increases as exercise intensity, frequency, or duration increases.

Proper conditioning will lead to the establishment of proper muscle balance, neuromuscular coordination, improvements in muscle strength and elasticity, and will toughen connective tissues such as tendon, ligament and bone, all of which can help reduce the probability of injury. For example, improper conditioning can lead to antagonistic muscle groups differing substantially in strength and placing unbalanced stresses on the joints. Many knee injuries are caused by an imbalance between well-developed quadriceps muscles and poorly developed hamstring muscles. In addition, proper conditioning can help maintain a normal body mass index. There is an increasing body of evidence that BMI's either below 18 or above 25 are associated with greater frequencies of injury.

"Health is my expected heaven."
John Keats, Poet, 1820

The use of improper technique in swinging a tennis racket can lead to tennis elbow, a chronic inflammation of the connective tissue structures at the elbow. Similarly, improper throwing or punching technique can lead to rotator cuff inflammation or tears at the shoulder joint. Whether using natural motions or equipment-assisted motions it is important to know and use proper technique.

Many sports and some exercise activities use equipment to facilitate the activity or to specifically protect the participant against injury. In strength training with free weights, a weight-lifting bench and the barbell would be examples of the equipment typically used. A poorly constructed or damaged bench, or a bar with improperly functioning weight clamps can lead to very serious injuries.

Finally, as discussed in Chapter 2, overtraining or overuse injuries will often result if a body system is worked too hard, pushing it well past the point of overload or, if sufficient rest is not allowed for tissue rebuilding between bouts of training or competition.

Common Injuries

The following is a summary of the injuries and conditions associated with exercise and athletics.

Amenorrhea (dysmenorrhea): A cessation or irregularity in the menstrual cycle common in women athletes with body fat percentages below 17%. Although not necessarily a serious condition, the prolonged exposure to reduced estrogen levels, the underlying cause of amenorrhea, can hasten bone calcium loss and osteoporosis. Treatment generally includes reducing exercise intensity. The menstrual cycle and associated conditions will return to normal as activity level decreases.

Athletes Foot (and "Jock Itch"): A fungal infection of the skin characterized by severe itch. Prevention and cure both involve keeping the area dry and paying careful attention to hygiene. The application of antifungal agents is the typical treatment.

Blister: A fluid filled separation between the upper and middle layers of the skin which develops in response to friction. Most blisters will heal in a few days as the fluid is reabsorbed into the blood. If a blister ruptures, cover the area with a sterile bandage and reduce activity on the area.

Burner (also called a Stinger): A burning or stinging pain that occurs in the neck, shoulder or arm that may be accompanied by a loss of sensation (numbness) and muscle control (paralysis). This injury occurs most frequently in football, gymnastics and hockey and results from collisions or falls that stretch or compress nerves of the brachial plexus located in neck and shoulder area. The immediate numbness and paralysis usually subside within minutes but residual pain and weakness may remain for several days. Rest is the recommended treatment.

Bursistis: An inflammation of a bursa, the fluid filled sac associated with many joints. Bursitis may be caused by trauma to the bursa, overuse or bacterial infection. The bursa becomes swollen and the area red and painful. Tennis elbow often involves bursitis at the elbow joint. Rest, antiinflammatory drugs and aspiration of excess fluid are recommended treatments.

Contusion: A contusion is a bruise caused by a direct blow to the body. Contusions usually involve bleeding into the damaged tissue which can result in pain, swelling and discoloration. The severity of the contusion can vary from mild (typical black and blue mark) to severe (involving skin, muscle and bone damage). Immediate compression will slow the bleeding and reduce the severity of the injury.

Cramp: A spasm (strong, sustained contraction) of a muscle associated with pain. Usually caused by injury or dehydration. Stretching and massage will usually relieve the cramp.

Dehydration: A condition brought on by excessive water loss, primarily through sweating. Characterized by dizziness, nausea and muscle weakness. Associated conditions are heat exhaustion and heat stroke. Preventative measure is drinking plain water prior to and during activity.

Dislocation (subluxation): The separation of two or more bones from their normal alignment at a joint; it does not involve a fracture or breakage of a bone. Realignment (reduction) and immobilization of the joint are required treatment for a dislocation. In a subluxation the bones realign on their own.

Exercise Induced Asthma: Intense exercise in cold, dry air can induce episodes of severe asthma; the abnormal constriction of air passageways in the lungs. Exercising in warmer and moister environments and taking prescription medications can prevent EIA and allow athletes to compete at world-class levels.

Fracture: A break in a bone caused by a fall, direct blow or overuse.

Stress fracture: a small fissures or fractures in the outer surface of the bone often not evident in X-rays. Stress fractures usually develop following highly repetitive loading activities even if the load is submaximal. Stress fractures are most common in the lower leg, lumbar vertebral and pelvic bones. Rest and, where necessary, splinting is the most common treatment.

Simple fracture (closed fracture): a complete but clean break in the bone with no penetration of the skin. Reduction and immobilization are required treatment.

Compound fracture: similar to the simple fracture but with the broken bone penetrating through the skin. Other internal tissues are often torn as well. Surgical reduction is often required along with antibiotics to prevent infection

Comminuted fracture: a shattering of the bone into many pieces.

Depressed fracture: typical in flat bones this involves a pushing in of the broken portion of bone.

Heart Attack: Approximately 75,000 of the 1.5 million heart attacks that occur each year are the result of heavy exertion; some job related and some exercise related. The risk of exercise-induced heart attack is greatest in sedentary individuals who engage too quickly in intense physical activities. Isometric activities involving short but intense muscle contractions can briefly raise blood pressure to dangerous levels and cause temporary spasms in the blood vessels feeding the heart.

Hematuria: Blood in the urine. The result of overexertion or overuse damage. Typically occurs after muscle overuse damage (rhabdomyolysis), after distance running, or after contact sports.

174

Meniscal Tear: The meniscus is a pad of cartilage within the knee joint that serves to help cushion and dissipate the forces normally generated within the knee. There is a medial and a lateral meniscus. Meniscal tears most often occur when the knee is forcefully externally rotated while in a flexed position as might occur during a skiing fall, football tackle, or quick directional change while running and result in intense pain, a "locking" of the joint in certain positions and general joint instability. RICE is the immediate treatment. Small tears may heal on their own while larger tears generally require removal of the damaged meniscus through arthroscopic surgery. Occasionally, a tear of the medial meniscus will occur along with a tearing of both the medial and lateral collateral ligaments of the knee (*see sprains*), a condition referred to as ***O'Donoghue's Triad***.

Myositis: An inflammation of a muscle associated with swelling and soreness.
Usually caused by overuse and apparent 12 - 24 hrs after activity. Aspirin will provide relief and light exercise will aid recovery.

Rhabdomyolysis: A condition characterized by the degeneration of muscle cells accompanied by pain, tenderness, swelling and blood in the urine. It is caused by overexertion in resistance training particularly with eccentric contractions.

Separation: (see dislocation)

Shinsplints: A painful condition along the front of the lower leg. Shinsplints may be the result of tiny stress fractures of the tibia or injury to the flexor muscles and tendons of the anterior shin. Shinsplints may result from overuse or sustained hard contact from running or jumping.

Sprain: An injury to a ligament caused when an excessive force is applied to a joint at a velocity and direction greater than the ligament can resist resulting in overstretching or overtwisting the ligament. Ligaments are the connective tissue bands connecting the bones and forming the joint capsules. A sprain often involves tears in the ligament which can range from small to nearly complete ruptures. Since ligaments are poorly vascularized, these injuries tend to heal slowly. Sprains are best treated by limiting motion of the injured joint and taking non-steroidal antiinflammatories. The restoration of full movement may require 4 weeks.

Strain: An injury to a muscle or tendon (the band connecting muscle to bone) usually involving a small tear resulting from overuse or stress. These are only moderately painful and are generally not considered serious injuries however, a small tear can enlarge if aggravated. Inactivity for 48 hrs, followed by a slow return to normal levels is advised.

Tear: See sprain and strain.

Tendonitis (Tendinitis): The inflammation of a tendon characterized by pain and swelling. Usually the result of overuse or from excessive strain or pressure on the tendon. Ice and anti-inflammatory medicines will help.

Selected Readings:

Arendt, E. **Common Musculoskeletal Injuries in Women**, *The Physician and Sportsmedicine*, Vol. 24, No. 7, July 1996,
http://www.physsportsmed.com/issues/jul_96/arendt.htm

Noakes, T.D., **Sudden Death and Exercise**, *Sportscience*, Vol. 2, No. 4, 1988,
http://www.sportsci.org/jour/9804/tdn.html

Schwellnus, M.P., **Skeletal Muscle Cramps During Exercise**, *The Physician and Sportsmedicine*, Vol 27, No. 12, November 1999,
http://www.physsportsmed.com/issues/1999/11_99/schwellnus.htm

Thornton, **Pain Relief for Acute Soft Tissue Injuries**, *The Physician and Sportsmedicine*, Vol. 25, No. 10, October 1997,
http://www.physsportsmed.com/issues/1997/10Oct/thornton.htm

Fitness Assessment Activities

The following series of activities will allow you to explore and measure the status of your own physical fitness and health. Each activity relates to a specific chapter in the text (see the last page of each chapter) and will allow you to determine a specific characteristic of your current fitness level. After determining your personal fitness profile for body composition, metabolic rate, flexibility, muscular strength, power and endurance, reaction response time, respiratory fitness and cardiovascular fitness you will be able to compare your personal values against the standard expected values for acceptable fitness. The final activity will lead you through the development of a personal exercise prescription for improving your fitness status.

Activity 1. Evaluating Exercise Readiness

Activity 2. Evaluating Activity Level

Activity 3. Rating of Perceived Exertion

Activity 4. Evaluating Body Mass Index

Activity 5. Evaluating Body Fat Percentage

Activity 6. Evaluating Body Fat Distribution Pattern

Activity 7. Somatotype Analysis

Activity 8. Evaluating Metabolic Rate and Energy Requirement

Activity 9. Evaluating Flexibility

Activity 10. Kraus-Weber Test of Back Fitness

Activity 11. Evaluating Muscular Strength

Activity 12. Evaluating Musculoskeletal Mechanics

Activity 13. Evaluating Muscular Power

Activity 14. Evaluating Muscular Endurance

Activity 15. Evaluation Core Muscular Fitness

Activity 16. Evaluating Posture

Activity 17. Evaluating Proprioception

Activity 18. Evaluating Reaction Response Time

Activity 19. Evaluating Respiratory Fitness

Activity 20. Evaluating Cardiovascular Fitness

Activity 21. Evaluating Cardiovascular Disease Risk

Activity 22. The Exercise Prescription

Evaluating Exercise Readiness

Procedure:

For each of the following questions, answer yes or no and indicate your answer in the check box at the right of each question.

	NO	YES
1. Are you presently involved in a regular exercise program involving vigorous cardiovascular activity for at least 15 minutes twice a week?	☐	☐
2. Are you presently over 35 years of age?	☐	☐
3. Do you have a history of any cardiovascular problems? (high blood pressure; abnormal heart rhythm; murmur; angina; heart attack)	☐	☐
4. Do you experience frequent fainting or dizzy spells under normal conditions or after exercise or exertion?	☐	☐
5. Do you ever experience pain or pressure in the left or mid-chest area, left side of neck or left shoulder or arm after exertion?	☐	☐
6. Do you ever experience swelling of the ankles or feet?	☐	☐
7. Do you experience shortness of breath after mild activity or exertion?	☐	☐
8. Are you more than 20 pounds overweight?	☐	☐
9. Do you have any problems with your joints, back or bones such as arthritis or rheumatism?	☐	☐
10. Do you presently have any other injuries or medical conditions requiring treatment or special attention (including diabetes, thyroid condition, asthma)	☐	☐
11. Are you currently taking any prescription medications?	☐	☐
12. Do you have any relatives who have had a heart attack or stroke before the age of 60?	☐	☐
13. Do you presently smoke cigarettes or have you only recently quit smoking?	☐	☐

If you answered yes to any of questions 2 - 13 it is advisable that you obtain a physicians clearance to begin an exercise program.

Data Sheet

Exercise Readiness

Name:_____

Course Section:_____ **Date:** _____

Number of questions, 2-13, answered with a YES

Number of questions, 2-13, answered with a NO

YES   NO

Is a physician's clearance recommended?

Describe why, for each of questions 2-13, a yes answer might be associated with an unacceptable risk for engaging in unsupervised exercise or athletic activities.

ACTIVITY 2

Evaluating Activity Level

Procedure:

Answer the following questions as honestly as you can. For each answer, select the frequency score value associated with that answer and enter it into the corresponding box on the right. Determine your activity level score by adding the numbers in the three boxes.

How frequently do you exercise?

Typical Number of Exercise Sessions per Week

	Frequency Score
Less than one time per week	0
1 time per week	1
2 times per week	2
3 times per week	3
4 times per week	4
5 or more times per week	5

Enter Score ☐ **A**

How long is your average exercise session?

Typical Length of Each Exercise Session

	Duration Score
Less than 5 minutes long	0
5 to 14 minutes long	1
15 to 29 minutes long	2
30 to 44 minutes long	3
45 to 59 minutes long	4
60 minutes or longer	5

Enter Score ☐ **B**

How hard do you exercise?

Typical Exercise Session Results In

	Intensity Score
No change in resting pulse rate	0
Little change in pulse (1-10 beats/min increase)	1
Slight change in pulse (10-20 bpm) and slight increase in breathing	2
Moderate increase in pulse (20-40 bpm) and moderate increase in breathing	3
Large increase in pulse (40 or more bpm), moderate Increase in breathing and moderate sweating	4
Large increase in pulse with heavy breathing and heavy sweating	5

Enter Score ☐ **C**

Exercise Activity Score = Product of the three scores   A x B x C = ☐

Activity Index Summary Score	Personal Activity Level
Greater than 61	Highly Active
41 – 61	Active
25 – 40	Moderately Active
15 – 24	Lightly Active
Less than 15	Sedentary

Data Sheet

Exercise Activity Index

ACTIVITY 2

Name:_____

Course Section: **Date:**

Exercise Activity Index Score ⬚

Personal Activity Level ⬚

Evaluation and Conclusion:

Briefly discuss the health implications related to your current exercise activity level.

Rating of Perceived Exertion

The ability to accurately determine your rating of perceived exertion (RPE) is an acquired skill that must be developed by practice. In this activity you will have the opportunity to gain experience and practice in determining your RPE for various activities.

Procedure:
1. Perform the first of the four exercise activities (casual walk), continuously, for a period of three minutes. After performing the activity for a period of three minutes, stop and determine your heart rate by taking a carotid (neck) or radial (wrist) pulse, counting the number of pulse beats over a ten second interval, and multiplying by six (to get a 60 second pulse, or heart rate). Enter this value into the data table.

2. Using the descriptive cues on the Borg RPE scale below, try and determine the RPE for this activity.

3. After a 15 minute period of rest, or on separate occasions, repeat steps 1 and 2 with each of the other three suggested activities as well as with any two of your own choosing.

Data Table

Activity	Heart Rate (beats per min)	Rating of Perceived Exertion (Borg scale rating)
Casual walk (3 minutes)		
Slow jog (3 minutes)		
Moderate jog (3 minutes)		
Fast Run (3 minutes)		
Option 1		
Option 2		

Borg Rating of Perceived Exertion Scale

6	7	8	9	10	11	12	13	14	15	16	17	18	19	20
very, very light			very light			fairly light		somewhat hard		hard		very hard		very, very hard

Analysis of Results

The RPE scale, as developed by Borg, is supposed to roughly correlate with your exercising heart rate and to provide a quick and easy way to estimate exercise workload. If a zero were added to the end of the RPE value at the end of each activity, it should be approximately what the heart rate would be in performing that activity. In order to be in the exercise benefit zone, you should try and achieve an RPE of between 12 and 16 during exercise.

Data Sheet

Rating of Perceived Exertion

ACTIVITY 3

Name:_____

Course Section:_____ Date: _____

Plot a graph showing the relationship between measured heart rate and the Rating of Perceived Exertion.

RPE																					

RPE values: 20, 19, 18, 17, 16, 15, 14, 13, 12, 11, 10, 9, 8, 7, 6, 5, 4, 3, 2, 1

Heart Rate: 50 55 60 65 70 75 80 85 90 95 100 110 115 120 125 130 135 140 145 150

Heart Rate

Evaluation and Conclusion:
Describe how accurately the Borg RPE scale reflects actual aerobic exertion.

How effectively do you believe the Borg RPE scale can reflect anaerobic exertion, such as lifting loads of varying weight?

Evaluating Body Mass Index

ACTIVITY 4

The body mass index is a ratio of body weight to height and is used as an indicator of weight status. The body mass index is calculated from the formula below:

$$BMI = \frac{\text{weight (kg)}}{\text{height}^2 \text{ (m)}}$$

A body mass index of between 20 and 25 is considered acceptable, greater than 30 is considered to be an indication of obesity.

Procedure:

1. Record an accurate measure of your body weight in pounds (without clothing). Enter this amount in box A:
   $\boxed{} A$

2. Record an accurate measure of your height (without shoes). Enter this amount in box B:
   $\boxed{} B$

3. To determine your body weight (W) in kilograms divide A by 2.2 :
   $A \boxed{} \div 2.2 = \boxed{} W$

4. To determine the square of your height in meters , Multiply your height in inches B, by .0254 :
   $B \boxed{} \times .0254 = \boxed{} H$

5. Determine H^2, the square of your height measurement:
   $H \boxed{} \times H \boxed{} = \boxed{} H^2$

6. Divide the values of W (weight in kg) by H (height² in m)
   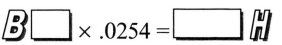
   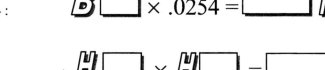
   $W \boxed{} \div H^2 \boxed{} = $ **BMI**

Compare your Body Mass Index with the table on the back of this page.

BMI	Classification	Disease Risk
< 18.5	Underweight	Increased
18.5-24.9	Normal Weight	None
25.0-29.9	Overweight	Increased
30.0-34.9	Clinical Obesity Class I	High
35.0-39.9	Clinical Obesity Class II	Very High
>40	Clinical Obesity Class III	Extremely High

Adapted from Grundy, S.M., et.al. Physical Activity in the Prevention and Treatment of Obesity and Its Comorbidities. Medicine & Science in Sport & Exercise. Vol. 31, No. 11, November 1999

Data Sheet

Body Mass Index

Name:_____

Course Section:_____ **Date:** _____

	Measured Value	Expected Value
Body Mass Index Value		
BMI Classification Status		
Disease Risk		

Evaluation and Conclusion:

Briefly describe the value of the BMI measurement relative to the previously used standard tables for height and weight.

In what situations is the BMI prone to give an erroneous conclusion?

Describe your own personal BMI evaluation and any implications it has on your overall state of health and fitness.

Evaluating Body Fat Percentage

ACTIVITY 5

Body fat analysis can be conducted a number of ways, the most common of them being underwater weighing, the use of skinfold calipers, the measurement of electrical impedance, and the application. This latter method measures the thickness of the subcutaneous fat layer that accounts for the majority of bodily fat.

Excessive body fat interferes with flexibility, endurance, temperature regulation and strength. It can lead to or exacerbate conditions such as hypertension, diabetes and heart disease.

Procedure:

1. Measurements of subcutaneous body fat are taken using skin fold calipers. Pinch the skin and underlying fat and lift away from the muscle below. Place the open jaws of the caliper over the skin fold and gently close. Your instructor will demonstrate the proper way to record skinfold measurements. Record the measurement in millimeters.

2. Males should obtain two measurements, one each from the anterior mid thigh *(a)* and one from the subscapular region *(b)*. Females should also obtain two measurements, one each from the suprailiac region *(c)* (lateral waist) just above the crest of the hip bone and one from the tricep region *(d)*. All measurements should be taken from the same side of the body.

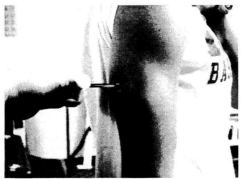

Tricep Skinfold Measurement

Males

Thigh skinfold measurement

Subscapular skinfold measurement

Females

Supriliac skinfold measurement

Tricep skinfold measurement

3. Using the nomogram charts below, mark the measurements on the respective lines, and connect the two measurement points with a straight line. The point where the line intersects the middle scale will indicate the body fat percentage value for that individual.

Male   Female

Data Sheet

Body Fat Percentage

ACTIVITY 5

Name:_____

Course Section:_____   **Date:** _____

	Measured Value	Expected Value
Body Fat Percentage by Skinfold		

Evaluation and Conclusion:

Describe your body fat percentage relative to the expected normal values.

Evaluating Body Fat Distribution

Waist-to-Hip Ratio:

The waist-to-hip ratio is an indicator of the body fat distribution pattern. General patterns can be either android, apple-like or thicker around the waise, or gynoid, pear-like or thicker on the hips, buttocks and thighs.

$$\text{ratio} = \frac{\text{waist measurement (in or cm)}}{\text{hip measurement (in or cm)}}$$

Procedure:
1. Determine, in either inches or centimeters, the circumference around the waist and the circumference around the hips.
   -The measurements should be made with a flexible measuring tape on the bare skin.
   -The waist measurement should be made at the level of the umbilicus (belly button).
   -The hip measurement should be made at several different points around the buttocks and the largest measurement should be used in calculating the ratio.

2. Divide the waist measurement by the hip measurement: $\dfrac{\text{waist (in or cm)}}{\text{hips (in or cm)}}$

Personal Body Fat Distribution Pattern =

In females, the average ratio is between 0.70 and 0.90 (gynoid pattern). In males, the average lies between 0.90 and 1.00 (android pattern).

Data Sheet

Body Fat Distribution

Name:_____

Course Section:_____   **Date:** _____

	Measured Value	Expected Value
Waist-to-Hip Ratio		
Body Fat Distribution Pattern		

Evaluation and Conclusion:
Describe the nature and implications of any variation in your waist-to-hip ratio from the range designated as normal for your gender.

ACTIVITY 7

Somatotype Analysis

The Heath-Carter Somatotype Rating Method serves as a widely accepted method of describing body type and has been used extensively in classifying the body types of athletes in a variety of sports. The somatotype rating method provides a three numeral description of three important components of body build. The first numeral in the rating scale provides an indicator of the degree of endomorphy or body fat content, the second provides an indicator of mesomorphy or musculoskeletal development and the third provides a measure of ectomorphy or linearity of the body.

Procedure:

To perform a somatotype assessment, one must use the Heath-Carter Somatotype Rating Form on which will be recorded various body measurements and subsequent calculations.

1. To determine the Endomorphic Component Value, the first number in the Somatotype Score:

    a.   using skinfold calipers, measure the tricep(t), suprailiac (si) and subscapular (ss) skinfold measurements.

        tricep skinfold   = [   ]

        suprailiac skinfold = [   ]

        subscapular skinfold = [   ]

    b.   determine the sum of the three skinfold measurements:

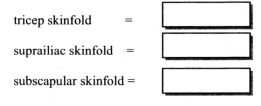

$$X = t + si + ss$$

$$X = \quad [\quad\quad\quad]$$

    c.   using the value of X form above, determine the Endomorphic Component Value using the following table:

If the value of X =	Then the Endomorphic Component Value is
0-19	1
20-27	2
28-36	3
37-46	4
47-59	5
60-73	6
74+	7

Endomorphic Component Value = [   ]

2. To determine the Mesomorphic Component Value, the middle number in the Somatotype Score:

   a.   determine the following values by measurement:

height (in) =

ht (height)

humerus biepicondylar distance at elbow (cm) =

H

femur biepicondylar distance at knee (cm) =

F

bicep circumference, fully flexed (cm) =

ac

tricep skinfold (mm)

ts

calf skinfold (mm)

cs

Humerus biepicondylar width

   b.   determine the muscle value of the arm by substracting the tricep skinfold from the bicep cicrcumference. The tricep skinfold must first be converted into cm from mm.

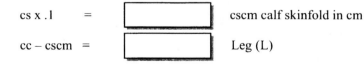

ts x .1   =   tscm   tricep skinfold in cm

ac – tscm   =   Arm (A)

   c.   Determine the muscle value of the leg by subtracting the calf skinfold from the calf circumference. The calf skinfold must first be converted into cm from mm.

cs x .1   =   cscm calf skinfold in cm

cc – cscm =   Leg (L)

d. Using the values determined above for height (ht), humerus biepicondylar distance (H), femur biepicondylar distance (F), muscle value of the arm (A) and muscle value of the leg (L), select and record the corresponding column number from the table below.

	1	2	3	4	5	6	7	8	9	10	11	12	13	14	15	16	17	18	19
ht	53	55	57	59	61	63	65	67	69	71	73	75	77	79	81	83	85	87	89
H	5.	5.2	5.4	5.6	5.8	6.0	6.2	6.4	6.6	6.8	7.	7.2	7.4	7.6	7.8	8.	8.2	8.4	8.6
F	7.1	7.4	7.7	8	8.3	8.6	8.9	9.2	9.5	9.8	10.	10.3	10.6	10.9	11.2	11.5	11.8	12.1	12.4
A	22	23	24	25	26	27	28	29	30	31	32	33	34	35	36	37	38	39	40
L	27	28	29	30	31	32	33	34	35	36	37	38	39	40	41	42	43	44	45

from the table above, determine the column number that best corresponds with your height in inches (ht)

from the table above determine the column number that best corresponds with your humerus biepicondylar distance (H)

from the table above determine the column number that best corresponds with your femur biepicondylar distance (F)

from the table above determine the column number that best corresponds with your arm muscle measurement (A)

from the table above determine the column number that best corresponds with your leg muscle measurement (L)

e. calculate the mean of the column values for H, F, A and L. For example if H was 7 its column number is 11. If F is 9.5, its column number is 9. If A is 33, its column number is 12. If L is 39, its column number is 13. The average would then be

$$(11 + 9 + 12 + 13) / 4 = 11.3$$

f. Calculate the difference between the average value calculated in e and the height (ht) column. For example, if the height is 5'9" (69") the column number is 9. The difference between the average in e (11.3) and the height column (9) is:

$$11.3 - 9 = 2.3$$

g. The Mesomorphic Component Value is determined by adding the number calculated above in step f, to 4.

$$4 + 2.3 = 6.3$$

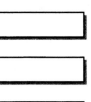

(round this number off to a whole number, in this example, to 6)

Mesomorphic Component Value =

3. To determine the Ectomorphic Component Score:

    a.   Divide your height in centimeters by the cubed root of your weight in kilograms:

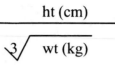

$$\frac{\text{ht (cm)}}{\sqrt[3]{\text{wt (kg)}}}$$

    b.   Using the value calculated in step 3a above, determine the Ectomorphic Component Score from the table below:

If the value from 3a is:	The Ectomorphic Component Value is
0 – 12.3	1
12.4 – 12.8	2
12.9 – 13.7	3
13.8 – 14.7	4
14.8 – 15.6	5
15.7 – 16.4	6
16.5+	7

Ectomorphic Component Score = ☐

Data Sheet

Somatotype Analysis

Name:_____

Course Section:_____ **Date:** _____

Endomorphy Component Value

Mesomorphy Component Value

Ectomorphy Component Value

Evaluation and Conclusion:
Describe, in words, your personal somatotype.

Is your somatotype consistent with the expectations for your gender?

By looking at members of your immediate family and taking into account your personal exercise of athletic activites, do you believe that your somatotype is more related to genetics or to lifestyle?

ACTIVITY 8

Evaluating Metabolic Rate and Energy Requirement

Normal daily activities such as breathing, heart beat and nerve conduction are energy requiring processes. The rate at which the body utilizes energy to perform these functions is known as the Basal Metabolic Rate (BMR) and is often expressed in Calories, a unit of heat energy. Additional activities also add to the daily energy demand and may include normal activities at work, at home and during recreation.

The following worksheet will allow you to calculate your daily metabolic energy requirements.

Procedure

1. Determine your body weight, in pounds, without clothing.   `136` lbs

2. Determine your standing height, in inches, without shoes.   `5'4"` inches

3. Factor the values above into one of the following formulas:

   women : BMR = 655 + (4.36 x weight in lbs.) + (4.32 x height in in.) – (4.7 x age in yrs)

   men: BMR = 66 + (6.22 x weight in lbs.) + (12.7 x height in in.) – (6.8 x age in yrs)

4.   **Personal daily BMR =** [   ] **kcal/day**

5. Determine the total daily Calorie expenditure by adding to the BMR the energy required for normal daily activities. Multiply the BMR value determined above by the appropriate daily activity factor shown below to derive the total daily energy requirement.

Typical Activity Level	Activity Factor
Light (normal activities)	1.3
Moderate (exercise 3-4 times/wk)	1.4
Very Active (exercise more than 4x / wk)	1.6
Extreme (exercise daily for 1 hr or more)	1.8

Daily BMR   x   **Daily Activity Factor**   =   **Daily Energy Requirement**

$$\boxed{} \times \boxed{} = \boxed{} \text{ kcal/day}$$

Data Sheet

Metabolic Rate and Energy Requirement

ACTIVITY 8

Name:_____

Course Section:_____ Date: _____

Data Measurement

Body weight (lbs)

Body height (inches)

BMR Calculation

Personal Daily Basal Metabolic Rate

Determine Activity Level Factor

Activity level Factor

Daily Energy Requirement Calculation

Personal Daily Energy Requirement

Evaluation and Conclusion:

Using the data obtained above and assuming no change in your current diet, determine the potential amount of weight loss that could be achieved by increasing your daily activity by one level.

ACTIVITY 9

Evaluating Flexibility

Flexibility pertains to the ability to have free movement of the limbs and trunk through normal ranges of motion. Flexibility is important in allowing an individual to participate in a number of exercise, athletic and everyday activities. Flexibility may become limited as tendons and ligaments loose their elasticity, muscles shorten or joint surfaces become irregular. Proper stretching, before and after exercise can increase and maintain flexibility.

Back and Trunk Flexibility:

One measure of overall flexibility is the ***Sit-and-Reach Test*** which measures flexibility of the trunk.

Sit-and-Reach Test:

Procedure: (requires a yardstick)

1. Place a piece of tape or draw a line on the floor in a clear, level area. The line should be at least 12 inches long.

2. Sit on the floor, legs extended, feet six inches apart with heels on the near edge of the line. Place the yardstick between your legs, perpendicular to the line with the 15" mark on the near edge of the line and the 1" mark closest to your body as shown below.

3. With a slow, steady movement, reach forward with both hands along the yardstick as far as possible without bending your knees. Hold the farthest position, touching the yardstick, for 3 seconds. Record the marking, in inches, of the farthest point reached. Repeat three times and take the best of the three readings. Compare with the table below.

Interpretation of the Sit-and-Reach Test

	Poor	Fair	Average	Good	Excellent
Male	< 9"	9-11"	12-14"	15-20"	>20"
Female	<12"	12-15"	16-20"	21-23"	>23

Back Arch Test:

The Back Arch Test provides an indication of the flexibility of the trunk (torso) by measuring the range of extension.

<u>Procedure:</u>

1. Lie on your stomach with your arms alongside your body.

2. Pressing your pelvis down to the floor, raise your head, neck and chest off the floor as high as possible and hold for 3 seconds.

3. Measure the distance from the floor to your chin and compare with the table below.

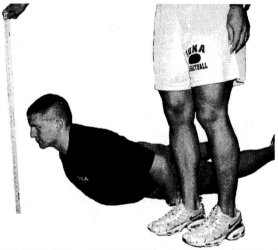

	Poor	Fair	Average	Good	Excellent
Male	<11"	12-15"	15-17"	17-19"	>20"
Female	<12"	13-16"	17-19"	20-23"	>24"

Hip Flexibility:

<u>Procedure:</u>

Lie on your back with your head on the floor, arms at your sides and palms touching the floor. Raise your knees up to your chest and determine the angle between your thigh and your abdomen. The angle will determine your score. Although it is best to measure the angle with a joint motion gauge, approximate measurements can be obtained by estimation.

Interpretation *of Hip Flexibility*

	Poor	Fair	Average	Good	Excellent
Male& Female	60°	55°	50°	45°	40°

Shoulder Flexibility:

Procedure:

Lie on your stomach with your chin touching the floor, arms outstretched in front of you and hands separated by a shoulders width distance. Grasp a rod or broom handle in your hands and lift it off the floor in front of you as high as possible. Do not lift your chin off the floor and do not bend your wrists or elbows. The distance, in inches, that the stick is lifted off the floor will determine your score.

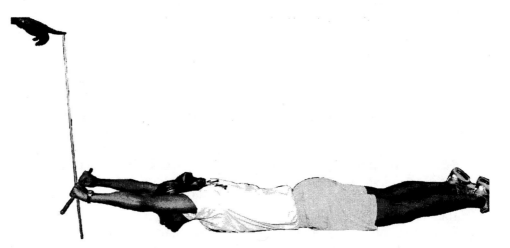

Interpretation of Shoulder Flexibility Test

	Poor	Fair	Average	Good	Excellent
Male	<10"	11-15"	16-20"	21-24"	>24"
Female	<12"	12-16"	17-21"	22-25"	>25"

Groin Flexibility:

The following activity will measure flexibility of the groin region.

1. Sitting on the floor, bend your knees so as to bring your thighs up against your chest with your legs held together and the soles of your feet placed flat on the floor in front of you.
2. Drop your knees to the sides and bring the soles of your feet together in front of you. Using just your leg muscles, press your knees as far down as possible.
3. Continuing to press your knees down towards the sides, grasp your feet with both hands and pull them towards your body as close as possible.
4. Measure the distance between your heels and your groin. Compare the result with the table below.

Groin Flexibility					
Measured Distance	25 cm	20 cm	15 cm	10 cm	5 cm
Flexibility Rating	Poor	Fair	Average	Good	Excellent

Your Distance [   ]   Your Rating [   ]

Rotational Flexibility:

The following activity will measure the rotational flexibility of the trunk and pectoral girdle.

1. Place a vertical line on a flat wall using a 12" piece of masking tape.
2. Stand approximately 18" away from the wall, with your back facing the wall, and your feet approximately shoulder width apart. Position yourself so that the midline axis of your body should be in line with the tape mark.
3. Extending your arms straight out in front of you, hands together, rotate your body towards the right, from the waist, and touch the wall at the farthest point that your rotation will allow you to reach. Be sure that your feet remain flat on the floor and facing away from the wall and your hands remain together. Mark this point on the wall with another small piece of tape.
4. Measure the distance between this point and the original tape line. If you did not reach the original line, indicate the distance as a negative number. If you passed the original line, indicate the distance as a positive number.
5. Repeat steps 2-4 rotating to the left.
6. Compare your results with the table below.

Trunk Rotational Flexibility					
Measured Distance	≤ 0 cm	5 cm	10 cm	15 cm	20 cm
Flexibility Rating	Poor	Fair	Average	Very Good	Excellent

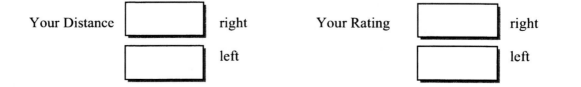

Your Distance [   ] right   Your Rating [   ] right

[   ] left   [   ] left

Data Sheet

Evaluating Flexibility

ACTIVITY 9

Name:_____

Course Section:_____ Date: _____

	Observed Value	Expected Value
Sit-and-Reach Distance		
Back Arch		
Hip Flexibility		
Shoulder Flexibility		
Groin Flexibility		
Rotational Flexibility		

Evaluation and Conclusion:

Evaluate the difference, if any, between the observed value (measured in lab) and the expected value (normal expectation) for each of the flexibility measurements. What might account for any difference? What type of exercise might improve flexibility?

ACTIVITY 10

Kraus-Weber Back Fitness

The muscles of the back play an important role in many types of exercise and sport activities. A sufficient degree of strength is required for maximal activity and to reduce the incidence of back injury. The Kraus-Weber Tests is a good indicator of the strength of the musculature of the back.

Procedure:

ACTIVITY	**SCORE**

1. Lie flat on your back with hands clasped behind your head. Lift both legs together, off the floor at an angle of 30° and attempt to hold for 10 seconds. Score 1 point for each second up to 10.

2. Remaining in the same position as above, have someone hold your feet and attempt to perform a full sit-up. Score 10 points for a full sit-up, 5 points for a partial sit-up.

3. Repeat activity 2, but this time with knees bent. Score as in activity 2 above.

4. Lie on your stomach, legs extended and hands clasped behind your neck. Raise your head, shoulders and trunk off the floor and attempt to hold for 10 sec. Score 1 point for each second up to 10.

5. Remaining in the same position as in 4, place your hand under your chin. Raise your feet and legs (from the hips) the floor and attempt to hold for 10 seconds. Score as above in 4.

6. Stand erect. Bend over at the waist and attempt to touch the floor at your toes. Measure the distance, in inches, from your fingertips to the floor. The score is calculated as 10 minus the number of inches measured to a low of 0.

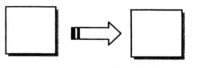

Total of scores
1 – 6

Total Kraus-Weber Score (sum of 1+2+3+4+5+ 6)

Results:

Enter your results in the box below.

	Kraus-Weber Point value
Actual	
Expected	

Interpretation of Kraus-Weber Score

Total Score	Back Fitness Level
60	Excellent
50-60	Good
40-50	Acceptable
Below 40	Poor

Data Sheet

Kraus-Weber Back Fitness

ACTIVITY 10

Name:_____

Course Section:_____ **Date:** _____

Enter your total Kraus-Weber Back Fitness Score

Evaluation and Conclusion:

Identify any areas of the test in which you scored less than 10 and describe how this may adversely affect overall back fitness.

ACTIVITY 11

Muscle Strength

Muscular strength is important not only for exercise and athletics but for everyday tasks as well. Opening a jar, changing a tire or carrying heavy articles all require muscular strength as do weight lifting, football or figure skating. Proper muscle fitness is also necessary to maintain proper posture and to prevent hazardous movements of joints. Muscular strength and power are primarily related to fast-twitch muscle fiber diameter. Muscle endurance is largely a function of the biochemical adaptation of slow-twitch fibers.

STRENGTH
Forearm Strength by Dynamometer:

While measurement of the strength of all the major muscle groups is often impractical, an adequate measure of overall muscle strength may be obtained by measuring *grip strength*.

Procedure:

To isolate the forearm muscles responsible for grip strength, hold the grip tester (hand dynamometer) in one hand with the forearm parallel to the floor. Squeeze as hard as possible and record the grip strength (in kilograms or pounds of force). Repeat three times, resting for one minute between attempts, and average the three measurements. Perform the test with right and left hands.

Results:

Record your results in the box below.

	Dynamometer Reading of Maximum Strength	
	Right Hand (kg or lbs)	Left Hand (kg or lbs)
Trial # 1		
Trial # 2		
Trial # 3		
Average Strength		
Expected Strength		

Table 1. Grip Strength Interpretation by Hand Dynamometer

	Male	Measured 1-RM (lbs)				
Test	Age Group	Poor	Fair	Average	Good	Excellent
Grip Strength *(dynamometer)*	<30 yrs	100	113	122	131	144
	30-50 yrs	91	102	110	118	129
	>50 yrs	80	90	97	104	114

	Female	Measured 1-RM (lbs)				
Test	Age Group	Poor	Fair	Average	Good	Excellent
Grip Strength *(dynamometer)*	<30 yrs	55	63	68	73	81
	30-50 yrs	46	56	61	66	73
	>50 yrs	44	50	54	58	64

Bicep, Upper Body, and Leg Strength by 1-RM:

A good indicator of the strength of an isolated muscle or muscle group is the one repetition maximum (1-RM). This is the maximum weight which can be lifted just once.

Procedure:

Start out by lifting a weight which can be handled comfortably. If the weight can be lifted more than once, add more weight. Continue adding weight until it is possible to correctly lift the weight only once, not twice successively. This weight is the 1-RM. ***Be careful to do this only with a partner***. The Table 1 lists the optimal 1-RM values for acceptable physical fitness. Perform the following activities to measure the strength of the various muscle groups.

Bicep Strength: Standing Barbell Curl
Upper Body Strength: Reclining Bench Press
Leg Strength: Seated Leg Press or Leg Extension

Results:

Record your results in the box below.

	1-RM value in lbs		
	Bicep Curl	Bench Press	Leg Squat
Trial # 1			
Trial # 2			
Trial # 3			
Average Strength			
Expected Strength			

Table 2. 1-RM Strength Interpretation

		Measured 1-RM (in lbs) as Percent of Total Body Weight				
		Poor	Fair	Average	Very Good	Excellent
Bench Press	Male	.6	.8	1.1	1.2	1.4
	Female	.3	.4	.6	.7	.9
Leg Press	Male	1.3	1.7	2	2.4	2.8
	Female	1.1	1.5	1.9	2.2	2.5
Leg Extension	Male	.6	.75	.9	1.1	1.25
	Female	.6	.7	.8	.9	1
Bicep Curl (barbell)	Male	.3	.36	.45	.55	.65
	Female	.2	.25	.32	.38	.45

Interpreting the table:

According to Table 1, above, a female who can bench press a weight that is only 30% of her body weight (.3) would rate as **poor** on this test. For a 100 lb. female, that would equate to a bench press 1-RM of 30 lbs (100 lbs x .3 = 30). Should a 100 lb female be able to achieve a 1-RM bench press of 70 lbs, her strength assessment would be **very good** (100 x .7 = 70).

For a 150 male, an average or acceptable 1-RM for the bicep curl would be about 68 lbs. (150 lbs x .45 = 67.5 lbs.)

225

Data Sheet

Muscle Strength

Name:_____

Course Section:_____ **Date:** _____

	Measured Value	Expected Value
Forearm Grip Strength		
Bicep Strength by 1-RM		
Upper Body Strength by 1-RM		
Leg Strength by 1-RM		

Evaluation and Conclusion:
From the data obtained in this activity, evaluate the current status of your strength relative to expected values and having a balanced level of strength throughout the body.

Determining Muscle Cross-Sectional Strength

ACTIVITY 12

In part, both the absolute and maximum strength of a skeletal muscle is determined by the muscle's size. Generally, human skeletal muscle has a characteristic strength per unit volume, with larger muscles being capable of producing greater force. Utilizing the forearm grip strength that was measured in Activity 11 and the muscle cross-sectional area of the arm that will be determined here, you will be able to estimate the cross-sectional strength of muscle in kg/cm^2.

1. Enter the average grip strength measurement from Activity 11.

2. To determine the cross-sectional area of muscle within the forearm:
   a) Using a tape measure, determine the circumference of the forearm from which you measured grip strength. Measure the circumference with the forearm muscles fully flexed and at the largest point. Be sure to enter this measurement in centimeters (cm).

   b) Using skinfold calipers, determine the thickness of a dorsal forearm skinfold measurement (midway between the elbow and wrist).

   c) Enter the value obtained for the forearm circumference (above) into the following formula:

$$\text{MAAcm}^2 = \frac{(AC - \pi\ SF)^2}{4\pi} \qquad =$$

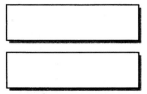

   where: MAA = muscle area of the arm (cm^2)
           AC is = circumference of the arm (cm)
           SF = skinfold measurement (mm)

3. To determine the cross-sectional strength, divide the average grip strength measurement from line 1 by the muscle cross-sectional area determined on line 4.

Length-Tension Relationship

ACTIVITY 12

When muscle is at its normal resting length (100%), there is a slight overlapping of the opposing actin filaments within each sarcomere that interferes with the action of some of the myosin cross brifges. As muscle is stretched slightly, this overlap is eliminated and muscle can contract more forcefully. If the stretch is taken too far, the actin begins to pull out from in between the myosin and the force of contraction weakens. This is all described in the length-tension curve. In this activity, we will explore the length-tension relationship.

1. Determine your baseline grip strength in accordance with the directions in Activity 11 with your hand held in a neutral position (the wrist is neither flexed nor extended.

   Enter the grip strength measurement in the neutral position. **A**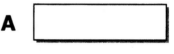

2. Repeat the grip strength measurement but, this time, do so with the wrist fully extended. In this position, the finger flexor muscles are pulled into a slightly stretched position relative to their normal resting length.

   Enter the grip strength with the wrist fully extended. **B**

3. Repeat, once again, the grip strength measurement but this time with the wrist fully flexed. In this position, the finger flexor muscles are compressed to a fractional percentage of their normal resting length.

   Enter the grip strength with the wrist fully flexed. **C**

4. Calculate the difference in grip strength from the extended wrist to the flexed wrist positions and enter the difference below.

   B - C =

ACTIVITY 12

Biomechanical Advantage

The 3rd-class lever system utilized at most of the major joints of the human skeletal system provides a mechanical disadvantage in that muscles must develop proportionally greater forces than the weight of the loads actually being moved as was discussed in Chapter 5. This, however, allows a much greater range of movement at the resistance point than is actually produced by the muscle at the effort point. In addition the speed, or velocity, of the movement at the resistance point is also enhanced, moving at a large multiple of the muscle's actual contraction velocity.

This lab activity will demonstrate this principle.

1. With your arm fully extended and hanging by your side, have your lab partner determine the length of your resting bicep muscle by palpation. (the muscle belly will be felt as a noticeable fleshy structure running almost the entire length of the arm, from axilla to elbow.

    Extended Bicep Muscle Length (cm) **A**

2. Fully flex your arm at the elbow by contracting the bicep muscle. Have your partner measure the length of the contracted bicep muscle.

    Flexed Bicep Muscle Length (cm) **B**

3. Have you partner measure the linear distance traveled by your hand as your bicep contracts and your forearm flexes.

    Linear Distance Traveled by Hand (cm) **C**

4. Determine the length by which the bicep muscle has actually shortened during the contraction by calculating the difference in length of the extended and contracted bicep muscle (A – B = D).

    Linear Distance of Bicep Movement (cm) **D**

5. Calculate the ratio of linear hand movement – to – bicep movement to determine the mechanical advantage with respect to range of motion.

    ## C / D = ratio

Data Sheet

Cross-Sectional Strength

ACTIVITY 12

Name:_____

Course Section:_____   Date: _____

	Measured Value
Average Grip Strength (kg)	
Muscle Area of the Arm (cm^2)	
Cross-Sectional Strength (kg/cm^2) (Personal)	
Cross-Sectional Strength (kg/cm^2) (Class Average)	
Cross-Sectional Strength (kg/cm^2) (Average for Females Only)	
Cross-Sectional Strength (kg/cm^2) (Average for Males Only)	

Evaluation and Conclusion:
Was there much variation between you own calculated cross-sectional strength and that of other class members? Explain.

Was there a noticeable variation between the average cross-sectional strength of males and females? Explain.

Data Sheet

Length-Tension Relationship

Name:_____

Course Section:_____   Date: _____

Grip Strength with wrist fully flexed

Grip Strength with wrist fully extended

Strength Reduction in flexed position

Evaluation and Conclusion:
Explain, using its impact on the actin and myosin interaction, the reason for the observed difference in measured grip strength when the position of the hand is changed.

Describe how this phenomenon may account for a portion of the strength deficit.

Data Sheet

Biomechanical Advantage

Name:_____

Course Section:_____   Date: _____

Linear Distance Traveled by Hand

Linear Distance Traveled by Bicep

Ratio of Hand-to-Bicep Movement

Evaluation and Conclusion:
Explain the reason why the observed phenomenon occurred.

Describe how this phenomenon may account for a portion of the strength deficit.

Evaluating Muscle Power

Power is the application of strength over time. A more powerful contraction results when the force of contraction is exerted over a shorter period of time. The speed of muscular contraction is the prime determinant of the explosiveness or power of athletic performance. Explosive performance is related to white fiber percentage whereas endurance is related primarily to red fiber percentage. The ability to perform a high vertical standing jump is directly related to the explosiveness or speed of contraction of the quadriceps (thigh) and gastrocnemius (calf) muscles.

Procedure:
A. Vertical Jump:

1. Standing with toes against a wall, feet flat on the floor and facing the wall, reach up along the wall as high as is possible with fingers extended and mark the wall (with tape if available) at the highest point which can be touched.

2. Step back one foot from the wall and, with legs together and no running start, jump as high as possible with one hand extended over your head and touch the wall. It is allowable to jump from a crouched position. Perform the jump three times and use your highest reach. The distance between the two measured points, that is between the highest point you can reach standing flat-footed and the highest point you were able to reach jumping, is your jump height score.

Jump Height Distance = ⬚ in meters or ⬚ in feet
  JH(m)   JH(ft)

3. To determine the power you were able to generate, factor your jump height distance and body weight into the following formula:

Power (kg-m/sec) = W(kg) x JH(m)   = ⬚
  where W(kg) = body weight in kg
    JH(m) = jump height in meters

Power (ft-lbs/sec) = W(lbs) x JH(ft)   = ⬚
  where   W(lbs) = body weight in pounds
    JH(ft) = jump height in feet

4. The Lewis Factor score provides another way to measure power. The Lewis Factor is calculated by the formula:

Lewis Factor Score $= 4 \times (\sqrt{JH}(ft) \times W(lbs))$

$=$

Lewis Factor Score	Horsepower	Fitness Evaluation
>1300	>2.3	Excellent power
1001 – 1300	1.8 – 2.3	above average power
701 – 1000	1.2 – 2.2	average power
<700	> 1.2	below average power

B. Horizontal Jump: Standing Long Jump:

1. Straddling a line on the floor (or a tape measure laid on the floor), with feet parallel and about shoulder-width apart, from a squatting position jump horizontally as far forward as possible landing with your feet, once again, straddling the line.

2. Measure the distance between the starting point and landing point, using the position of the toes in each case.

Horizontal Jump Distance =

3. Compare the measured value for the standing horizontal jump with the values in the table below.

	Female	Male
Excellent	> 6'4"	>8'3"
Good	5'10" – 6'4"	7'9" – 8'3"
Average	4'11" – 5'9"	6'11 – 7'8"
Fair	4'4" – 4'10"	6'1 – 6'10"
Low	0 – 4'3"	0 – 6'0"

Data Sheet

Evaluating Muscular Power

Name:_____

Course Section:_____   **Date:** _____

	Measured Value	Expected Value
Muscle Power (kg-m/sec)	☐	
Muscle Power (ft-lbs/sec)	☐	
Muscle Power (Lewis Factor)	☐	☐
Horizontal Jump Distance (in)	☐	☐

Evaluation and Conclusion:

Enter your measured values in the appropriate boxes for each of the muscle power evaluation tests. From the tables above, enter the values for the Lewis Factor and Horizontal Jump Distance for an average person.

Describe how your measured value compares with the average expected value.

What type of exercise or training program would be recommended to improve these power measurements?

Evaluating Muscular Endurance

Muscular endurance refers to the ability of a muscle to contract repeatedly over a period of time or to maintain a sustained contraction without fatigue. Muscular endurance is primarily a phenomenon of the slow-twitch fibers. Aerobic or endurance exercise will develop this potential by increasing blood supply to the muscle and producing more respiratory enzymes within the muscle. Muscle soreness following activity is usually a sign of poor muscle endurance capacity. The following tests will determine the endurance of the abdominal (rectus abdominus, internal and external obliques), upper body (pectorals and triceps) and leg (quadriceps and gastrocnemius) muscles.

Abdominal Endurance

Procedure:

Perform as many bent knee sit-ups as possible in 60 seconds. Hands should be clasped behind the neck, feet flat on the floor and held down. Sit-up and touch your elbows to your knees. Record the number of sit-ups performed in 60 seconds and use the table below to interpret the results. This is a test primarily of the rectus abdominus muscle and to some extent, the internal and external obliques.

Results:

Record your results in the box below.

	# of Consecutive Sit-ups in 60 sec.
Actual # of Sit-ups	
Expected # of Sit-ups	

Upper Body Endurance

Procedure:

Perform as many consecutive push-ups as possible (no time limit but, no resting between pus-ups). Legs should be straight back, hands separated a shoulder width apart, fingers forward and chest should touch floor. (Women should support themselves on their knees). Record the number of push-ups performed and use the table below to interpret the results. This is a test primarily of the pectoral muscles and the triceps.

Results:

Record your results in the box below.

	# of Consecutive Push-ups in 60 sec.
Actual # of Push-ups	
Expected # of Push-ups	

Biceps Endurance

Procedure:

A good test for measuring the endurance of the biceps and associate muscles is the pull-up (for males) or the flexed-arm hang (for females). For the pull-up test, grasp a chinning bar with palms facing forward. Raise the body by flexing the arms so that the chin is lifted above the level of the bar and return to a hanging position. Perform as many consecutive pull-ups as possible.

To perform the flexed-arm hang, grasp the bar as above and raise the body by flexing the arms so that the chin is lifted above the level of the bar. Hold this position for as long as possible.

Results:

Record your results in the box below.

	# of Pull-Ups	Flexed-Arm Hang Time (sec)
Actual		
Expected		

Quadriceps Endurance (Static)

Procedure:

Standing with your back flat against a wall and your feet spread apart to the width of your hips, slide down the wall until your trunk forms a 90° angle with your thighs and your thighs form a 90° angle with your lower legs (sitting position).

Support your total weight on your feet only, do not lean your back against the wall for support, only to help with balance. Determine the total number of seconds you can support your weight in this position and compare with the values on the table which follows.

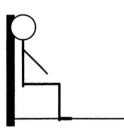

Results:

Record your results in the box below.

	Phantom Chair Time (sec)
Actual	
Expected	

Quadriceps Endurance (Dynamic)

Procedure:

From a standing position, lower yourself into a squatting position with your knees and hips each forming right angles (the same position as that held in the phantom chair test). Return to the upright position to complete one full squat.

Perform as many consecutive squats as possible until muscle fatigue prevents you form doing any more. Record the maximum number of squats performed.

Results:

Record your results in the box below.

	Consecutive Squats (#)
Actual	
Expected	

Table 1. Expected Endurance Values

Test	Male Age Group	Measured Values Poor	Fair	Average	Good	Excellent
Abdominal Endurance *(60 second sit ups)*	<30 yrs	26	33	37	47	52
	30-50 yrs	20	23	29	34	37
	>50 yrs	12	15	19	25	29
Upper Body Endurance *(# of consecutive push-ups)*	<30 yrs	8	20	38	50	55
	30-50 yrs	5	15	26	35	40
	>50 yrs	3	6	12	26	32
Bicep Endurance *(# of consecutive Pull-ups)*	<30 yrs	4	6	10	13	17
	30-50 yrs	3	5	9	11	15
	>50 yrs	2	4	7	9	11
Static Leg Endurance *(Phantom Chair time)*	<30 yrs	40	60	75	100	120
	30-50 yrs	33	54	68	90	110
	>50 yrs	26	49	60	80	96
Dynamic Leg Endurance *(# consecutive squats)*	<30 yrs	23	30	35	42	48
	30-50 yrs	15	20	25	32	39
	>50 yrs	10	12	17	25	30

Test	Female Age Group	Measured Values Poor	Fair	Average	Good	Excellent
Abdominal Endurance *(60 second sit ups)*	<30 yrs	18	27	30	43	48
	30-50 yrs	12	18	22	30	36
	>50 yrs	8	11	15	20	26
Upper Body Endurance *(# of consecutive push-ups)*	<30 yrs	3	10	26	39	45
	30-50 yrs	2	7	13	23	34
	>50 yrs	0	1	3	7	15
Bicep Endurance *(flexed arm hang time- sec)*	<30 yrs	17	21	28	35	40
	30-50 yrs	13	18	25	31	35
	>50 yrs	8	12	16	23	28
Leg Endurance *(Phantom Chair time)*	<30 yrs	25	35	45	60	70
	30-50 yrs	22	31	40	53	60
	>50 yrs	15	23	29	37	48
Dynamic Leg Endurance *(# consecutive squats)*	<30 yrs	18	22	28	35	40
	30-50 yrs	10	14	18	24	30
	>50 yrs	3	9	12	15	20

Data Sheet

Muscle Endurance

ACTIVITY 14

Name:_____

Course Section:_____   **Date:** _____

	Measured Value	Expected Value
Abdominal Endurance		
Upper Body Endurance		
Bicep Endurance		
Quadricep Endurance (Static)		
Quadricep Endurance (Dynamic)		

Evaluation and Conclusion:
Evaluate your overall muscular endurance relative to expected values.

Evaluating Core Musculature Fitness

ACTIVITY 15

The body's core musculature, commonly referred to simply as "the core", is an important group of muscles essential for generating power. Simply put, the core includes many of the major muscles located between the bottom of the sternum and the top of the knees. These core muscles are engaged at some level during all exercises, even when the exercise is being performed at distances away from your core; most importantly, they help support and maintain proper posture. Some types of exercises require you to use your core to maintain your posture in one position without movement. These types of exercises are commonly referred to as *static core exercise.* Exercises that demand gross movements such as the squat, deadlift and even bicep curls, rely on precise interactions between the different core muscle groups. These types of exercises are known as *dynamic core exercises.*

<u>Procedure</u>:

A. Evaluating Static Core Function:

1. Move into the basic push-up position with the legs extended, back flat, but resting on your elbows and forearms. This is called the *plank position*. Hold this position for 60 seconds.

2. Continuing to hold this position, lift your right arm off the ground and hold for 15 seconds. Return for resting on both forearms.

3. Continuing to hold this position, lift your left arm off the ground and hold for 15 seconds.

   Return for resting on both forearms.

4. Continuing to hold this position, lift your right leg off the ground and hold for 15 seconds. Return for resting on both feet.

5. Continuing to hold this position, lift your left leg off the ground and hold for 15 seconds.

   Return for resting on both feet.

6. Maintain the basic position for an additional 30 seconds.

Results:
Record your results in the box below.

Procedure	Measured Value	Expected Value
1. Standard Plank		60 seconds
2. Plank with Right Arm Raised		15 seconds
3. Plank with Left Arm Raised		15 seconds
4. Plank with Right Leg Raised		15 seconds
5. Plank with Left Leg Raised		15 seconds
6. Standard Plank		30 seconds

B. Evaluating Dynamic Core Function:

1. Using the proper stability ball for your size, Lie face down on the ball and support yourself with your hands and feet. Elevate your legs so only your waist is on the ball and your hands are on the floor. Now, walk out using your hands so that the ball rolls down to your ankles keeping your feet together. Next, walk back using your hands until the ball reaches your waist again keeping your feet together. When you reach the staring position, do not let your feet touch the floor. Perform this exercise for 10 repetitions.

2. Using the proper stability ball for your size, sit on the ball and grab two dumbbells to perform shoulder presses. While holding both of the dumbbells in front of you at shoulder height, extend one leg straight out in front of you while the other leg remains securely on the floor. Now, press the weight over head with the opposite shoulder of the extended leg. Perform this exercise for 10 repetitions.

Results:
Record your results in the box below.

Proceedure	Measured Value	Expected Value
1. Stability Ball Walk		10 repetitions
2. Stability Ball Shoulder Press		10 repetitions

Data Sheet

Core Muscle Fitness

Name:_____

Course Section: _____ Date:_____

Evaluation and Conclusion:

Evaluate your overall core muscle strength and endurance relative to the expected values.

What are the core muscles being utilized during these activities?

ACTIVITY 16

Posture Analysis

Each student has been provided with a copy of their personal posture analysis. All observations will be made from the analysis sheets.

In this exercise you will determine the presence of any tilt or distance deviation from the sternal midline plane in your posture from the frontal view analysis.

1. On the frontal view, relative to a point on the sternal midline, determine whether there is a deviation from the horizontal of the right (r) vs. left (l) acromion process, right and left elbow, right and left iliac crest, right and left knee, and right and left ankle. Also, determine whether there is a right or left tilt to the head relative to the sternal midline plane. Enter these observations on the Posture Analysis data sheet.

2. In addition, and also on the frontal view, determine whether there is a variation in the distance of each of these right and left-side body structures from the sternal midline plane.

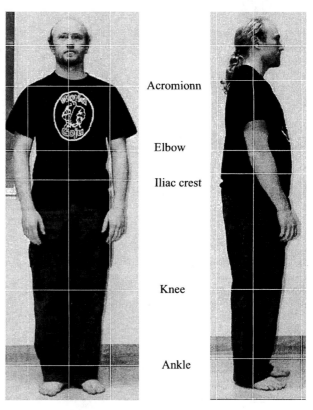

Acromionn

Elbow

Iliac crest

Knee

Ankle

In this portion of the exercise you will determine the presence of any postural deviation from the acromial plane using the lateral view analysis.

1. On the lateral view, the ear, elbow, iliac crest, knee, and ankle should all lie on a plane defined by a line drawn through the center of the

2. Enter onto the data sheet any deviation, anterior (A) or posterior (P) from this acromion plane.

ACTIVITY 16

Posture Analysis

Name:_____

Course Section:_____ Date: _____

	Observed	Expected
Head (Anterior)		
Head (Lateral)		
Shoulders (Anterior)		
Shoulders (lateral)		
Pelvis (Anterior)		
Pelvis (Lateral)		
Knees (Anterior)		
Knees (Lateral)		

Evaluation and Conclusion:

Evaluate the difference, if any, between the observed value (measured in lab) and the expected value (normal expectation) for each of the flexibility measurements. What might account for any difference?

Evaluating Proprioception   ACTIVITY 17

The ability to maintain static equilibrium (stationary balance) requires a high degree of coordination between the nervous and musculoskeletal systems. Information about the position of the body and it movement is relayed to the brain and spinal cord by the receptors of the **visual system** (*retina*), **cutaneous receptors** (*pressure receptors on the sole of the feet*), **proprioceptors** (*muscle spindle fibers, Golgi tendon organs, joint capsule mechanoreceptors*), and **central vestibular sensors** (*utricle, saccule, and semicircular canals*). This information is used to adjust muscular contractions to maintain a stable position. The following series of activities will help to assess the proprioceptive system.

Proprioceptive Finger-to-Nose Test
1. With the subject's eyes closed, the examiner lightly touches one of the subjects fingers on the right hand and asks the subject to touch that finger to the subject's own nose. This action is repeated three times.
2. The examiner notes the subject's success for each of the three tests as a (+) or (-) and summarizes the score for each hand as 3/3 (3 successes out of three attempts) 2/3, 1/3 or 0/3.
3. The test is repeated with the left hand.

	Test 1	Test 2	Test 3	Summary Score
Result Right				
Result Left				

Proprioceptive Movement Test
1. With the subject's eyes closed, the examiner moves the subject's middle finger on the right hand up or down, grasping the finger lightly on the sides (thereby avoiding the most sensitive pressure receptors). Test is repeated three times with the examiner randomly selecting the direction of movement.
2. The examiner notes the subject's success for each of the three tests as a (+) or (-) and summarizes the score for each hand as 3/3 (3 successes out of three attempts) 2/3, 1/3 or 0/3.
3. The test is repeated with the left hand.

	Test 1	Test 2	Test 3	Summary Score
Result Right				
Result Left				

Proprioceptive Space Test
1. With the subject's eyes closed, the examiner places the subject's right hand in a random selected position either in front or at the side, at a selected height, and degree of rotation. The subject is instructed to keep the hand in this position.
2. The examiner then asks the subject to imitate this position with the opposite hand.
3. The test is repeated three times, using different positions. The examiner notes the subject's success for each of the three tests as a (+) or (-) and summarizes the score for each hand as 3/3 (3 successes out of three attempts) 2/3, 1/3 or 0/3.
4. The test is repeated with the left hand.

	Test 1	Test 2	Test 3	Summary Score
Result Right				
Result Left				

Past-pointing Test

1. Examiner and subject face eachother standing approximately 2 feet apart.
2. Examiner holds up two index fingers, holding them approximately 6" apart at shoulder height and approximately 18" in front the subject.
3. Subject is asked to lift arms overhead and bring them down, hands facing palm down, to touch the examiners index fingers, once with each hand.
4. With eyes closed, the subject repeats this motion.
5. Record subjects success at repeating with eyes closed.

	Test 1	Test 2	Test 3	Summary Score
Result Right				
Result Left				

(adopted from The University of West Alabama, Athletic Training and Sports Medicine Center, Proprioception Tests)

To evaluate static equilibrium (balance)

The Stork Stand Test

1. Standing comfortably on both feet, without shoes, first place your hands on your hips and at your sides.
2. Lift your right leg and place your right foot against your lower left thigh so that your toes are resting against your lest kneecap.
3. At the direction of your partner, keeping your right foot raised and placed against your left knee, raise the heel of your left foot so that your are standing, balanced, on the toes of your left foot. Your partner will begin timing as soon as you are elevated onto your left toes.
4. Maintain this position for as long as possible without letting your left heel touch the floor and without removing your right foot from its position on your left knee.
5. Record the length of time that you are able to maintain this position.
6. Repeat steps 1-5 for the opposite leg.

Excellent	Above Average	Average	Below Average	Poor
> 50 sec	40 – 49 sec	26 – 39 sec	11 – 25 sec	< 11 sec

Your Stork Stand Test Time = [   ]

Stork Stand Test Position

Data Sheet

Proprioception Tests

Name:_____

Course Section: _____   Date:_____

Summary Score

R / L

Proprioceptive Finger-to-Nose Test

Proprioceptive Movement Test

Proprioceptive Space test

Past-pointing Test

Stork Stand Test   seconds

Describe the results obtained relative to expected values (3/3 is expected for the proprioceptive and past pointing tests, the "average" value is expected for the stork stand test. Explain what elements of the nervous system may contribute to any observed deficit.

Evaluating Reaction Response Time | ACTIVITY 18

Many sport and exercise activities require the ability to process sensory information and to integrate the appropriate motor response in as short a time as possible.

The following worksheet will allow you to calculate your daily metabolic energy requirements.

Procedure

1. Rest your arm on a table so that it is bent at the elbow at a 90° angle and your hand extends over the edge.

2. A partner will hold a meter stick ruler from above your seated position so that the lower end (the 10 cm mark) is positioned between your thumb and index finger as they protrude off the end of the table. Keep your fingers separated so that they do not touch the ruler but, closely enclose it.

4. Your partner will determine a time when the ruler is to be dropped, without your prior knowledge, so that it falls straight down and passes between your fingers. As soon as you detect the ruler beginning to fall, you will attempt to catch it between your fingers as quickly as possible. The quicker your reaction time, the shorter the distance the ruler will fall before you catch and stop it.

5. Your reaction time (t) can be determined by the following equation or by using the table below:

$$t = \sqrt{2y/g}$$

where t = reaction time

         y = distance in cm of fall

         g = acceleration due to gravity (980 cm/sec^2)

Distance of Fall (cm)	Reaction Time (milliseconds)
5	100 ms
10	140 ms
15	170 ms
20	200 ms
25	230 ms
30	260 ms
40	320 ms

6. Repeat the exercise three times and use your average reaction response time score.

Data Sheet

Evaluating Reaction Response Time

ACTIVITY 18

Name:_____

Course Section:_____ Date: _____

Data Measurement

	Distance of Fall (cm)	Reaction Time (ms)
Trial 1		
Trial 2		
Trial 3		
Your Average		
Class Average		

Evaluation and Conclusion:

Compare your measured reaction time with that of the class average. Describe the anatomic structures and physiologic processes that are likely to influence reaction time.

ACTIVITY 19

Evaluating Respiratory Fitness

Cooper Twelve-Minute Run:

The VO_{2max}, the ability of the body to deliver oxygen to the muscles, is the limiting factor in endurance activities and is considered by some to be the best overall indicator of physical fitness. The normal procedure for assessing the VO_{2max} requires the use of sophisticated instrumentation in a laboratory setting. A substitute test, which provides results comparable to the laboratory test, is the Cooper Twelve-Minute Run (developed by Dr. Kenneth Cooper and adapted by Dr. Bud Getchell)

Procedure:

Perform the test on a hard, level running surface. After warm-up and stretching, begin a timed, twelve-minute run at as fast a pace as can be maintained. Try to avoid periods of sprinting and slow jogging. Stop running after twelve minutes and determine the distance covered. The distance covered in twelve minutes will determine your VO_{2max}.

Interpretation of Cooper Twelve-Minute Run

Distance covered in 12 minutes	VO_{2max} (ml/kg/min) male	female
1.50 (miles)	<45	<40
1.60	47	44
1.70	49	47
1.80	52	51
1.90	56	56
2.00	59	58
2.10	63	
2.25	68	

Heller Institute/Queens College Test:

An alternative test to estimate VO_{2max} using a step-up bench and a stopwatch is the the Heller Institute Test for males and the Queens College Test for females. The modified test below represents a synthesis of these two tests.

Procedure:

Step up and down on a 15' bench or platform making 25 complete ascents/descents per minute in a four count sequence (left up - right up - left down - right down). Males will continue stepping for six minutes and females three minutes.

After completing the exercise, remain standing and count your pulse for 15 seconds beginning 5 seconds after the exercise stepping is finished (ie. take pulse from 5 to 20 seconds after exercise).

Evaluate the score in the table below.

Interpretation for Males (Heller Test)

Pulse count (5 - 20 sec)	Estimated VO_{2max} (ml/kg/min)	Astrand Classification of Fitness
>39	<39	poor
38 - 39	39 - 43	low
35 - 37	44 - 51	average
32 - 34	52 - 56	good
<32	>56	high

Interpretation for Females (Queens College Test)

Pulse count (5 - 20 sec)	Estimated VO_{2max} (ml/kg/min)	Astrand Classification of Fitness
>50	<28	poor
43 - 49	29 - 34	low
31 - 42	35 - 43	average
25 - 30	44 - 48	good
<25	>48	high

Alternatively, the following formulae can be used to calculate VO_{2max} from the pulse rate obtained immediately after performing the stepping activity:

Women: $VO_{2max} = 65.81 - (0.185 \times \text{heart rate in beats/minute})$

Men: $VO_{2max} = 111.33 - (0.42 \times \text{heart rate in beats/minute})$

Assessing Vital Capacity

The vital capacity provides a good indicator of the condition of the lungs and respiratory muscles (primarily the diaphragm and intercostals). Measurement of vital capacity requires the use of a special apparatus which is available in many forms, ranging from sophisticated electronic recording equipment to simple and inexpensive calibrated balloons.

Procedure:

To measure the vital capacity one must first inhale as deeply as possible, filling the lungs with as much air as possible. Now, exhale into the measuring device as forcefully as possible emptying the lungs of as much air as possible. Depending on the device used, read the vital capacity value.

Compare your measured vital capacity with your expected vital capacity.

To determine what your vital capacity should be, take you height (in cm), "H", and age (in years), "A", and use them in the following equations.

Females   Vital Capacity =((0.041)H - (0.018)A - 2.69)) x 1000

Males   Vital Capacity =((0.052)H - (0.022)A - 3.60)) x 1000

Vital Capacity = [   ]

Assessing Respiratory Reserve

Heymer Test of Respiratory Reserve

The test of respiratory reserve will give an indication of the functional reserve capacity of your respiratory system.

Procedure
The test is performed in the standing position.

1. Take five deep breaths, performing a maximal inhalation followed by a forced, maximal exhalation.

2. Perform a third maximal inhalation and hold your breath for as long as possible, recording the total time for which your breath can be held..

Average Values	Male 20-30 yrs	Female 20-30 yrs
	50-70 sec	50-60 sec

Your Value =

Data Sheet
Respiratory Fitness

Name:_____

Course Section:_____   Date: _____

	Measured Value	Expected Value
VO$_{2max}$ (ml/kg/min)		
Vital Capacity (ml)		
Respiratory Reserve (sec)		

Evaluation and Conclusion:

Write a brief assessment of your current state of respiratory fitness as measured by VO$_{2max}$ and Vital Capacity. Comment on what anatomic structures and what physiologic processes may be involved in contributing to your current status.

Evaluating Cardiovascular Fitness

ACTIVITY 20

One of the most important measures of overall physical fitness is the ability of the cardiovascular and respiratory systems to provide working muscles with oxygen and nutrients over a prolonged period of time (Cardiorespiratory Endurance CRE). The **_Modified Harvard Step Test_** and calculation of CRE or recovery time are two ways of measuring CRE. Both involve stepping up and down on a 16" - 20" step at a rapid pace for 3 to 5 minutes. Both tests are concerned with measuring the extent to which the heart must speed up to supply the exercising muscles and the time required to return to normal.

Procedure: (requires an accurate stopwatch)

1. Stand in front of a bench or step of suitable height. Step up with the right foot and then down, up with the left foot and then down. Continue stepping, alternating feet with each step, at the rate of 30 steps per minute (1 step every 2 seconds). Continue for three minutes straight or until it is no longer possible.

Person's Height	Step Height
less than 5 ft	12 in
5' to 5'3"	14 in
4" to 5'9"	16 in
5'10" to 6'0"	18 in
over 6'0"	20 in

2. Sit down and record the pulse for 30 seconds at the following intervals; from 1 to 1.5 minutes, 2 to 2.5 minutes and 3 to 3.5 minutes after finishing the stepping. Also record the total time required for the pulse rate to return to resting level.

3. The index of CRE is computed from the formula below:

$$\text{CRE index} = \frac{\text{duration of exercise in seconds} \times 100}{2 \times (\text{sum of the 3 pulse counts})}$$

CRE Index	Fitness Level
above 90	excellent
80 - 90	above average
65 - 79	High average
55 - 64	Low average
below 55	poor

An alternative measure of cardiovascular fitness can be obtained by using the table below. In the column indicating your gender, find the values which correspond to the length of time (in seconds) which were required for your pulse rate to return to normal. The column at right contains the corresponding fitness level.

Fitness Level Calculated by Recovery Time

Male	Female	Fitness Level
>180 seconds	>200 seconds	Poor
165-179 seconds	175-199 seconds	Fair
145-164 seconds	150-174 seconds	Average
125-144 seconds	130-150 seconds	Good
< 125 seconds	< 130 seconds	Excellent

Modified Tension Time Index (MTTI).

The MTTI is a indicator of the amount of work done by the heart and has been shown to be closely correlated with the amount of oxygen consumed by the cardiac muscle. One goal of aerobic exercise is to increase the workload of the heart in order to achieve a cardiac training effect.

Procedure:

Measure and record both the heart rate (pulse) and systolic blood pressure (BP) at rest and immediately after exercise. The MTTI is computed from the following formula:

$$MTTI = \frac{HR \times BP}{100}$$

The value of MTTI should range from 75 - 90 at rest and 350 - 450 following exercise. MTTI values which are above these ranges indicate that the heart is working harder than it has to in supporting these activities.

Maximum Heart Rate and Exercise Benefit Zone:

During exercise or athletic performance the heart rate increases in order to supply a greater blood flow to the muscles, lungs and skin. A point can be reached where the heart rate will become to fast for proper function and health will be endangered. This is known as the Maximum Heart Rate. For exercise activities to be of benefit to the heart and circulatory system, the heart rate must increase to somewhere between 70% and 85% of the Maximum Heart Rate. This range is known as the exercise benefit zone.

Both the Maximum Heart Rate and the Exercise Benefit Zone can be determined from the following set of equations:

A. Simple Determination

1. Maximum Heart Rate (MHR) = 220 - Age(in years)

2. Calculation of Exercise benefit Zone
   Lower Limit = MHR x .70
   Upper limit = MHR x .85

B. Karvonen Formula Determination

1. Resting Heart Rate (RHR) = heart rate (pulse rate) at rest
   Maximum Heart Rate (MHR) = 220 - age
   Heart Rate Reserve (HRR) = MHR – RHR

2. Lower end of Exercise Benefit Zone = (HRR x .6) + RHR
   Upper end of Exercise Benefit Zone = (HRR x .85) + RHR

Data Sheet

Evaluating Cardiovascular Fitness ████ ACTIVITY 20

Name:_____

Course Section:_____ **Date:** _____

	Measured Value	Expected Value
CardioRespiratory Endurance (CRE) Index	☐	☐
Resting Modified Tension Time Index (MTTI)	☐	☐
Maximum Heart Rate	☐	

Exercise Benefit Zone (Karvonen Formula)

Upper EBZ ☐

Lower EBZ ☐

Evaluation and Conclusion:
Write a brief assessment of your current state of cardiovascular fitness as measured by above indicators.

ACTIVITY 21

Evaluating Cardiovascular Risk

This worksheet will help to estimate your individual risk of developing cardiovascular disease. For each item, select the response which most closely matches your situation or condition. Place the number associated with that response in the space at right of each item. Total the individual numbers to obtain the summary score. Compare your total score with the table at the end of the worksheet.

For each item in this column	Select the most appropriate response which correctly describes your current condition						Place the point value of each response below
	[1]	[2]	[3]	[4]	[6]	[8]	
Age	10-20 years	21-30 years	31-40 years	41-50 years	51-60 years	61+ years	
	[1]	[2]	[3]	[4]	[6]	[7]	
Hereditary: Parents & Siblings	No family history of CVD	One with CVD over 50 years	Two with CVD over 60 years	One death from CVD under 60	Two deaths from CVD under 60	Three deaths from CVD under 60	
	[0]	[1]	[2]	[3]	[5]	[7]	
Weight	More than 5 Lbs below standard weight	-5 to +5 lbs of standard weight	5 to 20 lbs over-weight	21 to 35 lbs over-weight	36 to 50 lbs over-weight	51-65 lbs over-weight	
	[0]	[1]	[2]	[4]	[6]	[10]	
Tobacco Smoking	Non-smoker	Occasional Cigar or Pipe	Cigarettes 10 or less/day	Cigarettes 11 - 20 per day	Cigarettes 21 - 30 per day	Cigarettes Over 31 per day	
	[0]	[1]	[2]	[4]	[6]	[8]	
Exercise	Intensive Job & Light Exercise	Moderate Job & Light Exercise	Sedentary Job & Intense Exercise	Sedentary Job & Moderate Exercise	Sedentary Job & Light Exercise	Sedentary Job & No Exercise	
	[0]	[2]	[3]	[5]	[6]	[10]	
Cholesterol	Low Fat Diet No Sugar Intake	Below Average Fat and Sugar Intake	Normal Fat and Sugar Intake	High Fat and Normal Sugar Intake	High Fat and High Sugar Intake	Excessive Fat and Sugar Intake	
	[0]	[1]	[2]	[3]	[5]	[7]	
Systolic Blood Pressure	Below 110 mmHg	111 - 130 mmHg	131 - 140 mmHg	141 - 160 mmHg	161 - 180 mmHg	Above 180 mmHg	
	[0]	[1]	[2]	[4]	[7]	[9]	
Diastolic Blood Pressure	Below 80 mmHg	81 - 85 mmHg	86 - 90 mmHg	91 - 95 mmHg	96 - 100 mmHg	101 and above	
	[1]	[2]	[4]	[5]	[6]	[7]	
Gender	Female	Female Over 45 yrs	Male	Bald Male	Bald Short Male	Bald Short Stocky Male	

	[1]	[2]	[3]	[4]	[5]	[7]	
Resting Heart Rate men	56 & under	57 - 64	65 - 70	71 - 77	78 - 81	82 & Over	
women	65 & under	66 - 70	71 - 75	76 - 82	83 - 86	87 & Over	

	[1]	[2]	[3]	[4]	[5]	[7]	
Stress	No Stress	Occasional Mild Stress	Frequent Mild Stress	Frequent Moderate Stress	Frequent High Stress	Constant High Stress	

	[0]	[2]	[4]	[6]	[8]	[10]	
Present CVD Symptoms	None	Occasional Fast Pulse/ Irregular Rhythm	Frequent Fast Pulse/ Irregular Rhythm	Dizziness on Exertion	Occasional Angina	Frequent Angina	

	[0]	[2]	[4]	[6]	[8]	[10]	
Past CVD History	None	CVD Symptoms Not MD Confirmed	History of CVD Symptoms	Mild CVD, No Present Treatment	CVD Under Treatment	Hospitalized for CVD	

	[0]	[1]	[3]	[5]	[7]	[9]	
Diabetes	None, No Family History	Latent Positive Fam Hist	Chemical Dietary Control	Mild, Oral Rx Control	Moderate, Insulin Control	Severe,	

	[0]	[1]	[2]	[3]	[5]	[8]	
Gout	None, No Family History	None, Positive Fam Hist	Elevated Uric Acid	New Onset Gout	Repeated Gouty Attacks	Gout with Renal Complicat.	

total your point score here and compare with the chart below

Total Score	Relative Risk Index
6 - 14	Risk well below average
15 - 19	Risk slightly below average
20 - 25	Average Risk
26 - 32	Moderate Risk
33 - 40	Risk dangerous; you must reduce your score
41 - 55	Risk very dangerous; you must reduce your score
56+	Risk extreme; medical treatment recommended

This risk evaluation formula was developed by the New York State Education Department

Data Sheet

Evaluating Cardiovascular Disease Risk

Name:_____

Course Section:_____   **Date:** _____

Total Score   [ ]

Relative Risk Index   [ ]

Evaluation and Conclusion:
Briefly describe any risk factors which your assessment has indicated as possible causes for concern.

The Exercise Prescription

ACTIVITY 22

With today's pharmaceutically and technologically-driven health care system we have become accustomed to facilitating physical improvement through the use of prescription drugs, surgical intervention, or device-based therapies. First-step treatment for conditions such as heart disease, obesity, respiratory impairment, joint pains, bone loss and muscle weakness often come in the form of prescriptions for medicines (vasodilators, respiratory inhalants, anti-inflammatory agents). Such prescriptions often indicate a dosage, route of administration, and frequency of administration. It is becoming increasingly apparent however that exercise can be an effective therapy for each of the above conditions when used in place of or in addition to other therapies. Given the observations of Hippocrates over two millennia ago this should not be surprising.

The following exercise will use the data obtained through the fitness evaluation activities in this book and the conceptual and practical knowledge learned within its chapters to develop a specific, individual exercise prescription for you.

Procedure

1. Complete the Fitness Evaluation Report (Table 22.1) by entering your current values for each of the assessment activities into the appropriate space. For each of these fitness assessment values, enter into the box immediately to the right a (+), (✓) or (-) depending on whether your personal current value is better (+), equal to (✓), or less than (-) the standard normal value for someone your age and gender. Determine a personal goal for each of the measurements that reflect your desire to either maintain or improve each of the physical fitness measurements.

2. In order to address and improve each of the areas above where improvement is desired, a specific exercise prescription is recommended. The letters in the last column of Table 22.1 correspond to a specific exercise prescription in Table 22.2 A-F that follows.

Name:_____   Date of Evaluation:_____

Instructor:_____   Class Section:_____

Data Sheet

Exercise Prescription

Table 22.1.	Fitness Evaluation Report			
Fitness Measurement	**Your Current Value**	**(+), (✓) or (-)**	**Your Goal**	**Prescription for Improvement**
Body Composition				
Body Mass Index				A, F
Body Fat Percentage				
Waist-to-Hip Ratio				
Somatotype				

Metabolic Rate				**A, C**

Flexibility				
Sit-and-Reach				B
Back Arch				
Hip				
Shoulder				
Groin				
Trunk Rotation				

Kraus-Webber Back Fitness				**B, C, E**

Fitness Measurement	Your Current Value	(+), (✓) or (-)	Your Goal	Prescription for Improvement
Muscle Strength				
Grip				
Arm (bicep)				C, F
Upper Body				
Leg				

Fitness Measurement	Your Current Value	(+), (✓) or (-)	Your Goal	Prescription for Improvement
Muscle Power				
Vertical Jump				D
Long Jump				

Fitness Measurement	Your Current Value	(+), (✓) or (-)	Your Goal	Prescription for Improvement
Muscle Endurance				
Sit-up				
Push-up				E
Quadricep Static (sec)				
Quadricep Dynamic #				

Fitness Measurement	Your Current Value	(+), (✓) or (-)	Your Goal	Prescription for Improvement
Respiratory Fitness				
VO2max				A
Vital Capacity				
Respiratory Reserve				
Nerve Function				
Finger-to-Nose Test				
Movement Test				
Space Test				G
Past-pointing				
Stork Stand				
Cardiovascular Fitness				
Step Test				
MTTI				A, F
CV Disease Risk				

Table 22.2 A, B, C, D, E, F, G

The following exercise prescriptions relate to the letters, A – F indicated in the last column of the Fitness Evaluation Report above.

A	Cardiovascular Fitness / Aerobic Endurance/ Body Fat Reduction
Activity	Aerobic exercise or sports activity (Aerobic Class, Running, Cycling (spinning), Lap Swimming, Stairmaster, Basketball, etc.)
Intensity	Begin at 60% MHR, 7 METs, or 11 RPE
Volume	Begin with at least 20 minutes of continuous activity per session
Frequency	Begin with at least three sessions per week
Progression	Gradually progress intensity to 85-90% MHR, 14-16 METs, or 17-19 RPE Gradually progress volume to 60 minutes of continuous activity per session Gradually progress frequency to five sessions per week

B	Flexibility
Activity	Slow, steady stretching of all major joints
Intensity	Begin with stretching to the end of the normal range of motion
Volume	Begin by holding each stretch position for 10-30 seconds
Frequency	Begin with three stretching sessions per week
Progression	Gradually progress to pushing the stretch to the point of slight discomfort Gradually progress to holding each stretch position for 60 seconds Gradually progress to stretching every day Gradually introduce PNF stretching with proper supervision and partner

C	Muscular Strength
Activity	Resistance training activities for all major muscle groups stressing balance (Nautilus, Universal, Keiser, Fitlinx, Cybex, Free Weights)
Intensity	Begin with weights equal to 30-40% of the 1-RM for each muscle group
Volume	Begin with one set of 8-12 repetitions for each muscle group
Frequency	Begin with 2-3 sessions per week but not on consecutive days
Progression	Gradually progress to three sets of 8-12 repetitions per session every other day Gradually progress to 60-80% of 1-RM for each muscle group

D	Muscular Power
Activity	Begin with the prescription of muscular strength training but using rapid contractions Progress to plyometric training with supervision when power gain plateaus
Intensity	Follow the prescription for muscle strength training Begin with the gradual introduction of plyometrics
Volume	Follow the prescription for muscle strength training Gradually introduce plyometrics beginning with 5-10 repetitions
Frequency	Follow the prescription for muscle strength training Gradually introduce plyometric training two times per week
Progression	Follow the prescription for muscle strength training Gradually increase plyometric training to 12-15 repetitions, 4 times per week

E	Muscular Endurance
Activity	Resistance training activities for all major muscle groups stressing balance (Nautilus, Universal, Keiser, Fitlinx, Cybex, Free Weights)
Intensity	Begin with weights equal to 30-40% of the 1-RM for each muscle group
Volume	Begin with one set of 12-15 repetitions for each muscle group
Frequency	Begin with 2-3 sessions per week but not on consecutive days
Progression	Gradually progress to three sets of 15-20 repetitions per session every other day Do not exceed 60% of 1-RM for each muscle group Concentrate on gradually increasing the number of repetitions and sets performed

F	Nutrition
Carbohydrate	Consume an average of 6g of carbohydrate per kg of body weight per day
Protein	Consume an average of 1.2 g of protein per kg of body weight per day
Fat	Consume an average of 1.2 g of fat per kg of body weight per day
Calories	Consume no more calories per day than an amount equivalent to your daily dynamic energy requirement (metabolic rate evaluation)
Progression	For participation in long-duration aerobic activities, increase daily carbohydrate intake to 10 g/kg and protein intake to 1.4 g/kg For resistance training participation and the development of strength, increase daily protein intake to 1.6 – 1.7 g/kg Drink sufficient fluids (preferably water) to balance fluid lost through respiration and sweating

G	Agility / Coordination
Activity	Sport Specific Activities : eg. Golf driving range; baseball batting practice; skiing slalom practice; tennis volley practice; etc.
Intensity	Begin with low-level activities in a safe environment
Volume	Begin gradually practicing 15-20 min per day
Frequency	Begin with 2 – 3 sessions per week
Progression	Gradually progress in both the number of repetitions and the frequency of training sessions

Suggested Readings:

Gauer, R.L. and F.G. O'Connor How to Write and Exercise Prescription. *Uniformed Services University of Health Sciences* http://hooah4health.com/toolbox/exRx/default.htm

Data Sheet

Name:_____

Course Section:_____ Date: _____

Summarize the specific areas identified in your fitness assessment that you need or desire to improve (attach a copy of the data table 22.1).

Describe a specifically tailored exercise and nutrition program that you have designed to address your specific fitness goals. Be sure to provide an adequate explanation of why your exercise prescription contains the activities it does.

Index

Sensory input
Visual
Sight